COLORED *Amazons*

A JOHN HOPE FRANKLIN CENTER BOOK

POLITICS, HISTORY, AND CULTURE
A series from the International Institute at the University of Michigan

SERIES EDITORS
George Steinmetz and Julia Adams

SERIES EDITORIAL ADVISORY BOARD
Fernando Coronil
Mamadou Diouf
Michael Dutton
Geoff Eley
Fatma Müge Göcek
Nancy Rose Hunt
Andreas Kalyvas
Webb Keane
David Laitin
Lydia Liu
Julie Skurski
Margaret Somers
Ann Laura Stoler
Katherine Verdery
Elizabeth Wingrove

Sponsored by the International Institute at the University of Michigan and published by Duke University Press, this series is centered around cultural and historical studies of power, politics, and the state—a field that cuts across the disciplines of history, sociology, anthropology, political science, and cultural studies. The focus on the relationship between state and culture refers both to a methodological approach—the study of politics and the state using culturalist methods—and a substantive approach that treats signifying practices as an essential dimension of politics. The dialectic of politics, culture, and history figures prominently in all the books selected for the series.

COLORED *Amazons*

Crime, Violence, and Black Women

in the City of Brotherly Love,

1880–1910

KALI N. GROSS

Duke University Press   Durham and London   2006

© 2006 Duke University Press

All rights reserved

Printed in the United States of America on acid-free paper ∞

Designed by Heather Hensley

Typeset in Adobe Garamond by Tseng Information Systems

Library of Congress Cataloging-in-Publication Data appear on
the last printed page of this book.

For June Maria Gross

CONTENTS

ACKNOWLEDGMENTS

THIS PROJECT HAS TWO BIRTHS. Its empathy for the *unrespectable* is a penchant of my own—arguably bred into me but unwittingly nurtured by women in my family. Women determined and sharp enough to not simply get by, but also to push past obstacles and effectively *get over*. Its subject matter, however, came from my interaction with a group of students in Muncy, Pennsylvania. Just as I am grateful to the women in my immediate family, I find myself also indebted to the women at SCI-Muncy for teaching me more than I ever taught them.

The History Department at the University of Pennsylvania profoundly tested and honed my resolve. My committee, Mary Frances Berry, Kathleen M. Brown, and Farah Jasmine Griffin, provided invaluable training and guidance throughout the dissertation process. I also thank the many scholars, peers, and friends who enhanced my education: Luther Adams, Jackie Akins, Giselle Anatol, Elijah Anderson, Erica Armstrong, Jessica Davis-Ba, Ed Baptist, Herman Beavers, Deborah Broadnax, Stephanie Camp, Drew Faust, Rhonda Frederick, Leticia Hernandez, Ross Johnson, Tanaquil Jones, Robin Leidner, Marie Manrique, Murray Murphy, Leslie Patrick, James Peterson, Kirby Randolph, John Roberts, Nichole Rustin, Barbara Savage, Thomas Sugrue, Hayley Thomas, Rhonda Williams, and Rafael Zapata.

The Pennsylvania Historical and Museum Commission supported my research with grants in 1997 and in 2001. It is not an exaggeration to say that without these grants and the assistance of the Commission's archivists, this project could never have been completed. A special thanks to Judy Duritsa, Ruth Hodge, Anne Marie Ickes, Karen James, Linda Ries, Michael Sherbon,

Linda Shopes, Jonathan Stayer, and Robert Weible. I would also like to thank Natalie Caldwell and Ward Childs at the Philadelphia City Archive—their expert assistance helped me locate many of the proverbial needles in this haystack. Richard Boardman and Paul Savedow of the Free Library of Philadelphia came through for me at the eleventh hour with images, maps, and permissions, as did Brett Bertollino of the Eastern State Penitentiary Historic Site—thank you.

Between 1998 and 2000, my work benefited from the Consortium for A Strong Minority Presence Doctoral and Postdoctoral Fellowship at Occidental College. I thank Cecilia Fox for reading this manuscript in its early stages. Betsy Perry, a friend and colleague, graciously read draft after draft of this book long after I left Oxy. I remain indebted to her for her time and thoughtful comments. Arthé Anthony, Regina Freer, P. Gabrielle Foreman, Donna Maeda, and Movindri Reddy—all provided guidance and wonderful sisterhood during my time in Los Angeles. They reminded me of the importance of activist teaching and scholarship.

As a postdoctoral fellow at the Schomburg Center for Research in Black Culture in 2000, I was fortunate enough to work with a remarkable group of scholars. In addition to the Center's rich collections, fellowship seminars expanded my thinking, enhanced my writing, and sharpened my skills as a historian. Many thanks to Kim D. Butler, Jacqueline Goldsby, Cecilia Green, Robin D. G. Kelley, and Genna Rae McNeil. I also thank Aisha al-Adawiya and Diana Lachatanere. I owe a special thanks to Colin Palmer for his stewardship of the program, his astute comments on earlier drafts, and his support. His mentorship was invaluable—indeed, almost as good as his cooking.

The Ford Foundation Minority Postdoctoral Fellowship allowed me to fill in crucial research gaps, and my time in the Program in African American Studies at Princeton University in 2001 extended my opportunity to work with Colin Palmer. Nell Painter graciously read early chapters and offered encouragement and key insights. In 2003, I spent a wonderful summer concluding my research at the Library Company of Philadelphia and the Historical Society of Pennsylvania. Resources in the Library Company especially helped me complete chapter 1—thank you Jenny Ambrose, Linda August, Cornelia King, Phillip Lapsansky, Cathy Matson, Charlene Peacock, Erika Piola, Nicole Scalessa, Sarah Weatherwax, and Wendy Woloson.

Raphael Allen understood my vision and placed a great deal of confidence in my abilities, and I am truly grateful. Valerie Millholland, Miriam Angress, and Mark Mastromarino at Duke brought the project to fruition—thank you. C. Dallett Hemphill read several sections of this manuscript. Her input and time are greatly appreciated. Nikki Childers also read, critiqued, and copyedited drafts of this work—thanks a bunch little sister. Many thanks to Stephanie Camp and Rhonda Frederick for reading sections of my work even as they were both in the final stages of submitting their own manuscripts to publishers. Over the years Roger Lane has been a historical godfather of sorts—lending his microfilm reader and personal copy of the William Dorsey Collection and, more recently, the benefit of his vast expertise. Thanks for reading the manuscript and for your keen observations; most of all, thanks for your off-the-chain sense of humor—clearly, great minds really do think alike.

My colleagues in History and Politics at Drexel University also helped bring this project to completion. I thank Donald Stevens for his suggestions on the book and Richardson Dilworth for sharing his insights on key sections. A special thanks to Sharon Grinnage, Christian Hunold, Julie Mostov, David Munns (my future ex-husband), Joel Oestreich, Erik Rau, Amy Slaton, Kathryn Steen, and Gina Waters. Gabriella Ibieta and Abioseh Porter—thanks for your guidance and for lending an ear. I also thank Donna Murasko, the Dean of the College of Arts and Sciences, for her unwavering support of Africana Studies at Drexel University.

Cheryl D. Hicks spent months reading my work, and her studied review greatly improved the book. The benefit of her analysis is rivaled only by the richness of the friendship, sisterhood, and laughter that she shares. I am eternally grateful for the support, warmth, love, friendship, wine excursions, and meals with a host of family and friends, but especially: Stephanie Camp, Nicole Childers, Kneia DaCosta, Rhonda Frederick, Dianne Glave, Ross, Alison, and the entire Johnson family, Nzadi and Maghan Keita, Anisa and Kristine Lewis, Gwendolyn and Waviney Lyken, Inez and Dolores Ramos and the Ramos family, Charles and Tonya Rice, Maggie Ussery, Melissa Walters, Constance Wright, Maisha Yearwood and her family, and, my karmic-debt paramour, Irvin Martes. Sylvia Neal, my grandmother, encouraged me to complete this book and showed me how never to back down. Judith Lovell, my aunt, taught me that with will, you can get through a solid brick wall. Londa, Neal, Joselyn, the Lovells, and Craig continue to remind me of who I am and where I came from. Thanks.

June Maria Gross, my mother, continues to give me everything, including a model of perseverance, an iron core, and an unwavering commitment to education. You set me on this path long ago and believed in me when nobody else did. I love you and dedicate this book to you.

Introduction

NOTES FROM THE AUTHOR:
CRIME AND BLACK WOMEN'S HISTORY

As this place hath growne more popular and the people more increased,
Looseness and vice Hath also Creept in.

—Governor Markham, 1697 (quoted in Howard O. Sprogle,
The Philadelphia Police, Past and Present [Philadelphia, 1887], 31)

THIS BOOK AND ITS COLORFUL—if not irreverent—title stem from a series of events that occurred between 1995 and 1999, not the least significant of which was my discovery of an early twentieth-century news article detailing the crime of two "colored Amazons" in the City of Brotherly Love.[1] The most significant event, however, took place in the spring of 1995 when I team-taught a seminar to female inmates at the State Correctional Institution in Muncy, Pennsylvania. My participation in that course, a survey of African-American women's history, marked a fledgling attempt to bridge the gap between my political ideals and my professional training. By offering a class to women inmates—90 percent of whom were African American—I hoped to use my historical expertise to educate and empower these students.[2]

At the same time, I believed that passing history on in this way kept true to the legacy of black scholarship. African-American history, and much of Black Studies, for that matter, was resurrected, collected, and "preached" not solely for educational purposes but also for community empowerment, an empowerment that was political, social, and in many ways psychological.[3] Indeed, one only need consider the works of Ida B. Wells-Barnett, W. E. B. Du Bois, and Anna Julia Cooper or review Carter G. Woodson's epistle *The Mis-Education of the Negro* to see that African-American scholarship is as much about the liberation of black people as it is about documenting the experience of blacks in the United States and abroad.[4]

But in teaching that class at the correctional institution in Muncy, now a decade ago, I also faced the paradox of my training. I considered myself a teacher of African-American history, but my course rarely, if ever, represented the historical experience of my pupils. I found myself disseminating tales of noble suffering and perseverance—themes that dominate much of African-American history—to women who by these accounts would be considered failures. This realization shaped my research and led me to consider how the very legacy of black history had in more recent times begun to undermine its own mission.

Because so much of early scholarship directly resulted from black activism, its subject matter typically concentrated on figures and events that could dispel myths of black inferiority. Early scholars avoided controversial subject matter, fearing it might unwittingly validate racist stereotypes.[5] Those fears were not without merit. As a consequence, however, researchers muted a variety of experiences—most notably those that elucidate the complexities of African-American history and culture.[6] These experiences, of gays and lesbians, of the poor, of the insane, and of criminals, diagram the breadth of the black experience.[7] These histories also serve to highlight the contours of both freedom and democracy in a much larger sense.

Exploring the context of those on the margins teaches a great deal about those individuals and systems that customarily occupy the center. Investigating history from the bottom up ultimately creates a more holistic study and does so without overlooking or minimizing those who dwell on the fringes.[8] These projects also reveal just how powerfully the center is itself informed by those margins. Thus, when investigators bring groups such as black female criminals to the fore, history benefits from a more textured insight as well as from a valuable opportunity to map the inner workings of liberty and justice.[9]

Black female criminals spotlight the ways in which race, gender, and sexuality shape citizenship and criminal justice. Their cases make the boundaries of each particularly visible through the processes of lawmaking, law enforcement, the disposition of cases, and incarceration.[10] But the black female criminal experience does not simply show how race, gender, and sexuality are mediated. Rather it demonstrates how black womanhood is negotiated within the criminal justice system of the day. Moreover, contrasting glimpses of how white men, white women, and black men fared throughout these processes serve to bring the historical roots of present-day conditions into high relief. Black women's history of skirmishes with the law highlights the personal and outlines the margins for all those who move in and out of the legal system.[11] Though the value of the history of black achievement is undeniable and the body of work groundbreaking and impressive in its own right, it is not enough. A myopic concentration on the celebratory aspects of black history ultimately does a disservice to the field by neglecting important facets of both history and black studies.[12] By focusing solely on the heroic aspects of the black experience, the scholarship fails to address ongoing social problems.

Currently, black women are the fastest-growing prison population in the United States. Black women account for nearly half of all female prisoners in the country though they comprise less than 10 percent of the population nationwide.[13] And though black women have often been disproportionately represented in the criminal justice system, we have little insight into historical trends or their ramifications.[14] This epidemic cannot be successfully arrested without some sense of the historical scope of the problem.[15]

Colored Amazons is a step toward understanding the historical roots of black female crime, violence, and incarceration during the post-Reconstruction period. As such, it is also an examination of the intersection of race, gender, sexuality, and justice. This examination includes the study of black women and their crimes and an analysis of how their crimes are represented in press accounts and within the discourses of urban and penal reform. Ultimately this book seeks to understand how black female crime functioned in the lives of the perpetrators as well as in that of the society. It argues that the perpetrators and the apparatuses of the state jointly constructed black female crime. For some women, crime functioned as an extralegal source of income and, just as important, a means to attain personal and social autonomy. For the state, black female crime and its representations effectively galvanized, justified, and anchored a host of urban reform initiatives that affirmed white middle-class authority. At the same time, black female crime contributed to shifts in laws, policing, and confinement that disproportionately affected black women's crime rates.[16]

In understanding the nature and function of black female crimes, the book pays particular attention to the social context of crime and its perpetrators. By placing black women's lives at the center of my research, I seek to contribute to a growing body of work that focuses on the experience of poor and working-class African Americans.[17] In many ways, this book is as much about the shifting notions of black womanhood as it is about black women and crime. I study black female criminality, but I also use the women's crimes as a vehicle for gaining insight into the lives of otherwise marginalized black women.

Black female criminals cannot be regarded as complete anomalies within the black community at the turn of the twentieth century. Though arrest, conviction, and incarceration set them apart from their poor, working-class counterparts, the distinction does not negate a larger shared experienced.[18] On the contrary, the age, education, and economic status of black female criminals typified those of the larger group of African-American women in Philadelphia, though frequently women who committed crimes occupied the most disenfranchised strata of the community. Their crimes often illustrate circumstances and themes as well as motivating factors distinct from those of white female, white male, and black male offenders. Indeed, there was a method to their madness.[19]

With this in mind, I resist casting these women either as martyrs or as inherently deviant. Rather, the analysis sifts through the slippery matrix of what exists between propriety and pathology. This study is not a sanitized examination of black women and crime. Nor is it meant to either absolve or condemn the parties involved—whether those parties are the perpetrators, the victims, the courts, or the jailers. Indeed, many black women were railroaded by the criminal justice system. In other instances, black women's crimes reflected poverty and exclusion. In some cases, their crimes evidenced greed and ruthless materialism; in others, they suggested extreme levels of self-loathing and a disturbingly low threshold for violence.

However, black female criminals at the turn of the twentieth century are a particularly confounding population to study. Since most of the women were born just after abolition, their early histories are not documented in planters' records.[20] Because of their economic status and transient nature in the city, the women tend not to show up in customary historical records—census data, tax records, and property records yield precious few clues about them. Moreover, because black female criminals were predominantly unskilled wage laborers and semiliterate, few found themselves in a position to leave behind memoirs or diaries. For most, their criminal records serve as the only documentation of their lives. Although the records place otherwise invisible women on the historical map, they are frustratingly transitory. In-depth evidence about the women's lives remains elusive. It is difficult, if not impossible, to track the women after they are released from prison and cease to appear in prison and court dockets.

Paradoxically, prison and penitentiary records are at once detailed and scant. Though intake registers are exhaustive—most contain the perpetrator's race, age, height, weight, crime, sentence, marital status, and educational level—the documents contain only sparse information about the circumstances of the crimes. Penitentiary dockets list charges for which inmates have been sentenced, such as larceny or assault and battery, but nothing tangible about stolen items, where the crime occurred, or, if applicable, the victims. Though wanting for more substantive information, however, the records are close to ideal for compiling statistical databases on the city's offenders and for creating a general profile of black female criminals.[21]

To round out the evidence I combined quantitative data with evidence culled from all available trial transcripts, annual police and corrections reports, and daily periodicals—some generally reliable and forthright in their reporting, others careless and highly sensational.[22] Although transcripts are a rarity and annual reports only slightly richer than actual prison dockets, the city's newspapers and scandal rags proved plentiful. The juxtaposition of criminal data with Philadelphia's abundant collection of both judicious and vulgar periodicals made it possible to gather and verify otherwise missing information about black women and crime. Popular culture not only provides historical evidence of black women's crimes, but also displays a unique cultural lens that brings into focus a host of mainstream perspectives on black women, urban violence, and crime.[23]

Violence appears in this study in a number of ways. First, criminal violence committed by black women as well as the violence used against them is studied. Beyond the documentation of literal attacks, I also examined the social context of violence—here I refer to the ways in which crippling economic exclusion and social isolation constitute a tropic of violence that affected black women's lives, particularly the lives of black female criminals. The research also considers representative forms of violence—I refer to the ways in which racist images and representations of black women and black female criminals contributed to an overarching climate of racial antagonism.[24]

Perhaps even more important is the exploration of how contexts of violence overlap and affect black women's lives and their commission of crimes. My aim is to further address historical gaps, silences in the historical record.[25] Undoubtedly, the precise effects of violence are difficult to qualify, but it is nonetheless necessary for historians to broach the subject and to speculate about its impact on African-American lives. Although we do not have bounteous testimony to explain how negative images or a climate of racial hostility shaped the psyches of blacks in past generations, there can be little doubt that it did, or that its influence is important for black history and especially for histories of black crime and violence.[26] The dearth of scholarship on these historical issues is less a reflection of its importance than a function of limited sources attesting to emotional and psychological trauma.[27]

Rather than perpetuate the absences or re-create historical silences, however, historians must exploit new types of evidence.[28] This book, for example, employs interpretive analyses of both cultural mediums and criminal behaviors in an attempt to push past the limitations of the historical record. Thus, often in the absence of the women's own words, *Colored Amazons* uses black female crime—specifically, criminal acts—as evocative texts for historical analysis. I read black women's crimes not simply as evidence of illegal behavior but as texts possessing a palpable voice, one that effectively speaks of values, ambitions, and frustrations and also one that contains rare clues about black women's past experience of trauma.

Criminal acts, whether fueled by poverty, isolation, greed, or rage, constitute an incisive historical vocabulary. Using these crimes as audible texts affords these women greater historical agency and offers a more complete view of their social reality. Moreover, *Colored Amazons* is both descriptive and analytical: while it studies black women's crimes and their collision with criminal justice, the narrative is, whenever possible, somewhat indulgent in retelling the surrounding stories.

Race, Gender, and Prison in the City of Brotherly Love

Late nineteenth- and early twentieth-century Philadelphia presents an ideal period and location for this study. In 1780, the state of Pennsylvania passed an act for the gradual abolition of slavery and soon housed the largest population of free blacks before the Civil War. Yet despite its Quaker roots and reputation for liberal democratic ideals, Philadelphia witnessed some of the country's bloodiest riots against abolition, racial equality, and immigration in the decades following the American Revolution. The city's unique background affords a wealth of source material on everyday African-American life at the same time that Philadelphia's expressed opinions about blacks paralleled social attitudes prevalent in the nation. The mainstream perspective on race in the City of Brotherly Love never fully diverged from that held in other parts of the country—North or South.[29]

By 1900, Philadelphia was the third largest city in the country, and its legal system set trends for Massachusetts, New York, and Connecticut as well as a number of southern states.[30] The city also led the country in early forays into the rhetoric of biological criminality, including the notion of the "born criminal."[31] Moreover, the post-Reconstruction period marks the first wave of black migration from the South to the urban North and encapsulates an important historical moment by charting the intersection of newly minted black citizenship and early-modern penology.

Eastern State Penitentiary, the city's premier confinement facility, serves as both a literal and figurative symbol of the state apparatuses of power. Renowned for its architectural design, a close embodiment of the panopticon, as well as for its stringent philosophy of solitary confinement, the institution was more than a prison: it was a marker of the vigor and the extent to which reformers and lawmakers were willing to go to repress crime. As demonstrated at Eastern, the criminal justice system tried to enact social control through the almost complete regulation of prisoners' bodies.[32]

The treatment of black female criminals within Eastern presents another vantage point from which to gauge the institutional perception of black female crime. It also discloses how the criminal justice system regarded black women's citizenship. The penitentiary and black women's experience therein serve as another platform for understanding the boundaries of race, gender, and sexuality within the justice system. The warden's journals, in particular, are among the most valuable sources in this study and remain so up until 1910—just before the state abandoned the policy of solitary confinement in 1911 and also shortly before the Pennsylvania legislature passed an act to establish a separate institution for women in 1913.[33] The penitentiary and the period between 1880 and 1910 mark an ideal moment in the city's, the nation's, and, indeed, the prison system's historical evolution.

Turn-of-the-century Philadelphia underwent a number of dynamic social transitions. The fallout and backlash resulting from the Civil War and Reconstruction were substantial and mirrored changes occurring throughout the country. The granting of African-American citizenship, even if in name only, resulted in a profound displacement of traditional white entitlements. What it meant to be black and white in America had been powerfully altered by the Thirteenth and Fourteenth amendments in a way that not even "Redemption" could undo. The confirmation of black citizenship, though never fully actualized in day-to-day practices, resulted in tremendous anxiety for both whites and blacks. In the aftermath, both groups scrambled to reformulate or, depending on which side of the issue one was on, reestablish their former racial identities. These changes among others, when taken together, significantly impacted the remediation of crime.

Industrialization complicated these developments and gave birth to corporations that further tore the country's traditional social fabric. Labor moved from farms and the home to cities and factories. Native-born white men found themselves in competition not just with newly freed blacks and the ever-increasing populations of ethnic immigrants, but also with women. These changes ignited shifting notions of gender for both the bourgeoisie and the laboring classes.[34] The interplay between changing gender identities and sexuality played an integral part in the social change, as urban life witnessed a broader range of sexual identities and alternative sexual practices.[35] And whites were not the only Philadelphians grappling with the multiplicity of social transformations. The city's black community and black women in particular struggled with who they wanted to be and how they would actualize citizenship.

The disjuncture between black women's notions of citizenship and the prevailing discourse on black womanhood aided the construction of a black female criminal context. Rigid employment and housing discrimination dogged black women's efforts to become socially mobile at the same time that emerging definitions of criminality incorporated the stereotypical physical and cultural attributes assigned to blacks. Emerging definitions of criminality inscribed deviance as something inherent to all social others and in opposition to white middle-class cultural values. The rhetoric of crime control marked a codified middle-class cry for a return to the traditional social order—one that situated mainstream whites as social custodians.[36] The rhetoric, moreover, served as the ideological playing field upon which reformers and politicians competed for power in the city.[37]

Ultimately, the cultural and historical context of urbanization in Philadelphia makes it an ideal locale for exploring the complexities of crime and the layered social factors that contributed to black female offending. Perhaps equally important, the city's history embodies the contradictory themes of liberty and oppression in American history. The historical presence of blacks in Philadelphia serves as the allegorical nexus of an ongoing tug-of-war between democracy and a racial caste system.[38] Turn-of-the-century Philadelphians struggled with their commitment to the highest ideals of freedom and democracy at the same time that their actions belied an inability to fully divorce themselves from attitudes and practices that prevented a true implementation of their lofty ideals. Philadelphia's history magnifies the taut relationship between the noble desire to create a government built on justice and equality and the fundamental inability to relinquish the very privileges that impede such a democratic vision.

Mapping Colored Amazons

Colored Amazons locates black women and their crimes within a tangle of shifting social circumstances. Thematically arranged, the chapters are designed to provide a layered view of the subject. Chapter 1, "Of Law and Virtue," moves through key periods in Pennsylvania's early legal history. Using the case of Alice Clifton, an enslaved woman accused of murder in 1787, this chapter spotlights how race, gender, and sexuality took meaning through colonial slave laws. In doing so, it maps how those early notions affected justice for blacks during the Republican and Antebellum eras. In addition, chapter 1 foregrounds Pennsylvania's history of turbulent race relations and draws attention to the impact of that history on the evolution of criminal justice. Through an examination of mainstream responses to black citizenship and changing social demographics, the chapter foreshadows the interplay of race, gender, sexuality, and justice at the turn of the century.

"Service Savors of Slavery," chapter 2, maps the congested cultural grid of the city as well as the overall characteristics of black women and their crimes in the post-Reconstruction era. Through an investigation of black female labor, housing, and leisure activity, black women are situated in the city among native-born whites, European immigrants, and elite, middle-class African Americans. The chapter also examines how domestic service work factors into black female crime.[39] Specifically, it argues that poverty and alienation created the stark conditions that contributed to black women's crimes — overwhelmingly larceny.

"Servant theft," in particular, appears to reflect black women's frustration at being barred from industrial work and more lucrative forms of employment. An analysis of these crimes reveals how black women understood and regarded their social context. But also, this chapter demonstrates how black women's attempts to exercise personal freedom and social autonomy collided with the moral objectives of both black and white social reformers, reformers whose response to the increased presence of single black women amounted to a series of "moral panics" that ultimately impacted laws, policing, and black women's confinement.[40]

The third chapter, "Tricking the Tricks," builds upon the methodology in the previous chapter, though it concentrates on black female violence and black women's sex crimes. Investigating the specifics of fistfights, domestic disputes, and other instances of felonious assault, chapter 3 explores the relationship between black female violence and a black woman's inability to attain the social accoutrements of womanhood, such as protection and respect. The chapter also uses black female violence and instances of sexual exploitation to read violence back into the perpetrators' lives. Although most black women repressed their inner turmoil and anger, effectively invoking a veil of silence, I argue that black female crime, violent crimes in particular, is evidence of those who did not, or perhaps could not, dissemble the vicissitudes of poverty and discrimination.[41]

The next two chapters investigate popular and institutional responses to urban black women and their crimes. "Roughneck Women, Pale Representations, and Dark Crimes," chapter 4, spotlights how popular culture exaggerated black female crime and contrived false notions of illicit sex and danger in the city.[42] The chapter traces the press construction of the "Colored

Amazon."[43] Contrasting popular images of black female criminals with those of white male, white female, and black male criminals, I demonstrate how the caricature embodied racist notions of criminality. These images contributed to the mainstream ideology of white supremacy and to popular notions of pathological black urban dwellers. Moreover, the representations supplied a new and growing commercial trade in blackness. Replacing the literal sale of blacks, everyday merchandise relied on cartoonist representations of racial stereotypes. News accounts in particular created a space for the public to purchase stories of black depravity, and the sexual aspects of the Colored Amazon caricature provided a white male audience voyeuristic access to black women's bodies.

Chapter 5, "Deviant by Design," examines early criminologists' interpretations of black female crime. Specifically, it explores the effect of scientific notions of hereditary criminality. Here I show how reformers, police, and theorists implemented surveillance and policing tactics that ultimately created the very criminal—or "crime class"—they hoped to repress. Investigating the transformations in criminal identification practices, this chapter traces a larger ideological shift—a move from regarding criminals as individuals who committed crimes and could be rehabilitated to identifying individuals who were inherently criminal and ultimately in need of containment.

The exploration also reveals how mainstream bias shaped black women's experience at Eastern, as well as details black women's maneuvers to evade coercive prison practices. Perhaps more important, this account further highlights the relationship between the public outcry for black female containment and the theme underscoring this rhetoric—the protection of customary white cultural hegemony. It does so by juxtaposing prison administrators' apathetic "rehabilitation" of black female inmates with the same administrators' persistent and often brutal attempts to "correct" the behavior of white men imprisoned for sodomy. Prison workers obsessed over white male sodomites because their existence challenged the foundation of reform ideals. Inherent pathology explained blacks' criminal actions, but this very notion simultaneously disallowed the existence of a native-born white male degenerate. Prison administrators aimed desperately to "cure" these men above all other prisoners because white male sodomites represented a fundamental challenge to the rhetoric of biological criminality and, ultimately, white superiority.

The conclusion, " 'She was Born in this Prison,' " is less a summation than a series of final observations about black female crime and its determinants. Quoting the warden's journals on the death of a black female inmate born in the facility some two decades earlier, the conclusion uses this notation as a larger metaphor. " 'She was Born in this Prison' " addresses both the literal and figurative barriers encapsulating black women's lives during the late nineteenth and early twentieth centuries. Arguably, black female criminality was birthed both by the perpetrators themselves and by the broader structural inequalities played out in the legal system. Black women were not the only casualties of those inequalities, but they were among the most adversely affected by them.

Considering the historical implications of past black female criminality, the conclusion probes how this past relates to more recent incidents of black female crime. Through an examination of two infamous crimes that occurred in Philadelphia in the 1940s, the conclusion focuses on how the legacy of the Colored Amazon continued to influence popular opinion about black female criminals as well as the adjudication of their crimes.

Both phenomena—black female crime of old and its more recent incarnation—are implicitly connected to the limits of liberty. Crime operates as a powerful social prism. It reveals the complexities of individual lives as well as plots overarching social dynamics. The history of black female criminals teaches us more than their individual experiences and more than those experiences shared by black women or the black community. Black women's crimes speak more broadly of the rift between the political rhetoric of democracy and the legal reality of marginalized populations. The crimes examined attest to the subjective nature of race, gender, and sexuality within criminal justice and to the centrality of black women's experience therein.[44]

Chapter One

OF LAW AND VIRTUE:
BLACK WOMEN IN SLAVERY, FREEDOM,
AND EARLY CRIMINAL JUSTICE

> *In every human Breast, God had implanted a Principle, which we call love*
> *of Freedom; it is impatient of Oppression, and pants for Deliverance.*
>
> —Phyllis Wheatley, 1774

UNFREE LABOR ACCOUNTED FOR nearly one-third of the labor force in colonial Pennsylvania.[1] Slavery and indentured servitude coexisted at the time of
the colony's founding and ended together in the decades just after the American Revolution.[2] The number of Africans in Philadelphia rose from approximately 150 in 1684 to almost 2,500 in 1790—at that time blacks accounted
for 5 percent of the city's inhabitants.[3] Divided almost equally according to
sex, the black population combined those imported from the Caribbean with
native-born blacks and, toward the middle of the eighteenth century, slaves
shipped directly from Africa. Largely the property of merchants and artisans,
enslaved blacks lived with their owners in numbers of fewer than three to a
household. Most slaves led hard, isolated lives punctuated by hunger, disease,
and degradation. Their disproportionate mortality rate, 50 percent higher than
European Americans, spotlights the harsh realities of slavery in the North.[4]

Early abolitionists such as free blacks and Mennonites decried the inhu-
manity of slavery almost from the time of Pennsylvania's founding. When the
colony stirred with the rumblings of insurrection, black Pennsylvanians hoped
that revolutionary ideals would make their own liberation inevitable. Although

the struggle for independence did not end slavery, it ushered in swift changes that profoundly altered the quality of life for most blacks in the region. More than political rhetoric or revolutionary banter, liberty was an infectious principle that roused many. It breathed new life into the cause of black freedom and it prompted slaves to "steal themselves." It also engendered intense debate about the political and moral implications of a democratic society that tolerated slavery. In Pennsylvania, Independence invigorated the antislavery movement, expedited abolition in the state, and radically transformed justice and punishment. Yet liberty also proved temporal, fraught with strife, and, ultimately, fleeting.[5]

The trial of Alice Clifton, an enslaved woman accused of murder in 1787, acts as a historical conduit through which we can look backward as well as forward in Pennsylvania's history. Balanced on the axis of key social contexts, Clifton's trial occurs at a historical crossroads. Positioned between slavery and gradual abolition and corporal punishment and the emergence of the prison system, the case accompanied the birth of two nations—a burgeoning republic and a fledgling freed black community. The circumstances of Clifton's crime hearken back to the days of slavery, yet her trial is poised at the threshold of the future. The hearing, then, attests to the transformation of justice as well as to blacks' social status in the wake of the Revolution.

Perhaps most important, Clifton's trial diagrams how legislation regulating slavery shaped broader notions of race, gender, and sexuality. Ultimately, the statutes created impossible binaries in black women's lives. The circumstances of the case also highlight the impact of race relations on the development of criminal justice. Specifically, social mores established by slave laws criminalized blacks and erected systemic inequalities in the justice system. By using Clifton's case as a doorway into legal and social developments that came before her crime and those that followed, this chapter highlights three key periods in Pennsylvania's history. Mapping early enslavement, gradual abolition and industrialization, and early penology is crucial for understanding the interplay of race, gender, and justice in the late nineteenth century. Not to be lost is the symbiotic relationship between racial tension, social unrest, and the evolution of criminal justice. As this relationship becomes visible so too does a pattern of partial justice that leaves black women vulnerable to the vagaries of the legal system.

The Trial of Alice Clifton

Alice Clifton went on trial for the murder of her illegitimate child on April 15, 1787.[6] Clifton, seventeen years old at the time, labored primarily as a domestic servant for her owners, John and Mary Bartholomew, Philadelphia shopkeepers.[7] She stunned her owners on April 5, 1787, the day that Mary Bartholomew's sister-in-law discovered the lifeless body of a newborn girl stuffed in a trunk in the family's home. The Bartholomews soon learned Clifton had slashed the infant's throat, making a cut nearly four inches long and one inch deep with a razor purchased for a shilling.[8] Ironically, such a wound would typically constitute proof that the infant had been born alive, but Clifton's defense attorneys would argue that peculiarities surrounding the pregnancy pointed to a stillbirth. Her counsel tried in vain to convince the court that despite the reprehensible cutting, Clifton could not be found guilty of murder because she cut the child's throat postmortem.[9]

Formerly the property of Mrs. Bartholomew's father, Clifton lived with the Bartholomews for three years before her arrest.[10] Arduous labor, threadbare clothes, cruel punishments, and scarce food typified slaves' existence. Most likely Clifton would have been supervised by Mrs. Bartholomew and charged to perform a host of tasks from cooking and cleaning to laundry, sewing, and gardening. Clifton might also have been hired out to labor for other families or merchants in the area.[11] The close quarters in which slaves and masters lived rarely engendered pity or sympathy on the part of masters. Rather, slave owners often exploited the most basic human needs as a means to compel submission. Silvia Dubois, the slave of New Jersey and Pennsylvania innkeepers during the 1780s, said of her diet of potatoes, pork, beef, mush, and milk: "We didn't get a bellyful of these sometimes—I've often gone to bed hungry . . . was no use to complain—you had your measure and you got no more." Dubois also told of terrible beatings she received from her mistress, noting that she had been marked so badly that she would "never lose those scars."[12]

Slave owners also restricted spatial mobility, though bondwomen like Clifton routinely found ways to escape the master's watchful eye. Running errands that took her away from the home probably doubled as a means to meet with other slaves in the area. Evening jaunts likely provided avenues to socialize with members of the opposite sex.[13] During one of these excursions Clifton met

John Shaffer, a white man who lived nearby. The two developed an intimate relationship.[14] According to the record, Clifton conceived the first time "she was debauched" by him. Clifton met Shaffer regularly thereafter, and the two conspired to keep the pregnancy a secret.[15]

Despite repeated inquiries from the Bartholomews, who suspected the pregnancy, Clifton denied the charges. Even during labor, Clifton complained only of feeling ill. Mrs. Bartholomew checked on her routinely, but Clifton delivered between her mistress's visits and managed to conceal her daughter's birth. Although within earshot of Clifton, neither Mrs. Bartholomew nor members of her family heard the newborn cry. When Mrs. Bartholomew entered Clifton's room, the young woman, at that time up and about, asked for a change of clothes, claiming she felt much better.[16] Mrs. Bartholomew searched the house and enlisted the help of family members. Her sister-in-law discovered the infant under a roll of linen in a storage trunk. According to the testimony, Clifton initially claimed that, "she had laid on it, but could not help it."[17] The Bartholomews summoned the authorities.

Members of the inquest discovered the neck laceration, and shortly afterward Clifton confessed, though it remained unclear when she had cut the child's throat. Witnesses at the house could not say with certainty because the infant's head laid on its chest; in the absence of any blood, all believed that Clifton had smothered the child.[18] Clifton's multiple stories compounded confusion over the time of death. First claiming to have accidentally caused the infant's death and then taking responsibility for cutting its throat, Clifton later stated that the infant was stillborn. To support the latter claim, her attorneys offered evidence of an injury she had sustained a month prior to the birth. The Bartholomews' testimony corroborated Clifton's account of having fallen down the cellar steps a few weeks before she delivered. Because she fell with a log in her hands, the defense argued that this accident had gravely injured the fetus and precipitated a premature stillbirth.[19] Two doctors from the inquest testified that based on a preponderance of evidence—the fall, the small size of the fetus, the fact that Clifton delivered alone, and the lack of blood on the wound—they could conclude only that Clifton had made the incision postmortem.[20]

But Clifton's damning words and actions undermined her defense. Moreover, her reason for hiding the pregnancy supplied motive for the prosecution.

According to Doctor Foulke's testimony, Clifton said that Shaffer had persuaded her to kill the child. At the time she conceived, he planned to wed a "fine woman," and he feared the impact of a scandal. Shaffer had promised he would purchase her freedom if she killed the baby. He said she would live "as happy and as fine as his wife." Presumably taking advantage of the stillbirth, Clifton claimed to have cut the infant's throat in order to keep her agreement with Shaffer.[21] Neither Clifton nor Shaffer testified, and there is no indication that John Shaffer, who at the time of the trial was indeed wed to "Chavilier's daughter," faced criminal charges.[22]

At the close of the trial, when the chief justice informed the jurors of their responsibility, he took the liberty of offering his own opinion on the matter. He charged that, "so far as her efforts could effect [the infant's] destruction, [Clifton] exerted them unpitying, and void of maternal affection."[23] The jurors deliberated for three hours before finding Clifton guilty of willfully causing the death of her bastard child.[24]

Yet the verdict did not herald Clifton's ultimate demise. Before sentencing, Clifton's defense introduced an affidavit charging that Edward Pole, a juror, had stated prior to the trial that he did not see how the verdict could be anything other than guilty.[25] That Pole reached this conclusion before the hearing constituted cause, according to the defense, for the court to grant Clifton a new trial. The court denied the petition and sentenced Clifton to death. However, it appears that Clifton's sentence was overturned. The reason is omitted, but the record noted that Clifton's punishment was "respited by the Honourable Supreme Executive Council."[26] Perhaps the Bartholomews intervened, given that the outcome concerned their property. Beyond the abrupt cessation of the account, however, Clifton's fate is unknown; yet her ordeal sheds light on the social barriers bisecting black women's lives. Her case also explicates the role of the legal system in erecting those barriers.

Clifton's crime may behoove sympathy, but the broader circumstances cannot be overlooked, principally, that her best shot at freedom could be obtained only in exchange for the life of her child. Though her relationship with Shaffer appears to have been consensual, there can be little doubt of its exploitative nature. Clifton wielded some power by using her pregnancy as a bargaining chip, but her doing so more effectively discloses the extent of her powerlessness.

Clifton's behavior during and after the pregnancy maps her fragmented social context. Her crime embodies the tortured yearning that Phyllis Wheatley expresses in the epigraph to this chapter—"pant[ing] for Deliverance" epitomizes the actions of the young mother who pressed a razor into the throat of her newborn child.[27] The extremeness of her crime attests to the paradoxes of resistance; no matter how noble the desire for freedom, actually resisting slavery rendered any adherence to the law or conventional morality impossible. Yet accepting enslavement often translated into even greater injustices and moral transgressions. The laws that sanctioned slavery fundamentally outlawed the virtue of enslaved black women. Moreover, the legal system responsible for punishing Clifton itself bore no small measure of culpability in the circumstances leading up to her child's death.

The justice system in 1787 acknowledged the legal freedom of blacks born after 1780 at the same time it upheld the enslavement of those born before the gradual abolition statute. This circumstance is intimately related to the commission of Clifton's crime. Indeed the justice system wrought the legal and ideological void that restricted the liberty of black women like Clifton even as it would attempt to subject them to severe punishments for their efforts to obtain freedom. The contending forces that overlay Clifton's case, however, reflect the vestiges of colonial law and its initial negotiation of unfree labor. Early slave laws did not simply regulate the labor of imported Africans. Rather, it mediated broader aspects of social status and judicial access. As statutes crystallized slavery in the region, race, gender, and sexuality took meaning in ways that inscribed immorality and dishonesty onto black womanhood.[28]

Slavery, Law, and Black Women in Colonial Pennsylvania

Laws governing unfree labor structured social hierarchy in colonial Pennsylvania, and as a consequence slaves and indentured servants occupied the lowest rungs. It would not be the first time—or the last—that a legal system would bear the distinctive characteristics of those holding power and status. Yet the contours of social strata, particularly as they took shape through the evolution of slavery, severely affected black womanhood and black women's experiences in the justice system.

Slavery took root in Pennsylvania in much the same ways it did in colonies like New York and Virginia in that the early status of Clifton's predecessors remained legally ambiguous.[29] Brought by Dutch and Swedish settlers, both enslaved and indentured Africans toiled along the banks of the Delaware River in the 1660s. The prevailing legal code, the Duke of York's Laws, contained only a tacit sanction of slavery. The statute outlawed the enslavement of Christians, though it noted that conversion to Christianity did not grant freedom to blacks who converted after they had been purchased.[30] Upon his arrival, Penn attempted to treat blacks as indentured laborers. He included a provision in the Free Society of Traders stipulating that blacks should serve for fourteen years and thereafter become serfs. Most white Pennsylvanians, however, ignored this provision, and Penn himself instructed his steward in 1685 to purchase blacks to work on his farms because "a man has them while they live."[31]

Although slavery was antithetical to Quaker beliefs, the colonists eagerly purchased slaves. The new masters set blacks to work building houses, shops, wharves, and taverns. The colonial community numbered just over a 1,000 in 1684, so the influx of 150 Africans transformed the cultural landscape. Quakers were not the only immigrants in Pennsylvania and Philadelphia, and they were not immune to the bigoted assumptions firmly held by most European colonists. Rather, because of their tolerance of religious difference and their commitment to pacifism, the Quaker province attracted diverse settlers—both religious and political dissidents.[32] The native population, the Lenni Lenape, had been largely displaced before Penn and the Quakers arrived, but even with their numbers dwindling they too existed on the periphery of colony.[33] This mixed demographic together with the infusion of Africans reconfigured the severity of the more traditional European social divides.

Race, however, did not completely supplant customary class, ethnic, and gender divisions among European settlers; rather, it acted as a modifying agent.[34] The social and economic boundaries that distinguished "good wives" from "nasty wenches" and mistresses from maids were modified in that both types of women were Anglo and Christian. As such, white women were entitled to an elevated status, one separate and above that of Indian and African women. Colonists considered Indian and African women fundamentally barbarous and lascivious.[35] Women like Alice Clifton would occupy the lowest stratum in this emerging society. Landed gentry and yeomen, even indentured European men, shared a more contiguous definition of manhood, which was in opposition to that of indigenous and African men.[36]

Furthermore, Christianity, formerly the nexus of bitter social and political conflicts, served as a marker of civility that distinguished European immigrants from the heathen cultures of Indians and Africans.[37] Even conversion to Christianity could not raise either group to the social status of white colonists or white indentured servants—none of whom could be enslaved for life. As European religious and cultural values colored early impressions of Native and African peoples, so too would they play a key role in how racial differences correlated to criminality.

Specifically, differences in physical appearance and social rituals such as dancing and courting translated, for the English in particular, into unlawful behavior. Public nudity, polygamy, and the worship of deities beyond Christ and the Holy Father were punishable offenses in England.[38] Ethnocentric in their reasoning, Europeans viewed the culture of blacks and reds as one predicated upon lawless, amoral conduct. These notions contributed to a discourse that regarded criminality as characteristic of Native and African identities.[39] Such ideas proved highly damaging for black and red women because Europeans held females to an even stricter moral code. Appearing just as immoral as their men made African and Indian women seem far more depraved.

As African slavery gained a foothold in the colonial economy, slave laws reflected an ideology that increasingly scripted blacks as servile and untrustworthy.[40] Through the manipulation of punishment and protection, the justice system governed slaves and servants and their social conduct among the colonists, and in doing so it positioned blacks as fundamentally inferior. Differences in punishment, particularly the pattern of harsher discipline for blacks, conveyed blacks' powerlessness at the same time it implied greater criminal culpability.[41] Moreover, by failing to distinguish punishment for black men and black women, the laws especially devalued black femininity.

The first legislation to directly address enslaved Africans in Philadelphia serves as an example of how the legal system jeopardized black womanhood. The presentment of 1693 also marks increased apprehension over the growing number of blacks in the colony, and it represents a consolidation of slave owners' power over slave spatial mobility.[42] In Philadelphia and in places like New York, slaves, indentured servants, sailors, and other working-class colonists often labored in close proximity. Likewise the groups patronized common drinking hovels and taverns after hours. Blacks used these sites to assemble and discuss newsworthy events in the city and surrounding environs.[43] Troubled by this camaraderie and by blacks' movement after dark, the Court of Quarter Sessions directed constables and any "person whatsoever, to have power to take up negroes, male or female" found loitering without passes. Offending blacks were to be held overnight in the gaol, without food or drink, and publicly whipped the following morning with thirty-nine lashes "well laid on."[44]

Giving any "person whatsoever" charge over black females caught without passes is especially careless considering the strict social mores governing male and female interaction. Colonists knew that the public sphere often constituted dangerous terrain for women, and they generally proscribed female contact with men save family members and spouses.[45] Pennsylvania lawmakers essentially voided the need to protect black women. The lack of safeguards reinforced the notion that black female bodies had no value in a moral or Christian womanhood sense. They were not women. They were female laborers in much the same ways that African women in Virginia were taxed along with white and African men—as field laborers. White females in Virginia, often laboring women as well, were not "tithable." Despite their work, the legislature regarded them as dependent and in need of protection—these were women destined for domesticity.[46] The racialized gender distinction in the Philadelphia presentment foreshadows the social climate that Clifton would later inhabit as well as the overarching disregard that colonial society held for women like her.

The presentment of 1693 also contributed to the institutionalization of the city's racial hierarchy. Public corporal punishment typified colonial justice, but requiring passes within the city distinguished slaves from white indentured servants, who needed passes only when traveling outside of the county. In addition to erecting a greater social divide between the two groups, the language conflated the identity of blacks with that of slaves. Moreover, in other statutes directing the immediate arrest of individuals, the charge that suspects be denied food is omitted.[47]

Laws enacted between 1700 and 1706 varied criminal punishment and legal protection in accord with the race and gender of perpetrators and victims. The Act for the Trial of Negroes, passed in 1700, mandated separate Negro Courts. Established largely to appease slave owners who bemoaned the loss of labor when their slaves faced criminal charges, the Negro Courts, combining two justices of the peace and six freeholders, expedited cases against slaves. Although convened principally to try slaves, cases brought against all blacks, free and enslaved, male and female, were adjudicated in these courts and done so without benefit of council or of blacks having the right to testify against whites. The Negro Courts relied heavily on corporal punishments rather than extended labor, usually in lieu of fines or financial restitution.[48]

The act also contained harsher punishments for crimes committed by blacks. Blacks were hanged for murder, buggery, and burglary. The sole capital offense for whites was murder. Perhaps worse than the severe punishments, the Act for the Trial of Negroes eroded fundamental distinctions between free blacks and those who were enslaved. In doing so, it not only subordinated all blacks but canonized a separate and unequal system of justice. Moreover, in the same year, the legislature passed an act entitled "For the Better Regulation of Servants." By containing more humane forms of punishment than those available to slaves, it further distinguished the two groups. For example, servants convicted of theft could make financial restitution whereas slaves would be "severely whipped, in the most public place of the township." Such statutes also expose the role of law, race, and labor in establishing power relations in the colony.[49] Whether free blacks suffered those punishments earmarked for slaves is unclear. However, the ambiguity in the legal language, which often identifies blacks and slaves interchangeably, points to a precarious climate for free blacks.[50]

Laws governing sex crimes, rape, and attempted rape in particular, demonstrate the double standard of justice with respect to race and gender. Black men convicted of the rape of a white woman or girl were sentenced to death, while white men received thirty-nine lashes and seven years' imprisonment or extended indentured service. Free and enslaved blacks found guilty of the attempted rape of a white woman or girl were sentenced to castration, whereas white men were publicly whipped or branded. In a series of laws passed between 1705 and 1706, the punishment for the attempted rape of a white woman by a black man was changed to whipping, branding, imprisonment, and transportation—though it remained either whipping or branding for whites.[51]

In spite of the racial specificity for men who raped white women, however, the laws failed to acknowledge the rape of black women altogether.[52] Whether any men were prosecuted for raping black women is unclear, but the omission in the statute educes a number of key social values taking form, the most obvious being that the rape of black women either did not constitute a crime or did not merit serious attention. Lacking clear legal protection, black female virtue succumbed to the void in the sense that black women's bodies became the public domain of both black and white men.[53] The absence of punishment for the rape of black women reflects and serves the aims of slave masters, many of whom sexually exploited female slaves and profited from the assaults by claiming the offspring as property.

These practices had long-standing, disastrous implications for black womanhood and black humanity. Enslavement reduced black women to the level of human breeders, in addition to heightening their vulnerability to sexual assault, but society held black women accountable for their victimization. The double standard in the application of protection and punishment escaped reproach. In fact, popular attitudes promoted the notion that black women were so demoralized and libidinous that it was literally impossible to rape them.[54] A similar kind of cruel logic permeates the sentiments of the chief justice and jurors in Clifton's case. Entrenched bigotry allowed jurors like Edward Pole to assume Clifton's guilt before her trial. Moreover, although the nature of enslavement precluded domesticity and virtue for black women, the judge nonetheless chided Clifton for failing to live up to the proper standards of motherhood.[55]

Yet even as the legal absence of protection posed real threats to black womanhood, the consequences of possessing virtue were almost equally grave. Colonists closely scrutinized sexual morality. Men and women suffered stiff punishment for moral transgressions, but white women bore the brunt of punishments for bastardy, fornication, and other sexual infractions.[56] White rape victims had to be in good moral standing for perpetrators to be prosecuted, as the judiciary dismissed numerous rape charges against black and white suspects based on the common reputation of the accuser.[57] White women also endured special punishments. The ducking stool was a chair set up by the riverside for the purpose of dunking drunk and disorderly women and those charged with being "scolds."[58] This instrument specifically chastised women who transgressed "proper" gender roles and compelled silent submission to the boundaries of womanhood.[59]

Colonial laws erected social inequality along axes of race, gender, and sexuality, but labor and wealth also mediated judicial access. Wealthy whites could more easily avoid imprisonment and whippings by paying fines; indentured servants faced the possibility of fines and extended service as well as imprisonment and corporal punishment.[60] Yet that indentured servants had options beyond physical punishment placed them above blacks even if they enjoyed less power and privilege than free or landowning whites. Provisions made for their protection also distinguish white indentured servants. As early as 1682, criminal codes safeguarded them, noting that it was unlawful to keep any servants "longer than their time" and that "if any Master abuse his Servant on Complaint to the next Justices of the Peace he shall take Care to redress the Said Grievance."[61] Undoubtedly indentured servants suffered injustices, but they enjoyed protections unavailable to most blacks.

Justices relied on extreme whippings to make convicted slaves "examples of Terror to others of their Complexion."[62] The brutality of the whipping post and the pillory instructed not only the offending individual but the entire community who bore witness.[63] Violence in the justice system centrally shaped race relations. It sketched black powerlessness, and the harsh punishments further demoralized blacks — that black women endured them too especially demonstrated their subjection. Being stripped and whipped in a manner similar to black men erased the distinction between male and female — ultimately casting aspersions on black womanhood.[64]

Moreover, the legal system and its administration of justice essentially criminalized the black population. Later statutes would affirm this notion and act as a rationale to expand upon racist legislation. The preamble to laws in 1725 declared that "it too often happens that Negroes commit felonies and other heinous crimes." For the protection of society, laws passed between 1725 and 1726 banned interracial marriage, limited employment for free blacks, and authorized justices to bind out the children of free blacks without parental consent.[65]

These laws, however, could not stem the rising tide of abolition. By 1730, Quaker attitudes toward slave owning and the slave trade changed. The practice was regarded as a "disagreeable" one that members should avoid. In 1743, the importing of slaves became a punishable offense, and by 1758 the practice of owning slaves was condemned by Quakers. The decision to end slaveholding among members, however, did not evolve in a tidy, linear fashion. Conservative members challenged the decisions and frequently broke the rules.[66] Moreover, in addition to liberal Quakers, a small enclave of free blacks continued to agitate against enslavement. They aided runaways and purchased their own freedom as well as that of other blacks.

Over the next forty years, as colonists stepped closer to severing ties with what they considered a tyrannical monarchy, pressing questions about the role of slavery dogged the procession. Yet the institution endured even as Pennsylvania joined other colonies to declare independence. Racism and social inequality persisted long after Philadelphia would serve as the birthplace of the nation. The social dynamics of the city's past informed Alice Clifton's trial, but so too did the emergence of the prison system and the dawning of a newly freed black population in the city.

Alice Clifton's Trial in the Age of American Independence

The Clifton trial occurred just after the legal status of blacks in the state had undergone a radical transformation. Despite the constitutional acceptance of slavery, individual states retained the power to decide how best to mitigate ideals of freedom and democracy. Clifton's trial took place a decade after the American Revolution and just seven years after the Pennsylvania General Assembly passed the Act for the Gradual Abolition of Slavery in 1780. Pennsylvania was at the forefront of the movement to abolish enslavement in the North, and it led such states as New York, Massachusetts, and Connecticut in granting eventual black freedom. The legislation was the culmination of nearly a century of protest by runaway Africans, free blacks, German Mennonites, Quakers, and wage-earning whites who objected to unfair labor competition.[67]

The Act for Gradual Abolition approved black freedom insofar as it abolished slavery, but it stopped far short of advocating racial equality. In many respects the legislation almost perfectly embodied the contending forces underscoring America's dichotomous relationship with democracy and social inequality. The law marks one of the earliest and indeed most radical legislative steps toward disbanding enslavement at the same time that it represents a disappointing initiative that failed to guarantee the actual rights of blacks or to confirm black citizenship.

In effect, the statute accomplished just enough to inspire a conservative backlash and too little to provide blacks with adequate safeguards against it. Moreover, the revolutionary spirit that helped fuel the passage of the act was not so infectious as to dissuade slave owners from attempting to smuggle slaves out of state or to sell them down south to recoup their financial investments.[68] Though all slaves born after the passage of the abolition legislation were to be freed when they reached their midtwenties, the act did little for women like Alice Clifton—except perhaps to intensify their yearning for freedom.[69] Paradoxically, however, though the act did not pave the way for Clifton's freedom, it did allow for her to be tried as if she were a free woman. The 1780 legislation initiated dramatic changes in the state's criminal justice system. Specifically, the act outlawed the practice of using separate Negro Courts and imposed a uniform penal code for people of all races.[70] Given the circumstances, Clifton's case not only offers insight into the impact of slavery on black womanhood but also showcases the impossible position of women like her. Clifton sought to escape slavery by slashing her infant's throat and as a consequence found herself tried by a justice system that allowed for her enslavement even as it dismantled slavery for other blacks.

Ultimately Clifton's trial diagrams black women's powerlessness in the legal system before and in the aftermath of slavery. But the case also marks the complexities of early citizenship and race as well as the limitations and the potential of the justice system in the early republic. That Clifton's sentence appears to have been overturned indicates that a measure of justice was in fact possible. In some respects this gray area typified the administration of justice in the lives of black women following Independence. Its operation was not wholly corrupt but severely hindered by long-standing circumstances and racist attitudes that continued to shape and influence the law. As the justice system moved from corporal punishment to forced labor and confinement it initiated the disproportionate imprisonment of blacks, and within this group, black women proved most vulnerable.

Black Freedom and Institutionalized Incarceration

The experience of blacks in the justice system provides a unique record of the black community's growth and its resistance to legal and social exclusion. Despite the shortcomings of the Gradual Abolition Act of 1780, blacks in the

OF LAW AND VIRTUE

Philadelphia area seized upon its passage to strengthen themselves as well as the greater cause of freedom; though it did not come in Pennsylvania until 1847, when the last slave was freed, nor would it come nationally until 1865.[71] Even as gradual abolition meant that freedom was essentially a generation removed, its passage served as a watershed for black rights and for the black community's growth in Philadelphia. At the close of the eighteenth century the black population totaled 10,274, comprising roughly 3 percent of the state population and 5 percent of Philadelphians.[72] The city's groundbreaking legislation, its continued abolitionist agitation, and its proximity to the Mason-Dixon line all made Philadelphia a refuge for runaway slaves from Maryland, Virginia, and the District of Columbia.[73]

Between 1790 and 1800, the black population in Philadelphia rose from roughly 2,500 to almost 7,000, a growth rate nearly three times that of whites.[74] The increased number also stemmed from an influx of some 900 black Saint Dominguans who arrived with their masters in 1793. These newly arrived immigrants gained their freedom under a clause in the Gradual Abolition Act that declared any slave free after six months of residency in the state of Pennsylvania. Almost immediately indentured for long terms of service, however, these Caribbean immigrants nonetheless quickly joined abolitionist campaigns. Recent scholarship notes that their accounts of the rebellion in Saint Domingue reinvigorated the antislavery efforts of black Philadelphians.[75]

Composed of diverse constituencies, the emerging black community that Clifton was a part of developed in distinct, vibrant, complex ways. Nearly 2,000 free blacks in the city settled in the Seventh Ward, a narrow tract of land in the southeastern part of the city, and in neighboring Southwark and Moyamensing, areas battered by poverty—these were some of the roughest parts of Philadelphia (see map, below).[76] Though nearly a quarter of blacks remained enslaved, the community developed independent social, cultural, and religious institutions.

The founding of the city's first independent black church played a pivotal role in the community's expansion. The black church reflected the evolution of the community and called attention to the racial animosity that necessitated its development.[77] Before 1787, free and enslaved blacks worshipped at Saint George's Methodist Church, a predominantly white institution. As increasing numbers of blacks attended services, however, white parishioners sought to

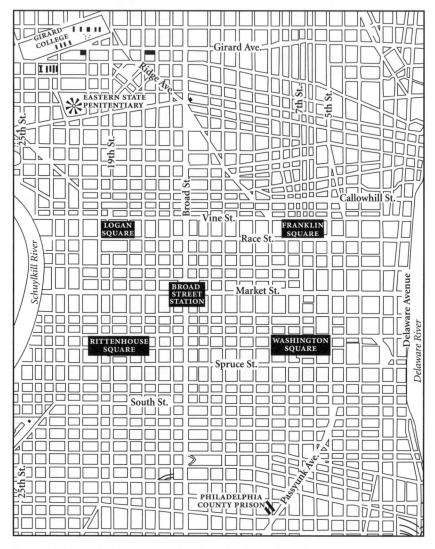

Map of Philadelphia (1892). Courtesy of the Map Collection, Free Library of Philadelphia.

Moyamensing: South of South Street, west of Passyunk Avenue.

Northern Liberties District: Girard Avenue to Vine Street, 6th to Delaware Avenue.

Seventh Ward: Spruce Street to South Street, 25th Street to 7th Street.

Southwark: Four blocks south of South Street, east of Passyunk Avenue.

Tenderloin: Callowhill Street to Race Street, Broad Street to 5th Street.

restrict blacks' seating to the church gallery. Blacks hotly protested the policy, and as they left the church two of Philadelphia's most influential black freedmen, Richard Allen and Absalom Jones, laid the foundation for the Free African Society. From this organization, Allen would found the African Methodist Episcopal Church in 1796, and Jones would establish the First African Church of St. Thomas in 1794.[78]

But even as the evolution of black churches signaled the burgeoning strength of the community, most blacks remained keenly aware of their vulnerabilities. In the decades following gradual abolition, manumitted blacks embraced freedom but had no possessions, no education, and few economic resources. Unlike indentured servants, newly freed blacks received no parting wages, bushels of corn, wheat, or clothing. Some black men cultivated skills such as tanning, carpentry, and blacksmithing that made them viable wage earners in the growing commercial economy, but most blacks performed unskilled labor. As a consequence, formerly enslaved women as well as a sizable portion of black men hired themselves out as indentured servants—often to the very masters who heretofore owned them.[79]

During the early part of the nineteenth century, however, African-American men enjoyed a monopoly in the barbering and catering fields. European immigrants eventually displaced black entrepreneurs during the 1830s and 1840s, but for a time nearly all of the barbers, caterers, and even a substantial number of bakers in the city were African American.[80] Black female labor principally revolved around domestic service, yet a few enterprising women carved out an economic niche by selling goods from pushcarts; the most famous were those who peddled pepper pot stew in the city's public squares. Visitors to the city frequently commented on the musical chants of black women hawking the stew in Head House Square, located near Second and Pine streets.[81] In rare instances black women became successful businesswomen. Rachel Lloyd, for example, a pioneering entrepreneur, operated a restaurant in the Walnut Street Theater from 1808 until she retired in 1850.[82]

Except for small enclaves, however, economic expansion among blacks remained limited and prosperity uneven. Compounding poverty and scant educational opportunities, most whites persisted in their distrust of African Americans. Regarding blacks as criminal, congenitally violent, and rebellious, many held these opinions in spite of blacks' often determined, though largely futile, efforts to allay white fears.[83] When blacks bravely helped bury the city's five thousand dead during a catastrophic outbreak of yellow fever in 1793, Mathew Carey, an Irish immigrant, marred their service by publishing rumors that black nurses and grave diggers robbed corpses.[84] That black community leaders had to publish a pamphlet refuting the charges evidences the breadth of the scandal. The entire ordeal perhaps foreshadowed the fate of race relations in the city.[85]

The Pennsylvania legal system emitted sparks from the friction between increased black agency, revolutionary idealism, and a conservative tradition that prevailed in large sectors of the city. Legislative initiatives between 1790 and 1820 marked increased hostilities toward urban blacks and spotlighted the ways in which race and citizenship collided within the justice system. In a move to disfranchise black men in 1790, conservatives lobbied to have the word *white* included among the qualifications for voting in the state's constitution. Though property-owning blacks retained the right to vote when the statute failed to pass, the move nonetheless testified to intensifying racist attitudes.[86]

The rising presence of blacks engendered mainstream apprehension and inspired more concentrated efforts to curtail it. Whites above all regarded the free black population as not simply a growing nuisance, but also as a growing danger. In 1813, the state House of Representatives sought to ban black migration, especially to Philadelphia.[87] Whites supported the measure and pressed for restrictions on native-born blacks. Although it was defeated, the call to compel any blacks convicted of a crime into forced labor contracts in order to compensate "the persons they may have plundered," demonstrates the fragility of black freedom.[88] James Forten, an affluent African American, denounced the proposed law, charging that it would essentially sell blacks "like the produce of the soil, to the highest bidder."[89] Even as African-American protest helped block the legislation, stereotypes of black criminality underscored mainstream efforts to circumscribe black freedom.

Pennsylvania's legislative history reflected nationwide social strife, especially those tensions surfacing in the urban North.[90] Most citizens celebrated Independence, but the vast changes ushered in by the Revolution and early industrialization created misapprehension and a climate of social unrest. Abolitionism in Pennsylvania became entangled in the web of social transitions because black freedom figured centrally in white middle-class anxieties. Many

OF LAW AND VIRTUE

characterized blacks as "habitual miscreants, cunning, libidinous, brutish, and drawn to insurrection." In anticipation of outrages committed by blacks, whites pressed local and state officials for increased surveillance of the city's black neighborhoods.[91]

The rhetoric of crime control merged with a social movement that, under the auspices of liberty, sought to reform judicial punishment and the penal code. In 1787, Dr. Benjamin Rush published "An Enquiry into the Effects of Public Punishments upon Criminals." His treatise criticized corporal punishment and called for a penal system that classified and housed prisoners in places of "repentance." Rush believed that convict labor would make the institutions self-supporting. Ideally, inmates would till gardens and produce their own food. Rush's ideas reflected European ideals of the Enlightenment and those of Cesare Beccaria, an Italian theorist. Beccaria's condemnation of torture in prisons and of the death penalty resonated with many jurists in the United States. And while Rush's vision never fully materialized—neither did Beccaria's—their ideas ignited changes in Pennsylvania's penal system. Convict labor initially replaced public punishment, and it seemed more humane. Inmates performed a valuable service for the city yet still suffered the humiliation of toiling publicly, in chains, on city streets.[92]

Rather than displaying shame or remorse, however, prisoners routinely assailed passersby with vitriolic tirades. Aside from hurtling lewd and profane insults, foul-mouthed ruffians initiated violent escapes that terrorized local citizens. It was not long before city officials moved convict labor inside the prison grounds. Philadelphia's Walnut Street Jail served as the primary confinement facility.[93] The movement toward penal reform swept through Pennsylvania with tremendous vigor, as it did throughout all the territories of the new Republic. Boston, New York, and New Jersey followed closely behind the penal developments in the Keystone State, and so did the South, which erected a flurry of institutions in South Carolina, Virginia, and Georgia.[94]

Incarceration sought to replace the barbarous punishments of old, but lengthy prison sentences proved quite perilous and arguably just as barbaric. Prisons always existed; however, institutions in the past only housed debtors and those awaiting trial. Ill-equipped for the masses of prisoners committed to its cells, the Walnut Street Jail quickly deteriorated into a late-century house of horrors replete with corrupt jailers, intermingling between the races and the sexes, and a troubling camaraderie among youthful offenders, debtors, those awaiting trial, and seasoned convicted felons.

With alcohol and tobacco available on the premises, and little else in the way of food or clothing rations, inmates and concerned citizens alike bemoaned the degradation occurring daily on prison grounds. In response to these unsettling developments, the Pennsylvania Prison Society for Alleviating the Miseries of Prisoners formed in 1787. Spearheaded by prominent judges, lawyers, journalists, and businessmen, the society's members railed against the squalid conditions of the facility and charged that rather than dissuading unlawful activity, the structure functioned as an institution of higher learning for depraved individuals.[95]

Rumors that the facility suborned prostitution, violence, and otherwise scandalous activities also elicited public condemnation. Escapes from the prison and bloody uprisings, against the backdrop of already aggravated social tensions, precipitated decisive action on the part of the state. Lawmakers responded in 1790 by passing an act to reform and expand the prison and transform its crumbling facilities into the country's first penitentiary. Expanding the Walnut Street Jail to include a separate building for felons, the legislation stipulated that the institution would house convicts, separate the sexes, and force inmates to perform sentences of hard labor on the prison grounds. Heralded as supremely progressive, the act was envisioned by reformers and legislators as a way to turn inmates away from crime through hard work and isolation from the forces that led them astray.[96] The transition promised to curtail rising crime — purportedly caused by runaways and wanton blacks. Walnut Street ultimately failed to accomplish its larger aims, yet the early confinement of blacks at the institution nonetheless holds important clues about race and systemic problems in the justice system.[97]

Although early penology developed under the banner of the Enlightenment, the subtext smacked of repression. Whereas the American Revolution and its spirit of liberty ushered in an end to corporal punishment and gradual abolition, the move to create the country's first penitentiary in 1790 marked a recession of already limited freedoms for blacks. The justice system sent blacks to the penitentiary at a higher rate than whites, and blacks received longer prison sentences. Even with colonial punishment disbanded, again blacks would experience justice as biased and unequal.[98]

OF LAW AND VIRTUE

Jacksonian America and Criminal Biases

Early industrialization, urban expansion, and shifting population demographics profoundly impacted crime in the city. As factories attracted greater numbers of foreign laborers, pockets of ethnic enclaves sprang up throughout the city. Populated mostly by immigrants and punctuated by poverty and cramped living quarters, the new neighborhoods epitomized urban squalor. The landscape also spawned a host of vicious street gangs. With names such as the Killers, the Schuylkill Rangers, and the Bouncers, street gangs plagued Southwark, Moyamensing, and Northern Liberties (see map, above). Delineating turf boundaries, the gangs engaged in bloody rumbles and played a significant role in urban crime. These groups, together with organized bands of street thieves, initiated smash-and-grab robberies in local stores and marketplaces in addition to picking pockets and lifting the watches of law-abiding citizens.[99]

Yet as new forms of crime took root, older forms of vice did not lose their appeal. Brothels, bawdy houses, and raunchy drinking hovels continued to attract patrons, and the sites routinely hosted lawless brawls.[100] Prostitutes and thieves, too, used the spaces to "roll" drunken patrons who took their eyes off of their valuables. Poor blacks and whites participated in this underside of city amusements along with well-to-do white male urban dwellers. Black prostitutes and vice parlors thrived, though they often bore the brunt of mainstream disdain. Even as a traveler noted that black prostitutes enjoyed greater patronage than their "fairer skinned rivals," he hastened to add that he held no objection to a "white man hugging a negro wench to his breast, provided his stomach is strong enough."[101]

Despite their popularity on the vice circuit, however, the majority of black women's crimes—and black men's for that matter—consisted of crimes against property, overwhelmingly theft. This pattern of criminal behavior was not new, but it became much more of a liability at the turn of the nineteenth century, when the judicial system intensified its enforcement of laws against theft and other property crimes. The shift amounted to a "low-level, selective campaign" within the criminal justice system that targeted blacks and other segments of the urban poor.[102] The focus on property crimes amounted to racial profiling in the sense that it rendered African Americans' "possession of almost anything of value grounds for a policeman's accusation of larceny."[103] The new measures in large part reflected broader social aims that sought to contain and simultaneously control blacks, immigrants, and the urban poor.[104] And its effects quickly appreciated. At the close of the eighteenth century, black crime accounted for less than 2 percent of the total crimes in Pennsylvania—a number that grew to just over 3 percent at the start of the nineteenth century and to 9.1 percent by 1864, during the Civil War.[105]

The sentiments motivating the stricter enforcement of larceny laws affected all aspects of criminal justice, but its impact proved most evident in Philadelphia's criminal courts. Blacks in the city found themselves unusually vulnerable to larceny charges and quickly comprised the bulk of Philadelphia's criminal commitments to the Walnut Street Jail. Though African Americans accounted for only 5 percent of the population, they composed nearly 15 percent of the penitentiary population. Of the 3,053 blacks who served terms at Walnut between 1794 and 1835—when the city closed the institution—2,596 received their sentences from Philadelphia courts. Or put another way, though only 35 percent of the inmates serving sentences at Walnut came from Philadelphia County, blacks accounted for almost 85 percent of those placements. Moreover, the Philadelphia justice system convicted blacks at a rate 19 percent higher than whites.[106]

Black women's experiences proved the harshest of all—nearly 72 percent of black women facing Philadelphia juries were convicted. African-American women had fewer cases dismissed than any other group in the criminal justice system, and they accounted for 47.5 percent of the women sentenced to Walnut Street. Black men accounted for only 29 percent of incarcerated men.[107] The pattern of disproportionate imprisonment remained consistent between 1843 and 1851, at which point blacks constituted 44 percent of all convicts in the Philadelphia judicial system, and black women 44 percent of first-time female offenders.[108]

The focus on crimes against property found black women highly vulnerable to arrest and conviction. Because of their concentration in domestic service fields, when they committed a crime there were generally witnesses around willing to testify against them. Conversely, black women were equally—if not more—vulnerable to false accusations of theft, whether the result of misplaced valuables or wage disputes gone awry. Justices and juries more often believed the word of their accusers, typically white employers, than that of black servants.[109] Indeed even the *Philadelphia Ledger* noted this disparity in the case of Mary Ann Costill, a young black woman tried, convicted, and imprisoned

FIG. 1. Edward Clay, *Life in Philadelphia Series* (1820), "Have you any *flesh* coloured silk stockings . . . ?" Courtesy of the Library Company of Philadelphia.

for larceny within two hours in 1841: "Unfortunately for Mary . . . she was not a noted forger or pickpocket or she might have fared better, and perhaps even escaped altogether."[110]

Black women's credibility suffered, too, from the long-standing social stigma concerning their morality—social attitudes that only intensified during the Jacksonian Era. Fundamentally, black women never fit the definition of republican womanhood. Slavery irreparably marred black female virtue, and their continued service in the households of others rather than in their own fundamentally devalued their femininity.[111] The stereotypical notions coloring justice permeated popular culture in the period as well—indeed the two mediums shaped and informed each other. Edward Clay, a political cartoonist, launched his infamous "Life in Philadelphia" series in 1820. The images, evidencing the racial retrogression of the period, ridiculed black womanhood by juxtaposing animalistic caricatures of black women dressed in gowns and attending social events typically considered the domain of white women (fig. 1).[112] The absurdity of black womanhood as depicted in the series mirrored racist stereotypes and social liabilities operating against black women negotiating the justice system. Echoing sentiments like those of the judiciary in Clifton's trial, black woman would continue to be marked as immoral, coarse, and unwomanly.

Obstacles impeded poor whites in the justice system too, though white women obtained release on bail and had cases dismissed more frequently than any other group. These entitlements may have weakened female autonomy, but chivalrous justices nonetheless spared them from serving long terms in prison either awaiting trial or as a part of sentences.[113] In contrast, racism and patriarchy left black women socially and economically vulnerable in ways that even black men might escape. Mainstream bigotry prevented black women from participating in the gallantries available to their white female counterparts. Among the most impoverished constituents in the city, most newly freed black women labored as indentured servants longer than black men. Even after black women served out their terms of indenture, few possessed the necessary job skills that might afford a minimal quality of life.[114]

Black womanhood contended with the chronic stigma of criminality and lawlessness—rhetoric that also functioned as part of a larger campaign against black freedom in the city. But while poor and working-class blacks suffered the brunt of these campaigns, the more elite sectors of the black community did not escape ridicule and racist scrutiny. In accord with the satirical Edward Clay series, early presses lambasted free blacks. In 1828, the *Pennsylvania Gazette*, describing an African-American ball, characterized the partygoers as "ladies and gentlemen of colour, dressed in 'character' in the most grotesque style." Typical of the sardonic pieces published about freed blacks, the article further warned, "It is indeed high time that some serious attention was paid to the conduct and pursuits of the class of persons alluded to . . . at this rate how long will it be before the masters and servants change places?" One elite Philadelphian further quipped that slaves "were a happier class of people" than free blacks, who "taint the very air by their vices and exhibit every sort of wretchedness."[115] A malignant fear pervaded the gibes, and the warnings aptly encapsulated white hostility toward black social mobility.

Throughout the 1830s and 1840s rising tensions over labor competition and abolitionism culminated in a spasm of violent racial clashes. In 1829, a bloody riot erupted after a Philadelphia abolitionist called for immediate emancipation and racial equality. Tempers would again flare in the wake of Nat Turner's rebellion in Southampton County, Virginia, in 1831. Anticipating masses of bloodthirsty blacks flocking to the city, white Philadelphians chastised free blacks for inspiring rebellion in the South and luring migrants to the city, which caused "crime and poverty within the city streets."[116] So intense were the fears that in 1832 the General Assembly narrowly defeated a petition to limit black migration to the city.[117] During routine violent outbreaks, whites attacked blacks on the streets and destroyed abolitionist literature; in one instance the mayor along with corrupt patrolmen and firefighters watched as rioters hurled abolitionist pamphlets into the Delaware River.[118] In 1838, antislavery activists stood by in horror as marauding whites stormed the abolitionists' newly constructed Pennsylvania Hall and burned it to the ground.[119]

Far from embodying brotherly love, Philadelphia was in danger of being torn apart by racial hostilities. As nativist campaigns gained support, an act that was defeated in 1790, nearly fifty years earlier, found a more receptive audience in 1838. With the Pennsylvania legislature's successful inclusion of the word *white* among voting qualifications, the 1838 constitution disfranchised black male voters at the same time it granted universal suffrage to white men.[120] Though working-class whites spearheaded much of the violence and perhaps the most blatant forms of bigotry, white elites, too, found African-American progress disquieting and supported disfranchising black voters.

Moreover, in spite of their antislavery advocacy, many Quakers conservatively delineated the boundaries of social interaction; Quaker meetinghouses, for example, had separate benches for blacks. It is no wonder that rumors that James Forten sought "to wed his daughter to a whiter species" infuriated the most liberal among them.[121] But emotions boiled over among both blacks and whites as the spate of violence took its toll. Robert Purvis, another prominent African American, decried the "wantonness, brutality and murderous spirit" of rioters who assaulted blacks celebrating the emancipation of slaves in the British West Indies in 1842.[122] The violence spilled over into immigrant communities as well. Throughout the 1840s, Irish immigrants battled nativist white Protestants in bloody riots over labor competition, political power, and social and economic access.

Race riots, the proliferation of street gangs, a woefully inadequate police force, and a startling connection between local fire companies and a series of riots in 1853 finally prompted the state legislature to pass the Consolidation Act of 1854. This act disbanded a number of the most corrupt fire companies — those known for intimidating police and citizens and for initiating violence. The statute also consolidated twenty-nine municipalities, which made Philadelphia the second largest city in the nation. More important, the legislation centralized and expanded the police department as a means of establishing law and order. The move ultimately curtailed the violence that had reigned in Philadelphia's streets for the past decade, yet as justice became centralized everyday citizens found their power to initiate prosecutions fundamentally usurped by the powers of the state.[123] Moreover, the virulent bigotry that precipitated the riotous outbreaks accompanied the evolution of justice. Perhaps the *Liberator* described the situation best when it noted in 1858, "All is not dark in Pennsylvania, but the shadow of slavery, oh, how drearily it hangs!"[124]

A Look Backward, A Look Ahead

When Alice Clifton went on trial in 1787, she straddled two worlds: one a society that embraced slavery and corporal punishment and the other a burgeoning republic that embraced freedom and democratic justice by degrees. Her experience bridges the relationship between black womanhood and the legal system before and after abolition. Clifton's case provides a provocative model of the complexities surrounding black female crime and the role of justice in shaping black women's behavior. By positioning blacks in the lowest social rung and by criminalizing blacks through laws and practices that denied their humanity, early laws projected an image of black women as dishonest and licentiousness — ultimately disallowing impartial justice for black female offenders.

As the city's freed black community took form, mainstream Philadelphians responded by expanding and centralizing criminal justice. Certainly a breadth of events accompanied both developments, but the evolution of black citizenship and that of early criminal justice are mutually constitutive. Given the history of slavery and racism in the region, it is no coincidence that blacks received harsher treatment in the legal system. Moreover, Philadelphia's experience following Independence and in the antebellum period parallels social transformations that occur in the city as well as nationwide after the Civil War. African-American citizenship would be constitutionally mandated by 1865, but the legacies of the past severely limited blacks' rights. The legal system would again limit black freedom and citizenship in the urban North, and the discourse would profoundly constrict black women's lives.

OF LAW AND VIRTUE

Chapter Two

SERVICE SAVORS OF SLAVERY:
LABOR, AUTONOMY, AND
TURN-OF-THE-CENTURY URBAN CRIME

*After the war and Emancipation great hopes were entertained by the Negroes
for rapid advancement, and nowhere did they seem better founded than in
Philadelphia.*

— W. E. B. Du Bois, *The Philadelphia Negro: A Social Study,* 1899

WHEN PENNSYLVANIA PASSED THE ACT for the Gradual Abolition of Slavery
in 1780, blacks viewed the legislation as a solid blow against enslavement in
the state, but they also knew its limitations. The act advanced the cause of
black freedom, yet most understood that, nationally, a larger battle loomed.
Secession led most African Americans to believe that swift, sweeping changes
would soon follow. And indeed, change did occur. The Civil War, the Emancipation Proclamation, and a national amendment would end slavery at last, but
the struggle to exercise the rights of citizenship had only just begun. Freedom
was bittersweet. Racist violence and exploitation saturated the years following
Reconstruction.

Indeed, the period bore many revelations about the future of black advancement—revelations that ultimately dashed much of the hope "entertained
by the Negroes." Emancipation and the Fourteenth and Fifteenth Amendments did not wholly fail African Americans, but legislation alone could not
erase the antagonism, bloodshed, and loss that accompanied the processes of
both enslavement and nationwide abolition. Nor would it be enough to clear

the roadblocks that stood in the way of African-American equality.[1] Thus, the period possessed an inherent cruelty. It raised black expectation at the same time that social conditions virtually disallowed the possibility of achieving anything more than second-class citizenship, and at times even this was remote.

Black female crime in turn-of-the-century Philadelphia has its origins in a knot of interwoven yet warring social themes. Striking parallels to the conditions surrounding Alice Clifton's case exist, but turn-of-the-century crime contains important distinctions.[2] Those differences reflected new expectations as well as new limitations. Rather than resulting from a single factor such as poverty or discrimination, black women's crimes took form within a layered context of contested sites. Social bias influenced employment, housing, and justice in a manner that created rigid polarities in black women's lives. Yet at their most elemental level, their crimes took root in the disjuncture between African-American women's expectations and their social reality in the urban North. Black women, those already in the city and those who migrated to Philadelphia, hoped to benefit from better employment opportunities and greater avenues for personal autonomy.[3] Operating under a misconception about the extent of Philadelphia's liberalism, however, few achieved their goals.

When labor, housing, and urban and penal reform are explored, black women's circumstances—and crimes—become visible; how crime functioned in the lives of the perpetrators and in the broader society is also revealed. It is not just that black women were so downtrodden that crime was their only means of survival—though this was certainly true in most instances— but in addition their crimes responded to a volatile mix of systemic bias, abject poverty, and obstructed dreams. Limited employment options and a complicated relationship with servitude lay at the heart of this conflict, but also black women struggled against the regulation of their womanhood in both the black community and mainstream urban sectors.

Servility and Fannie Smiley's Life of Crime

Discrimination permeated black women's lives. Their exclusion from the city's expanding commercial industries was a particularly devastating blow. Profound resentment accompanied their acceptance of positions as domestic servants, the work most readily available to black women.[4] Domestic service work was labor intensive and low paying, and black women complained bitterly that it reminded them of slavery.[5] Cleaning at the behest of white employers seemed like a step backward at a time when other groups—working white women and newly arrived immigrants especially—found ways to move forward. Factory work was not without exploitation and drudgery, but it nonetheless held a certain cachet among working women in the city, and black women wanted very much to participate.[6]

Domestic service powerfully contributed to the social context of black female crime by virtue of both poverty and proximity. Often the most poorly compensated laborers in the city, black women proved to be among the most isolated as well. Economic conditions forced many to live in substandard housing in dangerous parts of the city—areas rife with crime and the vicissitudes of urban poverty. Moreover, domestic service kept black women impoverished, though simultaneously the positions afforded easy access to valuables in employers' homes and nearby shops. Having few viable legal alternatives, some black women decided to use crime to improve their lives. African-American women accounted for roughly 4 percent of those arrested and held in the county prison.[7] Larceny, mostly petty theft, accounted for the majority of black female crime, and within this segment, black servants represented the majority of black female offenders in the city. Primarily driven by economic necessity, most stole sporadically.

Yet social circumstances also gestated a core of black women who used "servant theft" as their primary source of income. Servant-thieves donned servants' uniforms to gain access to the homes of potential employers, usually those of middle- and upper-class whites—homes they burglarized. Fannie Smiley, a black woman in turn-of-the-century Philadelphia, was the quintessential servant-thief. In 1887, Warden Michael Cassidy characterized Smiley as "thoroughly bad, commenced by being in the House of Refuge," a correctional institution for wayward minors. Though hardly an impartial opinion, given Smiley's prolific criminal career, clearly the warden's disparaging comments held more than a modicum of truth. By the age of twenty-two, when she served her first sentence at Eastern State Penitentiary, Smiley had already served three prior sentences—one at the Philadelphia County Prison, one at the House of Refuge, and one at the House of Correction.[8] Though her prior convictions were one- and two-month sentences in smaller detention facilities, her "theft of property valued at $55, from the home of Charles A. McCall" garnered Smiley her first lengthy sentence—two years and three months at Eastern.[9]

By all accounts Smiley was a model prisoner. Under Philadelphia's commutation law she received an early release on February 2, 1889.[10] Even the cynical Warden Cassidy noted that "she has been a well behaved prisoner," adding that Smiley "earned eighteen dollars while here."[11] In spite of her demonstrated work ethic at the penitentiary, however, seven months later Smiley was arrested and convicted again for "the larceny of a box containing $200, the property of Fielding Ford."[12] After serving another eighteen-month sentence, Smiley left Eastern on February 19, 1891.

Prison dockets show that Smiley was single, had no children or dependents, and was able to read and write.[13] According to her intake description, Smiley had no physical ailments or chronic addictions that might otherwise impede her securing and maintaining legal employment. Yet Smiley stayed true to her occupation—listed as "thief" in prison intake records—and was arrested again in 1900. In this instance, Smiley posed as a servant in two West Philadelphia homes. Hired by Percy V. Barber of 4911 Walton Avenue and one L. L. Prince of 505 South Forty-fifth Street, she relieved both employers of clothes, "cut glass," and silverware—the total number of items valued at two hundred dollars.[14] Although this case netted Smiley and the three fences that resold her stolen goods sentences at Eastern, she was arrested again and served another sentence at Eastern in 1908.[15] Apparently this was her last stay at the penitentiary. On August 11, 1909, Smiley was transferred to the State Hospital for the Insane at Norristown, Pennsylvania, the records of which are no longer available.[16] Whether Smiley feigned insanity, as many did to escape the severity of the penitentiary, is unknowable, yet her record of incarceration yields important evidence about black female crime.

Smiley was among a cadre of black women who made the decision to use crime, particularly servant theft, as their primary source of income. Smiley does not typify the majority of black female criminals in the city, 69 percent of whom were first-time offenders, but her record testifies to the existence of women who refused to obtain legal employment, such as it was for black women at the turn of the century.[17] Roughly 13 percent of the black women at Eastern had "thief" listed as their occupation.[18] Included in Smiley's cohort were women like Johanna Twiggs and Sadie Shotwell. Twiggs, a Virginia migrant and servant-thief, was a seven-time recidivist at Eastern, while Shotwell, alias Sadie Smith, operated as a "professional shoplifter."[19]

Prison administrators probably listed the women's employment as thieves under a legislative initiative to track members of the "crime class," but the women's own criminal records nonetheless demonstrate a pattern of theft in place of work—primarily in lieu of domestic service.[20] African-American women's experience in Philadelphia suggests that the decision to steal rather than work represented their frustration with employment discrimination as much as it evidenced a misguided effort to achieve social and economic autonomy. In masquerading as servants to gain access to wealthy white homes, career thieves provide a view of black women's own understanding of their prescribed social roles as well as the lengths to which some would go to defy those notions. To some extent the crimes suggest a hidden transcript that seems to contest racist limitations at the same time that it flies in the face of the prevailing ideology of respectability. The ways that servant-thieves decided to break the law demonstrates an alternative reasoning that has political and social characteristics unique to the perpetrators' experience.[21] In many ways servant-thieves echo, if not embody, the sentiments of one despairing black woman in 1907: "Unless I am willing to engage in a few menial occupations, in which the pay for my services would be very poor, there is no way I can earn an honest living."[22]

Career thieves, however, were exceptional. Their records were far more extensive than those of most black female criminals in the city. Yet their socioeconomic status typified the profile of black female criminals, and indeed, that of most single black women in the city. Between 1880 and 1910, the average black female criminal in Philadelphia was twenty-eight years old, single or widowed, semiliterate, and among the lowest paid workers in the city.[23] The overwhelming majority of their crimes, nearly 70 percent, were theft and other crimes against property. Roughly 5 percent were vice crimes such as prostitution or the illegal distribution of alcohol, while 23 percent consisted of violent crime, predominantly assault and battery and manslaughter.[24] Forty-three percent of the black female criminals at Eastern were southern migrants.[25] This statistic represents the dislocation of southern migrants as much as it reveals shifting demographics within the city's black community.

Southern Migration and Urban Aspirations

Following Emancipation, the black population in Philadelphia doubled, grow-ing from 22,147 in 1870 to just under 40,000 by 1890. Within this early wave of southern migrants, black women between the ages of twenty-five and twenty-nine migrated at nearly twice the rate of black men in the same category, out-numbering them by 2,500 in 1890. By 1910, black women outnumbered black men by 5,597.[26] Why black women chose to leave their homes for parts north is intimately related to the goals and expectations of those black women already residing in northern cities. As black women adapted to citizenship, the recla-mation and reconfiguration of their womanhood figured centrally in the pro-cess.[27] Having been victimized and morally stigmatized during enslavement, African-American women were eager to shake off this legacy. Slavery and work-ing conditions played a large role in the manufacture of negative myths about black female lasciviousness. Therefore labor, both what black women did and how they were compensated, significantly factored into how their woman-hood, citizenship, and autonomy would be actualized.[28]

Leaving southern rural and urban areas represented several interrelated goals. Aside from agricultural work, the only employment readily available to black women in the South was domestic service, an occupation that held real dangers for black women and girls. Contract and wage-labor disputes routinely culminated in violent assaults on black women, and their proximity to white men made them especially vulnerable to on-the-job sexual harassment and rape.[29] Moreover, justice was impossible to obtain, as southern judges made no secret of their contempt and disregard for black rights—a judge in one case stated explicitly, "This court will never take the word of a nigger against the word of a white man."[30] In this particular instance, a black domestic had re-fused the sexual advances of her employer. When her husband sought redress for the affront he was cursed, beaten, arrested, and forced to pay a twenty-five-dollar fine.[31]

Because it offered limited employment alternatives and few avenues for protection, domestic service in the South was highly perilous terrain, one that black women hoped to escape by heading north.[32] As late as 1904, Fannie Barrier Williams, a black northern activist, bemoaned the "significant and shameful fact" that she remained in constant receipt of letters from "the still unprotected colored women of the South." Women begging her to "find employment for their daughters . . . to save them from going into the homes of the South as servants, as there is nothing to save them from dishonor and degradation."[33] Perhaps even more telling than the letters Williams received was that single black women elected to make the journey north at all. Whether aided by employment agents who charged exorbitant fees or buoyed by news of financial opportunities, black women left rural and urban parts of the South, boarding trains and steamboats to reach northern destinations. Possessing little money and few personal belongings, some had the addresses of employers they expected to find upon arrival, while those departing without the aid of an agent made the trip planning simply to make do once they arrived.[34]

Black women's migration serves as both a literal and symbolic refusal to accept the wholesale disregard of their humanity and self-worth.[35] The movement also reflected a rejection of economic exploitation. Rather than risk the dangers of domestic service for low wages or end up essentially reenslaved by debt peonage contracts, 46 percent of black women surveyed in the early part of the twentieth century stated that they migrated to Philadelphia in search of better jobs and fair wages. At the very least, they knew that northerners paid almost twice what southerners did for domestic work.[36] Moreover, female southern migrants were not alone in their aims. Black women in the North, too, contended with the linkage between their womanhood and illicit sexuality. Like their sisters in the South, they hoped that the end of enslavement would lead to greater autonomy and greater protections—ideally akin to the safety and courtesies enjoyed by white women.[37]

Philadelphia appeared to be an ideal location for a number of reasons: it housed the largest population of free blacks before the Civil War, played a pivotal role in the abolitionist movement, and was fast becoming the industrial hub of the nation. In addition, employment for women and girls rapidly expanded and diversified. Black women, native Philadelphians, and migrants alike, hoped to move past domestic service into industry. Factory work held greater appeal in that it seemed more likely to distinguish them as wage earners. They went to work, put in a certain number of hours or produced the requisite number of items, and received compensation for their labor. Workers in a factory did not appear to suffer the same level of surveillance or supervision from white employers as domestic servants did. Young black women in particular hoped to escape what they considered menial labor, in the process avoiding the isolation and degradation that routinely accompanied such appointments.[38] Yet black women who chose Philadelphia as the place to begin anew found themselves again subject to an intricate matrix of exclusion and exploitation.

Racism, Philadelphia-Style

Although substantially different from those of the South, the cultural politics of the City of Brotherly Love proved racism to be both multifaceted and enduring. While plainly based on long-established stereotypes, urbanization and social reform added new dimensions to the "ever changing same."[39] Undergoing remarkable physical and technological expansion, the city's nineteenth-century landscape evolved from small brick homes and horse-drawn carriages to a skyline punctuated by stately concrete buildings, electric railway cars, and telephone wires. By the turn of the century, public waterworks and expanding roadways made Philadelphia the country's third largest urban center. Yet the fruits of this growth did not reach all of the city's inhabitants. The city's railroad, iron, and coal industries selectively employed native-born whites and, despite sporadic nativist campaigns, greater numbers of European immigrants. African Americans, displaced from traditionally held skilled and unskilled labor positions, found themselves barred from the expanding industrial and manufacturing fields.[40]

Racist exclusion was a constant feature on shop floors; both native-born blacks and newly arrived southern migrants found it a barrier almost impossible to surmount. Regardless of their level of skill and persistence in seeking better employment, rejection often proved as swift as it was bigoted. As a shopkeeper explained to one black applicant, "I wouldn't have a darky to clean out my store much less stand behind the counter."[41] When blacks did secure factory work, white employers often hired them only in an effort to dissuade immigrant and native-born white labor from striking. Even in this limited capacity African-American women faced alienation.

During a cloak workers' strike in 1890, a white factory owner, Gabe Blum, replaced Russian Jews lobbying for better wages with African-American men. Denying allegations that he hired black men only to discourage strikers, Blum asserted that African-American men, among the most "honest, intelligent and industrious" of workers, were often deprived of better jobs "because of no other reason than that their skin is black."[42] Unfortunately, his convenient sympathy for African Americans excluded black women. Anxiety over their increased presence together with competition from white ethnics, many of whom refused to work alongside blacks, culminated in a growing distrust and criticism of black female laborers in the North.[43] Perhaps indicative of these feelings, Blum deferred the employment of African-American women. Although he employed white women for piecework at home, Blum implied that black women lacked necessary job skills, claiming he would employ them "as soon as they become competent to do the work." This rhetoric—and suggestions of their limited abilities—plagued black women seeking diversified employment. The company eventually took applications from African-American women, but the number of positions offered could not accommodate the demand, and there is no record of extensive hires.[44]

White women, despite the restrictive gender codes of the era, enjoyed the lion's share of new jobs available to urban women.[45] Of the total population of working women in Philadelphia, 46 percent held jobs in manufacturing fields, 11 percent worked in trade and transportation industries, 38 percent were employed as house servants or domestics, and 5 percent occupied professional service positions. African-American women, 90 percent of whom worked as domestics, accounted for approximately 1 percent of those employed in industries outside domestic service and for 9 percent of those employed in manufacturing or mechanical fields.[46] The Reverend W. A. Lynch, in his address to the Women's Quaker City Beneficial Society, lamented in 1898, "One of the sad conditions of colored women in this city is that they are barred from avenues of industry that are generally open to other classes of females." Lynch continued, "Nowhere in stores, shops, factories or like places do we find colored girls or women; neither do we find them as clerks or stenographers in the business marts of our great city."[47] Lynch adequately assessed African-American women's employment at the close of the century and beyond.[48]

Yet while discrimination hindered blacks' ability to break into new fields of employment, the actual process of locating potential jobs further complicated matters. In certain cases, southern migrants entered labor contracts before they arrived in Philadelphia, usually agreeing to work for two or three months without pay to cover the cost of their journey. These young women might find themselves locked into wholly unsuitable or exploitative arrangements.[49] For women who roughed the journey north on their own or for those already in the city, part of the difficulty in locating work stemmed from the nature of racism and discrimination in the city itself. Prejudice in Philadelphia possessed opaque complexities that heightened African-American vulnerability. Most white Philadelphians generally abhorred blatant displays of bigotry, and the state supported laws protecting civil rights. But laws such as the Act to Provide Civil Rights for all People in 1887, which prohibited discrimination against blacks in hotels, restaurants, and businesses, were rarely enforced. Legislation did little to change daily practices and racist attitudes. African Americans navigated an urban landscape marred by uncertainty.[50]

Although few signs read "Colored Only," African Americans in search of work, restrooms, housing, and public recreation often wandered into business establishments and neighborhoods unsure of how they would be received. In some instances, blacks and whites enjoyed recreational sports, pubs, and other forms of entertainment together. In other cases blacks were, as Du Bois noted, "liable to insult or reluctant service in some restaurants, hotels and stores, at public resorts, theatres and places of recreation; and at nearly all barber shops."[51] Racial violence also factored into daily experiences in the city, as blacks crossed paths with groups of white toughs who might throw watermelons, racial slurs, or fists.[52]

Ultimately, residency in Philadelphia demanded that African Americans learn and adhere to a set of unspoken racial codes—subjecting many newly arrived migrants to the dangerous practice of trial and error. Under the circumstances, black women seeking employment had to be careful about where and how they found work. Crooked employment agencies were rumored to procure inmates for brothels and bawdy houses. Reputable agencies were in short supply.[53] Most black women secured jobs by word of mouth, but others occasionally undertook the more daunting task of knocking on doors. Job hunting in this manner, however, was a frightening ordeal, one that some black women tried to avoid—partly because of the potential dangers unknown employers posed and partly out of a fear of rejection.[54] But refusals became more frequent. The nation's economy fluctuated throughout the period, and economic upheavals such as the depression of 1893, as well as two prior panics in 1873 and 1883, resulted in widespread poverty and unemployment. The conditions only exacerbated racial tensions already prevalent in the city's job market.[55]

Even in areas of domestic service, where employers reportedly clamored for black female labor, rumblings of shifting social attitudes darkened the horizon. Just as blacks arrived in the city in droves, so too did ever-increasing populations of European immigrants.[56] They competed with blacks for jobs and, like native-born whites, often refused to work with black women, making black employability that much harder. Mainstream notions about black womanhood and crime, too, influenced their ability to obtain work. Black women experienced increasing hostility from white employers, who routinely complained of their laziness, dishonesty, and incompetence in handling the simplest household chores. Though overall public sentiment affirmed the reliability of "colored domestics," a growing number of whites hired ethnic immigrants, attesting to their greater efficiency. One black domestic noted during an interview in 1899, "If the mistresses had bad luck with one colored girl they won't have another. They think all colored is alike."[57] Antagonism toward black female domestics, however, may not have been purely symptomatic of growing white racism.

The sentiments also may have been a reaction to black women's own response to their limited employment options and evidence of their effort to exert autonomy within the domestic service field. In some instances, to offset unfair wages and harsh working conditions, black servants routinely claimed cooked leftovers, scraps, and a portion of "pantry staples." Laundresses occasionally "borrowed" their clients' garments for church services and other special occasions. Moreover, though many desperately needed work, greater numbers may have refused to work at the expense of their self-respect.[58] As one domestic pointed out, though "long-service" was generally preferred and more lucrative, "sometimes you can't stay at places; some of the ladies an' gentleman's not very pleasant."[59] Typically, most appointments lasted a little less than a year and a half.[60] Rather than accepting hostile or exploitative treatment from white employers, black women might have been more forthright in expressing their discontent with unfair employment practices and more proactive in leaving positions where the treatment was unsuitable.[61]

Despite a relatively taut job market, many black women sought work affording both status and a degree of personal autonomy. Parallel to developments in cities like New York, Boston, and London, domestic service evolved into a more professionalized field. In many ways, this helped make the work more palatable. "Grades of Service" distinguished household domestics—so-

FIG. 2. Frank Leslie's *Illustrated*, "War of the Races in the City of Brotherly Love—Colored Washerwomen Berating Chinese Laundrymen" (1875). Courtesy of the Library Company of Philadelphia.

cially and financially—in Philadelphia. Female domestic work had roughly twelve subdivisions ranging from bell or errand girls to children's nurse to general household servants.[62]

More specialized grades such as laundering and cooking offered better wages and more leisure time for women, though the jobs were labor intensive. Backbreaking in its requirements, laundry work included picking up and delivering clothes, washing the articles with soap made of lye, hanging them to dry, and pressing out wrinkles with heavy irons heated over coal and, later, gas-burning stoves. Yet laundresses, usually married women with children, enjoyed the freedom of working from home and could often solicit the help of children and other family members.[63] But black women's dominance in this area was also being jeopardized as a small but industrious number of Chinese immigrants sliced into a rather thin market (fig. 2).[64] Cooks also enjoyed greater personal freedom as well as overall prestige. Good cooks were revered for their culinary skills in preparing food and also for the skill required to regulate cooking flames. Waitresses also received decent wages, but positions in the better-paying establishments typically required a high degree of literacy and a basic knowledge of china, silverware, and dining room etiquette.[65]

The range of positions among cleaning women depended less on the type of work performed and more on the employment circumstances of the household. Philadelphia's well-to-do families employed large domestic staffs. These jobs paid the best wages, furnished decent living accommodations, and comprised more manageable duties since chores were divided among several servants. Such a domestic not only enjoyed a greater degree of leisure time, but also had greater opportunity to save her earnings. Annie Harvey, a black woman who worked for the Fisher family, one of Philadelphia's oldest elites, managed to save five thousand dollars, which she bequeathed to her church after her death in 1888.[66] Most households, however, employed a general servant or housekeeper and hired out specialized chores such as laundering and cooking. This type of service, too, employed a "better class" of domestics—better at least in comparison to a woman who worked as the sole employee in a household.[67]

Newly arrived and single native-born black women typically found themselves toiling in the "roughest single-handed places."[68] This type of servant, as one black woman explained, "drags the ashes, tends the furnace, cleans the front, and does every single thing."[69] Considered among the lowest and least desirable grades, general service, in addition to being labor intensive, paid the lowest wages, averaging around three dollars per week. Yet black female domestics' earnings in general were extremely low, both when compared to black and white men's wages and to those of white female domestics. Whereas black men employed in domestic service could earn on average weekly salaries ranging from three dollars to eight dollars, the typical black woman's weekly earnings fell between two dollars and four dollars. White female domestics annually earned an average of ten dollars more than black female domestics. White male domestics received higher wages than black women, black men, and white women, in addition to occupying almost all of the industrial and manufacturing jobs available.[70]

The impact of employment discrimination and racial prejudice in the city had profound implications for the quality of an African-American woman's life as well as for her proximity to urban crime. Most single domestics boarded with their employers, but roughly 40 percent of single black women went home in the evening.[71] Rooms in cramped lodging houses cost from three to six dollars per month, so black domestics who did not work as live-ins were forced by their low incomes, the cost of living, and de facto housing discrimination to live in the Fourth, Fifth, Seventh, and Eighth wards of the city, areas that contained some of Philadelphia's worst slums.[72] The Seventh Ward, one of the oldest black neighborhoods in the city, housed Philadelphia's largest concentration of African Americans in the 1890s (see map). African Americans experienced some spatial displacement as a result of fluctuations in immigrant settlement and a small measure of black residential mobility. But by 1910, of the city's thirty-nine wards, the Seventh was still home to the largest concentration of African Americans, 11,553.[73]

The Seventh Ward was the heart of Philadelphia's black community. AME Mother Bethel, one of the oldest black churches in the country, sat on the corner of Sixth and Lombard, while the long-standing Institute for Colored Youth was on the corner of Ninth and Bainbridge Streets. These two cornerstone institutions were, however, not far from an infamous black-owned saloon just south of Eighth Street on Lombard.[74] Blacks in the Seventh and adjacent wards often inhabited dark courtyards, narrow alleyways, and sewage-flooded streets.[75] Streets like Alaska, Minster, and the notorious Middle Alley were rife with illicit pastimes such as drinking, gambling, and prostitution.[76] The high concentration of single black women in such neighborhoods may have contributed to the mainstream's association of black women with crime. Du Bois characterized these sections of the city as "noisy and dissipated" and having an abundance of "Negro loafers" crowding the street corners day and night.[77] Still though, Philadelphia's streets in general were filled with the sound of firecrackers, fistfights, and domestic disputes. As one historian noted, gunfire "remained as much a part of the street scene as cobblestones and manure."[78] Yet somehow gunfire proved to be less of a danger to ward residents than the condition of the housing itself.

Though Philadelphia enjoyed a reputation for being the "City of Homes," housing conditions rapidly deteriorated by the turn of the century as masses of blacks and European immigrants streamed into the city. Streets decorated with large homes owned by the city's well-to-do stood prominently on main avenues and thoroughfares, obscuring the smaller houses of middle-class families and skilled laborers. Behind all of these, and least obvious, were the back-alley shacks and shanties of the poor. Philadelphia's housing conditions did not rival those of New York or Baltimore in decrepitude, but its slums still ranked among the worst in the nation.[79]

A 1904 exposé on conditions in the Seventh Ward revealed a disturbing element of urban life. The report cited crumbling, overcrowded, and unsanitary housing. Yet despite the city's miserable housing conditions, the study described black homes as being meticulously tidy. Researchers attributed this phenomenon to the high concentration of domestics in the neighborhood,

SERVICE SAVORS OF SLAVERY

perhaps failing to realize that despite the dilapidated conditions of the buildings, black women tried to create good homes.[80] But black women's best efforts could hardly counter the structures or the spatial arrangement that contributed to urban hazards.

To accommodate the growing population of working poor, the backyards of larger houses were subdivided and filled in with back-to-back rear dwellings. A seedy combination of "Trinities" and shanties culminated in a web of isolated courtyards and back alleyways.[81] The Trinity houses, containing one room per floor, might have suitably housed a small family but were poor shelters for the masses that often crowded into them. Moreover, tumbledown wooden shacks offered decrepit living conditions exceeded only by the damp cellar dwellings that existed throughout the slums. These cellars usually housed bakeries or butcher shops that also stored goats, pigs, chickens, and geese. Business traffic further congested already overcrowded tenements and rear walkways.[82] In 1895, 171 such alleys and courts filled the Fifth Ward, and 88 existed in the Fourth Ward. A single block in the Seventh Ward bounded by South, Lombard, Fifth, and Sixth Streets contained 15 alleys.[83]

Filled with human waste and refuse, the maze of isolated thoroughfares and overpopulated buildings generated a profusion of hazards, including the spread of disease. The structures were prone to deadly fires such as the one in 1897 that claimed the lives of a black woman and an infant who was sleeping nearby in a box in the kitchen.[84] Moreover, the alleys and courtyards provided ideal havens for unseemly urban pastimes. The Seventh Ward in particular served as home to notorious slum districts in whose chaotic and dangerous back corners an array of thieves and streetwalkers lurked.[85]

Although it is difficult to gauge the emotional impact of urban poverty, reports of African-American women's suicides may be one indication. The suicides and attempted suicides of young African-American women like Victoria Washington were routinely documented in the local press. Washington, a twenty-one-year-old migrant from Virginia, was found dead in her home with the gas "turned on at the full." Washington committed suicide after receiving notice from her employer that her position would be terminated. Other black women like Alverta Richards overdosed on laudanum, while Mattie Woods was found dead after "accidentally" ingesting a cup of mercury chloride.[86] Though the specific reasons behind each suicide are impossible to pinpoint, the recorded deaths suggest that large numbers of black women may have suffered from depression and, most likely, a profound sense of isolation. In addition to living in abject poverty, the work schedules of most domestics, who had only one afternoon or alternate Sundays off, left little time to cultivate a social life or to establish extensive support networks outside work.

In an attempt to respond to black women's impoverished conditions and their inability to gain admission to most white almshouses, AME Mother Bethel Church established a home for "fallen women" in the heart of the Seventh Ward.[87] The Protestant Episcopal Church of the Crucifixion also established a shelter on Lombard Street. According to the rector, Henry L. Phillips, "Here a door for homeless women and children, free of charge, and without regard to race or creed, has been kept open."[88] Despite their charitable initiatives, however, the almshouses could not accommodate the numbers of destitute black women.

Varieties of Crime

Exclusion and economic disenfranchisement often thwarted black women's ability to maintain anything above a substandard quality of life. Not only were black women barred from the opportunities presented by expanding industries, but also, even in areas of employment that most found degrading, they faced competition and marginalization. Furthermore, domestic service played a central role in their poverty and alienation and fundamentally influenced their crime. Some 68 percent of black women imprisoned at Eastern worked in some form of domestic service at the time of their arrest, while 52.5 percent were employed in the lowest grade as general servants.[89] The high percentages reflect black domestics' disadvantage in the justice system as well as in the social and political economy of the city.

As in the revolutionary era, black domestics at the beginning of the twentieth century often received convictions solely on the word of their employers and appeared before white magistrates, prosecutors, and juries. Sometimes charges of theft stemmed from misplaced items, but in other cases, as one black washerwoman explained, "White folks tend to lose what they ain't never had."[90] In still other instances, accusations of theft occurred when domestics and their bosses did not see eye to eye on the servants' habit of claiming table scraps and other *disregarded* household goods. But whether their arrests resulted from domestics taking too many liberties with leftover food and "borrowed" clothes or from bald theft, most of the servants arrested stole coats, shoes, and everyday household items such as umbrellas and watches. Others stole china or pilfered milk containers and food.[91]

The stolen merchandise showcases the conjunction of poverty and opportunity. Perhaps the thefts involved a fair amount of envy and greed, but the crimes perpetrated by domestics rarely indicated an organized pattern of thieving. The crimes differed from those committed by women like Fannie Smiley and Johanna Twiggs. Most servants were first-time offenders accused of stealing from their employers rather than women posing as servants for the sole purpose of burglarizing white homes. In rare cases, however, domestics committed more serious offenses in an effort to conceal their thefts: for example, women like Ida Washington, a Virginia native, who was convicted of larceny and arson in 1900, at the age of twenty-two. Washington created a great deal of trouble "by playing off robber and setting fire to the house" where she worked.[92] In a similar case, Louisa Brooks, though acquitted of arson, was convicted of stealing a dress from her employer. Brooks, a thirty-two-year-old Virginia native and a first-time convict, received a three-year sentence of hard labor at the penitentiary.[93]

Though most servants committed their theft at their place of employment, some shoplifted from markets, boutiques, and department stores. Hannah Primus, a twenty-eight-year-old native-born Philadelphian, worked as a servant before her arrest for stealing three jerseys from a store on Frankford Road in 1888 (fig. 3).[94] Primus served eleven months before being discharged in early January of 1889.[95] In rare instances, black women engaged in widows' pension scams or other forms of pension fraud.[96] Throughout the Seventh Ward, petty insurance societies preyed upon poorer blacks by selling "sick and death benefit" policies at higher prices than those sold by regular companies and those available to whites.[97] Perhaps because of their dubious nature in black neighborhoods, some African Americans regarded the companies as fair game. Whatever the case, these women—women such as Virginia Henry, Elizabeth Short, and Lizzie Smith—often teamed up with African-American men to make false affidavits in order to obtain money from widows' pension policies.[98] In 1892, Virginia Henry was convicted with Isaiah Miller for making a false

FIG. 3. Hannah Primus, *Rogues Gallery Books* (1888). Courtesy of the Philadelphia City Archive.

claim for widow's pension money—in Miller's case a false affidavit to assist Henry in illegally obtaining the funds.[99] Harriet Lee, a black woman from Schuylkill County, Pennsylvania, was convicted of perjury on a pension claim in 1898. The former scrubwoman, age fifty and a first-time offender, served nine months at Eastern.[100]

But while most black women were sent up for first-time petty theft cases, black female criminals paralleled the larger penitentiary population with a 30 percent rate of recidivism. As a group, recidivists shared a number of traits. Most were either servant-thieves or shoplifters, and nearly all adopted aliases as a means of dodging the authorities, who typically doled out longer prison sentences for repeat offenders. A first-time larceny conviction at Eastern usually garnered a twelve- to sixteen-month sentence. Members of the "crime class" —hardcore recidivists—usually received eighteen-month to three-year sentences.[101] The rate of black female recidivism largely reflected the actions of career criminals like Amanda Powell (fig. 4).

Early in her career, Powell, a native of Cumberland County, Pennsylvania, learned the importance of misinforming authorities. All but mastering the art

SERVICE SAVORS OF SLAVERY

FIG. 4. Amanda Powell, *Rogues Gallery Books* (1888). Courtesy of the Philadelphia City Archive.

of deception, she operated under the alias Annie Wilson in 1881, when she served her first larceny sentence at Eastern.[102] Though intake registers listed her formal occupation as a servant under the name Wilson, Powell had already served two terms at the Philadelphia County Prison for theft. If the true nature of her criminal record had surfaced, Powell might have entered Eastern as a "thief" and received a sentence longer than a year. However, it was not long before Powell was characterized as a thief in penitentiary registers. In addition to her yearlong term at Eastern in 1881, Powell would serve two more sentences at the facility. With an accomplice, also an African-American woman, Powell returned to the penitentiary on another larceny conviction in 1888.[103] After serving eleven months with commutation, less than three months later Powell was again convicted and sentenced to another eighteen months at the penitentiary for theft.[104]

Though extensive arrest records might raise questions about thieves' efficacy in their chosen line of work, comparisons of career thieves' attire upon arrest with that of other black female criminals suggest that crime allowed women like Powell to enjoy the finer things in life, including warm coats,

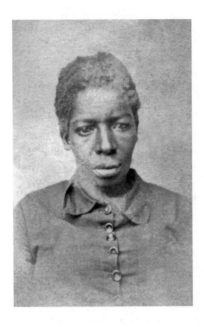

FIG. 5. Lizzie Brooks, *Rogues Gallery Books* (1880). Courtesy of the Philadelphia City Archive.

watches, earrings, and brooches (figs. 4, 5). Imprisoned with substantial sums of money on their persons, the benefits of their profession were palpable. But the consequences of the lifestyle were equally substantial. Prison life was brutal, and black female inmates often died from illnesses while serving their sentences; others took their own lives. Some went mad.[105] Yet in spite of the dangers and risks, crime offered real financial incentive and, perhaps more important, a means to be self-determining without having to acquiesce to the strictures of mainstream society.

Taking Back Their Bodies

Whether black career criminals or everyday working black women, few could resist the avenues of entertainment that city life offered. Economic factors typically precluded poorer blacks' participation in "reputable" mainstream forms of entertainment. Yet poor and working-class blacks carved out a unique urban culture and community, one that expressed itself through fashion trends, underground urban dancehalls, and raucous revelry. Reformers' wholesale condemnation of drinking, socializing on street corners, and frequenting of informal dancehalls (known as "jook joints") disregarded how southern migrants and poorer African Americans created social networks.[106] Much of the consternation seemed ignorant of the fact that even when blacks participated in mainstream amusements such as going to the theater, whites ushered them into crowded balconies that often hosted vice transactions.[107] Local clubs and bars were often the most accessible, affordable forms of entertainment, particularly for single, poor, and working-class black women.

African-American women's leisure and urban styles were intimately connected to their agency as well as to community formation. Servants sometimes befriended other domestics by meeting on errands, gossiping on porchfronts, and socializing while performing work chores.[108] Though finances were usually slim, buying secondhand clothing and other cheap goods gave black women an opportunity to benefit from their own labor. Crowding street vendors and secondhand clothing stores on their days off, urban blacks would stroll the city's shopping districts while splitting the costs of roasted peanuts and other cheap snacks. The rituals represented black women's participation in urban consumer trends at the same time that it reflected methods of self-identification and social networking. From scarves to wrappers to the hats they chose, clothing especially confirmed their lives outside of work, outside of the servant uniform.[109]

In wearing outfits of their own choosing, blacks not only signified their autonomy, but also employed style to help them recognize and be recognized by those from similar backgrounds. Hat styles, for example, may have allowed women from the South as well as from other parts of the country to recognize each other in an otherwise anonymous urban sphere. Black women from Philadelphia, Delaware, and the District of Columbia typically selected capotes draped with elaborate scarves or felt hats with flamboyant plumage— ostrich feathers in particular were in vogue in the 1890s (fig. 6a). Black southerners from states like Maryland, Virginia, and Georgia often opted for straw hats with wide brims and broad, black-band ribbons (fig. 6b). Although keeping abreast of fashion trends was a token of their adjustment to city life, the styles also provided an alternative means of exercising freedom and maintaining communal ties beyond their employer's households.[110]

Popular pastimes in the Seventh Ward included smoking cigars, drinking beer, and shooting pool. Pennsylvania lawmakers prohibited the sale of alcohol in establishments that played music or allowed dancing. Thus drinking in par-

FIGS. 6A AND 6B. Carrie Harvis (1883) and Lizzie Roberts (1895), *Rogues Gallery Books*. Courtesy of the Philadelphia City Archive.

ticular comprised much of Saturday night's activities. Taverns in the Seventh Ward served a range of constituencies. Blacks and whites could be found drinking together in most spots, though each bar usually served more of one group than the other. Saturday nights were the busiest time, and between eight and ten o'clock scores of men and women, black and white, would line up to be served and to socialize. Some patrons purchased beer to serve to guests at their own social gatherings.[111]

The mixed company in many saloons unnerved the more conservative sectors in the city, but most bars were friendly neighborhood spots, not dens of iniquity. Workingwomen popped into taverns on their way home with bundles of laundry or groceries in tow. For women whose work was filled with mundane drudgery, the late evenings were irresistible escapes. Certainly some saloons had a rougher clientele than others, but this was also determined, to some extent, by their environs—indeed, "a sharp class of criminals and loafers" patronized bars located near Middle Alley.[112] Ultimately, blacks could unwind in neighborhood haunts without being scrutinized by more uptight blacks or treated like deviants or second-class citizens.[113]

Yet while local pubs offered reasonably affordable outings to poor and working-class blacks, even more informal spots allowed blacks to engage in

SERVICE SAVORS OF SLAVERY

drinking as well as dancing—never mind gambling and shooting craps. Illicit dancehalls, businesses operating without liquor licenses, afforded patrons even greater freedoms. Admittedly these sites often were the scene of domestic squabbles and drunken shoving matches. Such altercations tended to be harmless bouts for the most part, but occasionally the skirmishes snowballed into brawls that only the authorities could sort out.[114] Nevertheless, their free or very low cost of admission made the spots a favored place to pass the time.

Reformers decried the overtly sexual nature of the dances and found the dresses and hats partygoers donned outrageous and distasteful. Yet the spaces nonetheless served as important centers for acculturation among many urban blacks.[115] The jook joints allowed black women and men to celebrate their bodies. The dancehalls also gave otherwise marginalized blacks an alternative means to obtain admirers, social status, and respect. Popularity could be based on the mastery of rhythmic moves and performance styles rather than solely on economic status.[116] Indeed, these outlets allowed otherwise disenfranchised black women to come alive and literally shake off the tensions of urban life.

Unfortunately for the women, however, their presence in these venues touched off a wave of anxiety that concentrated on containing the sites and redirecting black female leisure.[117] Urban reformers—both black and white—were extremely apprehensive about the shifting population demographics in Philadelphia, especially the growing number of unwed black women. Philadelphia possessed dangerous amusements for white women, but reformers generally regarded black women and girls as active agents in the city's moral demise. What is more, reformers failed to take responsibility for the ways in which their efforts contributed to the spread of the underground entertainment scene.[118]

The Black Elite and Urban Reform

It is perhaps no surprise that when black women exercised personal autonomy, particularly by participating in the city's underground nightlife, doing so landed them in a sea of social contention and strife. Urban reformers were preoccupied above all with the conduct of women from the South. According to black reformers in 1910, southern black women were especially vulnerable to the "scores of worthless well-dressed men who urge the girls to see the town, to earn easy money that they may wear fine clothes such as dazzle their unaccustomed eyes."[119] Regarding southern blacks as little more than uneducated countrymen "rushing from the hovels," elite and middle-class blacks saw migrants and their participation in urban pastimes as the gateway to crime.[120]

Urban poverty sank to new lows during the Gilded Age and Progressive eras, and the dangers of poverty, crime, and vice were real factors impacting black southern migrants. Within this group, single, black female migrants were highly vulnerable. Yet poor native-born black women appeared to be equally at risk. Among the top three crimes committed by black women, native-born blacks accounted for the greatest percentage of larcenies, while crimes such as assault and battery were equally divided between native-born Pennsylvanians and the largest southern migrant populations.[121] Yet most reformers regarded southern migrants as most susceptible to urban decay and also as most responsible for aiding its growth. As much as they feared the dangers and risks that jeopardized migrant women, black reformers feared the impact the migrant population would have on race relations in the city at large.[122]

Though black reformers packaged their rhetoric in the language of protection, their actions doubled as an effort to contain black female sexuality; they wanted to protect all that it jeopardized. Because whites used public spaces to define black womanhood as unfeminine—often refusing black women and girls seating on buses and refusing other courtesies customarily extended to white females—black reformers sought to use attire and public conduct to redefine mainstream notions of black morality. Unseemly public behavior on the part of poor and working-class black women not only threatened these efforts, but also could potentially lead to a rollback of the few advantages citizenship afforded.[123] In spite of racism and limited opportunity for black advancement, elite black Philadelphians enjoyed a few social and economic gains they were desperate to hold onto.

For a small cadre of blacks, Philadelphia did indeed appear to be the land of opportunity.[124] In 1885, Philadelphia was home to eight African-American doctors, two of whom were women, and an African-American lawyer, John D. Lewis—apparently the city's first—and an artist, David Bowser. By 1891, the city employed twenty black teachers, sixty black policemen, and one fireman.[125] Yet even as the *Times-Philadelphia* reported that the "colored people of this city are making more progress than is apparent to the casual observer," it did so under the anxious title, "Invading the learned professions."[126] Covering the Sixth Annual Reception of the Colored Barbers' Mutual Aid Association in 1886, a journalist noted that the outfits worn by the partygoers were costly, elegant costumes "that outshone some of those at white balls." [127]

Eerily reminiscent of attitudes displayed during the city's first experience with black freedom some fifty years earlier, the subtext of the articles marked the undercurrent of suspicion and renewed racial hostility that dogged elite and middle-class blacks. [128] The mainstream press closely monitored property ownership and the purported "growing numbers" of blacks "Engaged in Profitable Business." [129] The press not only exaggerated economic gains, but also failed to recognize that strides taken by African Americans did not occur without struggle. In 1890, a black man attending Jefferson Medical College battled a committee of white students demanding his expulsion. [130] While the unsavory display of bigotry was rationalized as resulting from the presence of a large southern white student body, school officials neglected to declare what steps would be taken to remedy the situation.

In the political arena, African-American legislators remained marginalized. The same city that had circumvented black voting rights in 1838 during Reconstruction underwent violent clashes as newly franchised black voters swelled the Republican Party. In 1871, a riot claimed the life of a prominent black activist and schoolteacher, Octavius V. Catto. Annual elections touched off the deadly skirmish, but ensuing bloody clashes ultimately reflected long-standing white resistance to black citizenship and advancement. [131] Though blacks overwhelmingly joined the Republicans, the party of Abraham Lincoln, in the 1870s, they rarely reaped the rewards typically granted to other voting blocs. Rather, white party members routinely ridiculed black voters and their politicians. As a report in 1896 exclaimed, "The Republican Recital A Success, The County Ticket Named Without Any Opposition, AFRO-AMERICANS NOT IN IT." [132]

Philadelphia's bigotry, in many respects, mirrored the national response to African-American freedom. [133] The city's residents promoted notions of freedom, democracy, and equality at the same time that they were overwhelmingly unwilling to relinquish the advantages that prevented the full implementation of those principles. Many Philadelphians celebrated the North's victory and abolition while at the same time believing that blacks would be better off either by returning to Africa or remaining in the South. In addition, though they feared that African Americans would become a burden on the city's resources, the prospect of black advancement seemed almost as disturbing. With the repeal of the Civil Rights Act in 1883 and the landmark decision *Plessy v. Ferguson* in 1896, which legalized racial segregation in the South, Philadelphia's resurgent racism followed a nationwide trend.

Lacking influence in state and local government, African-American activists shifted from the political realm to "racial uplift" initiatives within their own communities. For many black elites racial uplift centered on self-help, racial solidarity, and social purity. Because of the central role that women played in structuring the family and certainly the black community, reformers policed women's behavior in particular to help construct a public black identity that emphasized respectability, sexual propriety, temperance, hard work, and thrift.[134] But in enacting a strategy of racial uplift, African Americans also adopted a rigid, highly patriarchal, and often divisive social code.[135] Maintaining class distinctions figured centrally in their notion of social order and propriety, which ultimately stratified segments of the black community along lines of educational access, wealth, and skin color. Social stratification among blacks in Philadelphia was especially visible in the composition of church congregations.[136] The Protestant Episcopal Church of the Crucifixion, for example, had a more impoverished congregation than St. Thomas's "mulatto houseservants," and Berean Presbyterian's poor congregation starkly contrasted with the "older, simpler set of respectable" blacks from Central Presbyterian.[137]

Positioning themselves as moral custodians, elite African Americans chastised single black women for failing to conform to proper gender roles even as they used the plight of southern migrants to assert their authority over the urban black community.[138] Alarmed by the spate of urban places of amusement and the scores of single men and women crowding into them, urban reformers used the vulnerability of southern black migrants as a way to impose a more bourgeois notion of sexuality and social conduct. One part of the process included passing harsh judgment on the amusements and parlors themselves, while another aimed to control black women.[139]

Organizations such as the National League for the Protection of Colored Women, an interracial agency predominantly operated by elite blacks, aided newly arrived black female southern migrants.[140] Members met women at docks and bus stations and offered temporary housing and storage at fairly reasonable rates. In offering assistance, however, the organization usurped the women's agency and assumed moral control over the women's lives.[141] Insisting that "the Southern colored woman is very poorly equipped to grapple with this environment," reformers agonized over the corrupting dangers of taverns, dancehalls, and other illicit pastimes.[142] The Philadelphia chapter of the league asserted that were it not for their interception of women arriving at ports and bus stations, the "young women might have drifted to the bad district and become criminal."[143]

Not entirely off the mark in their critique, in part reformers sought to grant the same considerations enjoyed by white women to black women and girls. But in the process black reformers often affirmed long-standing stereotypes of black female immorality in addition to infantilizing migrant women.[144] Reformers fretted over the presumed increase in promiscuity that single black women would bring and the impact it would have on the community as well as how it would shape white attitudes about the race. Elite and middle-class blacks bemoaned the purported lack of respect for the marriage vow among lower-class blacks; but black women bore the brunt of their admonishments against premarital sex while black men's complicity largely escaped reproach.[145]

The notion that the migrants needed protection, though patronizing, proved to be among the more benign attitudes. Other native-born blacks proffered notions of rampant criminal vice among southern migrants. In 1899, William Truitt, a local African-American businessman, denounced corrupt black political leaders and black migrants as the cause of "rising crime." According to Truitt, southerners, "after arriving here[,] . . . are taken in charge by the politician. They are allowed to organize so-called political clubs which are nothing more than 'speak-easies' or policy dens."[146] Truitt's critique of ward politics was an accurate one, however; his assertion largely linked corruption and crime to black southern migrants, masking native-born blacks' participation in illegal enterprises and their own exploitation of black southerners.

Policing, Justice, and Mainstream Urban Reform

A growing cacophony of voices in the city—and indeed in the nation—regarded crime itself as the real "Negro problem."[147] Popular sentiment rehashed myths of African-American degeneracy, though turn-of-the-century proponents amended the assaults. According to their rhetoric, urbanization acted as a catalyst for a malignant rise in black crime. Black women existed as corrosive agents in this deterioration. White reformers argued that slavery demoralized the black family and that black women's immorality — their sexual impropriety and the fact that so many worked outside of the home — contributed to moral deficiency in the black community.[148] Charging that slavery obliterated blacks' capacity to participate in the industrial labor market, white penologists insinuated that thieving among blacks was a cultural problem.

This preponderance of black crime, according to Philadelphia's own Henry Boies, caused the criminal justice system to enforce stricter punishments against blacks.[149] Endeavoring to be sympathetic in his study, Boies concluded that "without conscientious scruples to deter them," blacks knew "no better than to steal rather than starve"; somehow these options appeared to hold a choice.[150] Boies's conclusion likely attempted to justify glaring disparities in the city's criminal sentences. White men served average prison sentences of 12.4 months as opposed to black men, who averaged 14.8 months. Black women typically served 14.1 months, a sharp contrast to the average 8.5 months that white women received.[151] In shifting blame for the disparities to blacks, urban reformers ignored the effect of racist social and economic exclusion.

Popular opinions like those published in an 1888 news article clung to the belief that "prejudice against color is slowly but surely dying out." Instead, an aversion "to industry and frugality" lay at the heart of the African American's inability to attain social mobility.[152] A Philadelphia criminal court judge in 1893 implored blacks, those "sincerely interested in the welfare of their race," to assess "what is radically wrong that produces this state of affairs and correct it, if possible."[153] The troubling "state of affairs" was the purported sharp increase in crime among African Americans. But black crime was not epidemic. Crime rates rose among all of the city's constituents, largely in accord with the growth of the population. Criminal convictions grew from just under 800 in 1880 to nearly 1,100 in 1894; this number climbed to just over 1,400 in 1909. At the same time the city's population swelled, moving from roughly 1.3 million to nearly 1.6 million and peaking at just over 2 million by 1910.[154]

However, blacks were disproportionately represented in the criminal justice system. African Americans accounted for nearly 20 percent of all those awaiting trial for criminal offenses though their population in the city never comprised more than 6 percent. White men comprised 67 percent of the city's criminal defendants, while white women accounted for another 13 percent.[155] The numbers of blacks at Eastern proved equally stark. Blacks represented roughly 20 percent of the penitentiary population. Black women accounted for only 1.1 percent of inmates but they represented nearly 40 percent of female prisoners.[156] White women comprised 1.7 percent of those at Eastern, while black men accounted for 18.5 percent, and white male inmates made up the remaining 78.8 percent.[157]

Crime in the city reflected a confluence of social circumstances. Parallel to circumstances that arose during the Jacksonian Era, labor strikes, women's increased role in the labor force, urbanization, and black citizenship comprised an untidy mix of destabilizing factors that stoked mainstream anxieties.[158] In addition to establishing settlement houses, orphanages, and refuges for the poor, reformers expanded upon earlier initiatives aimed at containing "casualties of the new society."[159] These reforms contributed to rising crime rates.

Changes in law and public policy largely reflected white middle-class Protestant values—values that were increasingly at odds with those of the masses of urban dwellers.[160] Less about halting the structural conditions that promoted crime than about preserving traditional aspects of the city's social hegemony, the elite's reforms largely safeguarded their own preeminence and situated them as rightful social custodians.[161] Urban reformers who would regulate social conduct targeted pubs and illicit amusements by lobbying for stricter legislation on the sale and distribution of alcohol. At the same time, state and city officials, together with members of the Pennsylvania Prison Society, bolstered the city's 1854 Consolidation Act, which centralized law enforcement and streamlined criminal justice proceedings.[162]

Although the City of Brotherly Love seemed to be awash in wine and spirits almost from its inception, the consumption of intoxicating elixirs had been hotly contested. For decades, the state legislature entered and reentered acts regulating alcohol.[163] Almost as often as rules hit the books, however, working-class communities, migrants, and immigrants responded with popular challenges to the laws. These challenges included blatant disregard of the statutes to near riots when authorities tried to enforce sanctions. Given the risks, night watchmen and ordinary citizens were loathe to swear out warrants against tavern owners and others who violated drinking prohibitions—partly because most did not support the initiatives and partly because doing so might win the plaintiff the wrath of citizens and proprietors alike.[164]

But temperance reformers renewed their efforts and successfully passed and enforced more restrictive legislation. Statutes prohibited serving liquor to minors and also outlawed liquor in businesses that offered other entertainment, such as singing and dancing. The legislature also ended the sale of liquor on Sundays. In regulating alcohol, reformers and legislators alike—perhaps unwittingly—found a way to more directly insert the apparatuses of the state into the daily lives of city residents. Laws that prohibited minors sixteen and under from consuming alcohol encroached upon parental authority. Laws prohibiting tavern owners from selling liquor to anyone known to be habitually intemperate further extended the reach of the state into the rights and prerogatives of city dwellers.[165]

Citizens could and did find ways to circumvent these initiatives, but changes made to liquor licensing laws profoundly impacted the flow of booze and the incidence of crime in the city. Prior to the 1880s, licensure for the sale and distribution of alcohol had been a relatively simple process—it required fifty dollars and a list of references. Relatively inexpensive and free of bureaucracy, getting a liquor license was a fairly accessible way for migrants and working-class men and women to become business entrepreneurs. By the late 1880s, however, reformers effectively lobbied the state to change the requirements so that a potential proprietor needed a two-thousand-dollar bond and a license fee of five hundred dollars. Even applicants with the necessary funds for licensure still contended with stricter scrutiny of their requisite list of references, and many who managed to apply were turned down as otherwise unsuitable.[166]

More than simply reinforcing regulation on the sale of alcohol, temperance reformers enacted an almost fanatical enforcement of the statute that most clashed with the social practices of blacks especially—the one prohibiting alcohol in establishments that played music and allowed dancing.[167] Because music played a central role in African-American leisure activities, many proprietors simply took their chances in violating the statute. And the risks were real. Aside from the police, temperance reformers formed their own watchdog committee. The Law and Order League inspected pubs and taverns and filed complaints against establishments that broke liquor laws. One of the Seventh

SERVICE SAVORS OF SLAVERY

Ward's most influential black saloon keepers, Gil Ball, was routinely cited.[168] Ball had enough money to pay the fines and enough clout to convey the usual graft that was the cost of doing business in Philadelphia, but others were not as fortunate, and even Ball eventually lost his license in 1890.[169]

The new licensing laws had a devastating impact. The number of successful liquor license applications dropped from nearly thirty-five hundred to just over one thousand, and the number of legitimate black-owned pubs dwindled.[170] But what proved more problematic about the shift in licensure is that the law did not stop the sale or distribution of liquor in black communities. Many businesses continued to sell and distribute alcohol without licenses—the new law effectively criminalized otherwise legitimate businesses and would-be entrepreneurs. Black women patronized and participated in the ensuing underground economy, though only 0.6 percent of black women at Eastern were serving time for breaking the liquor laws.[171]

Unlicensed businesses led to a multiplicity of illegal activities. Bribery and kickbacks to ward bosses who doled out protection from police raids became a new business expense. Often the money required to successfully operate above the law necessitated participation in still other illegal activities. Underground speakeasies and pubs housed more illicit operations on the upper floors—usually gambling and prostitution. It is not that these crimes did not occur in black, poor, or urban communities and even in the more well-to-do social circles before the licensing changes. Rather, the laws heightened inner-city corruption and forced a blurring of the line between legal and illegal, licensed and informal.[172]

At the same time, penal reformers focused on strengthening the police and the justice system. Under the 1854 Act of Consolidation, criminal justice shifted from arrests and prosecutions initiated by citizens to a system increasingly run by police and prosecuting attorneys. Prior to the 1854 act, citizens as well as constables initiated arrests and prosecutions by going to local magistrates to file charges against suspected criminals. Magistrates, depending on the merits of the charges and after obtaining a fee for their services, would issue a warrant to constables. The defendant would be brought before the magistrate to stand trial. Citizens exerted substantial control over arrests and over the extent to which a case would be pursued in court. Sometimes a complainant might issue a warrant against an offending neighbor or an unruly street tough as a means of mediating disputes rather than actually subjecting defendants to criminal sentences. Battered wives could use the process to remove abusive husbands from the home for a day or two—or permanently—under the threat of prosecuting assault and wife-beating charges to the limit of the law.[173]

Corruption permeated the fee-based system. Often justice could be bought. Given the fee incentive, magistrates rarely dismissed charges no matter how petty. To highlight the need for centralizing justice, reformers manipulated racism and sexism by claiming that African Americans, and black women in particular, clogged the system with "nuisance suits."[174] After consolidation, arrests would be made chiefly by police; prosecutions would be initiated primarily by prosecuting attorneys. Though consolidation passed in 1854, its evolution in praxis was slow. Renewed efforts in the late nineteenth century brought about expanded police forces and altered the roles of magistrates. Following the original act, the number of policemen and police districts rose from 650 and 16, respectively, in 1855, to 1,000 and 24 in 1871; by 1900 there were 1,250 police officers.

The number of officers in Philadelphia was smaller than that in other major cities such as Boston and Chicago, but the police nonetheless became a force to be reckoned with.[175] Patrolmen received instructions to detain "all persons from some place outside of the State and found loitering here without visible means of support." Idolatry, sobriety, attire, age, race—all became social indicators of criminal conduct, and as such justified police action. The subjective criteria proved particularly perilous for Africans Americans, immigrants, and Philadelphia's poor.[176] Moreover, legislation targeting tramps further threatened impoverished residents. Specifically, the fees court officers and constables earned for every tramp arrested and convicted increased from twenty-five cents per tramp in 1879 to one dollar in 1899.[177]

Reforms in criminal justice added more muscle to policing at the same time that liquor reforms unwittingly ripened the urban environment for illicit underground activities. These dynamics ultimately contributed to rising crime in the city. Additionally, the initiatives expanded the power of mainstream reformers. The Pennsylvania Prison Society had a direct line to the mayor's office, and the organization influenced police practices.[178] For example, their installation of female matrons in police precincts probably curtailed abuses of female prisoners; yet almost as much as this testifies to their charitable aims it sketches the breadth of the society's grasp on the justice system as a whole.[179]

The society's members exerted broad influence on city government and seemed especially adept at shaping public sentiment on crime, poverty, and vice. Founded in 1787, the group was instrumental in closing the country's first penitentiary and in erecting Eastern State Penitentiary. Referred to by Eastern's warden as "benevolent cranks" in 1886, the predominantly elite and middle-class Quaker group also lobbied on behalf of prisoners' rights.[180] Some of the beneficiaries were impoverished African-American adolescents, but for the most part their reform efforts failed to aid blacks. Unlawful segregation, housing discrimination, and antiblack violence may have been publicly denounced but led to few criminal arrests. Paradoxically, racist crimes allowed poor whites and white ethnics to insert themselves into the new emerging American identity—one that increasingly rested on whiteness rather than nativity. Although these crimes solidified blacks' exclusion from broadening notions of citizenship, arguably heightening urban decay, society members primarily worked to secure enough cells to hold prisoners and enough police to escort them there.[181]

The Next Level of Black Female Crime

Most blacks expected the latter half of the nineteenth century to be a watershed for economic prosperity and social access. By the dawn of the twentieth century, however, equality and the full rights of citizenship remained elusive. Crime powerfully shaped the lives of black women in Philadelphia, from providing illicit entertainment to contributing to social autonomy to aiding those simply struggling to survive. Moreover, criminal offending was born of complicated social dynamics, both for the black women who committed crime and for those who did not. Lawbreaking afforded some black women an alternate means to navigate the hardships of city life, but this fomented racist sentiments about black women and crime overall.

Yet black women's crimes also exist as an alternative record, a means of interpreting unspoken and otherwise undocumented sentiments. Poverty crimes and servant-theft speak powerfully about the perpetrators as well as about the criminal circumstances breeding them. Black female violence and sex crimes, though lesser in number, also contain important clues about the women's lives and experiences in the city and its criminal justice system.

Chapter Three

TRICKING THE TRICKS:
VIOLENCE AND VICE AMONG
BLACK FEMALE CRIMINALS

She would rob any white man who went with her; they might send her to
prison for it, but after she came out she would continue to play the game.

— *Philadelphia Public Ledger*, August 23, 1860

ON AUGUST 23, 1860, the *Philadelphia Public Ledger* covered an unusual exchange that took place in the city's Court of Oyer and Terminer. Georgiana
Coleman, a black woman accused of stealing ten dollars from a white man,
not only admitted her guilt but also declared her intention to repeat the crime
in the future. Arrested for playing the "badger game," a crime whereby women
posing as prostitutes lured, subdued, and robbed would-be patrons, Coleman
articulated a rather defiant stance.[1] She promised to victimize "any white man"
who attempted to purchase her services. Normally, this kind of press coverage
would point to journalistic hyperbole rather than to actual comments made
by a perpetrator. In this instance, however, what seems even more surprising
than her purported declaration was Coleman's sentence. Rather than eliciting
severe punishment for her crime or lack of racial deference, Coleman went
home a free woman — and this was not the first time. Some five months earlier,
another judge had dismissed similar charges against Coleman.[2]

Apparently agreeing with her sentiment, justices routinely "ignored"
charges against black female badgers. Magistrates often adopted the attitude
that white men who would patronize black prostitutes got what they deserved.[3]

Judge Allinson dismissed badger theft charges against three black women in 1881, announcing to the court and the white plaintiff, Mick Albright, that "if there was anything which would justify the reestablishment of the pillory and whipping post it would be that such a man might be publicly and properly punished."[4] In the justice system's eyes, worse than the defendants' theft was Albright's failure to adhere to customary racial and sexual mores. Albright's solicitation of black prostitutes constituted, at least publicly, a morally reprehensible transgression of white masculinity. But among the black women involved, badger theft marked a significant social development. Theirs was a bold crime and one that appears to have been largely directed against white men.

Larceny typically resulted from financial hardship and, in the more pronounced cases of servant-theft, from the stresses between those hardships and black female autonomy. Badger theft, however, demonstrated a more volatile combination of financial, social, and emotional motivating factors. More than the crimes discussed previously, badger theft, sex crimes, and felonious assaults constitute unique texts for historical analysis. Because precious few firsthand accounts are available, these crimes present rich evidence for gaining insight into the psyches of black female perpetrators. The nature of these criminal acts speaks of the women's desires, fears, and vulnerabilities as well as of their triumphs, disappointments, and rage.[5] In some cases, black women turned to violence as a last resort, when protection or justice seemed otherwise unobtainable. In other instances violence occurred when their efforts to attain the social accoutrements of womanhood, such as marriage and respectability, were thwarted. But more than mapping the patterns, the present examination reads violence back into black women's histories. Grounding the discussion in the collective history of black female exploitation, this investigation uses factors surrounding sex crimes and felonious assaults to unearth important clues about the perpetrators' own experience of violence.[6]

Race, Violation, and Representation

Rape and the sexual victimization of black women irredeemably stain American history. During enslavement black women endured brutal, demoralizing assaults perpetrated by both white and black men. Even after Emancipation, black women found themselves especially vulnerable to white men. White men used rape and the exploitation of black female bodies as a means to reinscribe their former positions of power and authority over southern society.[7] African-American women who asserted independence or laid claim to entitlements traditionally reserved for white women risked particularly savage assaults. Gang rape and other forms of sexual torture became common instruments used to teach black women their place.[8] White and black northerners perpetrated assaults against black women as well. In addition to employing physical violence, northerners undermined black female agency by manufacturing and objectifying damning representations of black womanhood.[9]

These representations conflated black female identities with notions of urban degeneracy and vice. They essentially maligned black female virtue and made all black women visual metaphors of female immorality. Popular entertainment and crime reporting relied on depictions of accentuated black female promiscuity, and emerging technologies and art forms contributed to this defamation. Black women's bodies functioned as negative tableaus, blank tablets upon which the notions of whiteness and masculinity could be fleshed out and clarified.[10] Journalists, emerging scientists, and even artists like Philadelphia's own Thomas Eakins made use of exploitative images of black womanhood.[11]

Eakins, a noted local artist and instructor at the Pennsylvania Academy of Fine Arts, exhibited a series of photographs of nudes in 1882. Included in the series were two photographs of a nude eight-year-old black girl reclining on a couch in his studio.[12] Her hand was placed suggestively on her hip, and she gazes seductively into the camera, "reminiscent of [the] French tradition" in early nude photography. The black girl is one of only two subjects in the entire series that looks directly at the camera with an overtly sexual gaze. Eakins's photographs magnify the conflation of black femininity and the mythology of black female hypersexuality.[13] Even a prepubescent black girl could be stripped, posed, and packaged as a seductive spectacle.[14] Notions of black female licentiousness also enabled a different set of social standards. Black women could not expect to be regarded—or protected—as "real" women or ladies.

Yet the late nineteenth and early twentieth centuries witnessed the passage of several laws, national and statewide, designed to protect women and children. Most concentrated on regulating labor, but the period suffered several "white slavery" scares. The country passed a spate of laws, including the Mann Act of 1910, against enticing young women and girls for "immoral purposes."[15] Philadelphia passed several such laws and further instructed police to keep a close watch on sex parlors operated by Chinese men or other ethnic minorities where white women might be present.[16] Largely designed to protect young white women from blacks, Chinese, and other ethnic immigrants purportedly seeking to sell their virtue on a seedy black market of "forced prostitution," the statutes regulated white women's movement in the city.[17] Though the scares reflected tensions surrounding white women's increased participation in the urban sphere and their growing sexual freedom, the rhetoric nonetheless affirmed the sanctity of white womanhood, and did so against an erasure of dangers facing black women. Unlike earlier laws that outlawed only the rape of white women, protective legislation did not explicitly exclude black women, but in praxis black women rarely benefited from any of the statutes' provisions.[18]

Even when black women could benefit from the new laws, verdicts still fundamentally circumscribed their victimization. In 1900, when three black male defendants received five years each for enticing two black minors, Annie Mathews and Mary Walker, the court, despite testimony of the sexual assault on the two girls, found the men "not guilty on other indictments charging felonious assault."[19] Young black women could be enticed for immoral purposes because the intent or the very act of enticing was illegal, but a conviction for a sexual assault upon them was apparently a different matter. Existing within a discourse of opaque femininity, black women remained vulnerable in much the same ways that they had been during enslavement. Notions of past immorality haunted their lives in the post-Reconstruction era.

Addie Hunton, a contributor to *The Voice of Negro* in 1904, noted that discussions of the "race problem" had begun to magnify the purported weaknesses of black womanhood. In characterizing the climate for black women, Hunton aptly described the situation when she wrote, "Everywhere her moral defects are being portrayed by her enemies; sometimes veiled in hypocritical pity, and again, in language bitter and unrelenting." Far from being the recipients of traditional protections extended to other women of the period, black women were vilified by the same detractors who were "ever secretly seeking to make these vilifications true."[20]

Black female writers often challenged the prevalent misconceptions about African-American womanhood and the hypocrisy of racial and sexual politics. Frances E. W. Harper upbraided the rhetoric of white sexual protection in Philadelphia in her book *Iola Leroy* in 1892. Harper implicitly indicted race and gender bias by placing Iola Leroy, a "white" mulatto, at the crossroads of the white slavery scare. Directly exposing the hypocrisy of white reformers' protective legislation, Harper invoked a "heroine [that] is everything an extended anti-white-slavery model acknowledges, except white."[21]

Yet African-American responses to violence against black women were ill equipped. Limited by their own adherence to respectable middle-class politics, black women warily confronted the impact of sexual assault. As ladies, it would have been inappropriate to fully immerse themselves in the ugliness of rape, incest, and family violence—either to confront the acts or to expose the atrocities publicly. In her address at the 1893 Columbia Exhibition in Chicago, Fannie Barrier Williams could only hint at the issues. Williams praised the "chivalric sentiment and regard from young men of the race that give to the young women a new sense of protection," adding, "I do not wish to disturb the serenity of this conference by suggesting why this protection is needed and the kind of men against whom it is needed." Cloaked in gentility, Williams's statement barely touches on the pervasive violence against black women.[22]

Although the combined physical and representational attacks comprised an almost complete assault on black womanhood, no "Red Record" chronicles the endemic rape or the emotional damage caused by sexual terrorism and social exclusion.[23] The destructive impact of the national climate of contempt, enmity, and exploitation is all but ignored in most historical documents.[24] Depression, anxiety, low self-esteem, suicidal tendencies, substance abuse, anger, and violence—all the likely outcomes suffered by the victims and by other members of the black community remained largely invisible in public discourse. Sex crimes against black women, especially those committed by white men, are scarcely documented in criminal prosecutions.[25]

Because so few black women could obtain legal protection or redress for injustices, many adopted internal strategies of protection. Enacting what Darlene Clark Hine coined "a culture of dissemblance," black women crafted public personas that downplayed their sexuality.[26] Black women closeted their emotions, sensuality, and pain in an effort to minimize their vulnerability. But this course of action produced serious consequences: it muted their experience of trauma, diminished public platforms on which to contest their victimization, and left precious little evidence of the psychological impact of social violence.[27]

Not all chose the path of womanly resistance and silent suffering, however. Most black women deployed the culture of dissemblance in the outside world while expressing their more private sentiments to each other in smaller, more intimate spaces. Black women relied on the church for strength and on their own independent black organizations.[28] But a small number of black women were either disconnected from these community support systems or found that they offered too little respite. Though the silence around the impact of black female violation is profound, black female crime provides a rare sounding of black women's feelings and emotional turmoil. Twenty-three percent of black female criminals sentenced to Eastern used some form of violence to defend themselves and to seize the things they wanted. The actual skirmishes—fistfights, stabbings, and shootings—were indeed messy, ugly affairs involving relatives, intended marks, or identified foes. Their crimes in late nineteenth- and early twentieth-century Philadelphia were not necessarily a direct response to specific incidents of sexual trauma or abuse. Rather, the illegal acts may indicate a broader resentment toward the prolonged denigration of their womanhood.

The World of the Badger

Badger crimes were not limited to black women or white male victims, but black female badgers were distinct in that the majority of their victims were white men.[29] Occasionally, opportunistic black prostitutes opted to rob especially drunken patrons rather than perform sexual services. However, most convicted badger thieves were serial offenders. This was their primary form of criminal offending, distinguishing them from prostitutes. Black women's badger crimes comprised a range of motivating factors such as greed, envy, and anger. The crimes thus open a unique window on the perpetrators and also offer an interesting challenge to negative stereotypes about black female sexuality.

Maligned as amoral and licentious, white men figured prominently in the manufacture of this narrative about black women. Historically, white men masked their attacks on enslaved black women by promoting the idea that libidinous black women were all but impossible to rape. Whereas white men used negative sexual myths to victimize black women with impunity, conversely, black badgers used the "pretense of sex" to victimize white men. By effectively "tricking the tricks," black badgers turned the older script on its head. Paradoxically, the crime allowed black women to capitalize on their own former exploitation. Manipulating theories of sexual degeneracy to entrap their victims, the women exposed white men's immorality in trying to purchase sex and in attempting to engage in interracial sexual intercourse. In doing so, black badgers challenged key aspects of the prevailing sexual narratives. These are not the black women that white patrons expect, as Arthur Beacham, who was relieved of $77 by Bessie Smith when he "made her acquaintance on the street one night," discovered.[30]

Actual statistics for the frequency of the crime are difficult to assess given the uneven record of prosecution. Records at Eastern State Penitentiary indicate that in addition to larceny, badger theft—typically falling under the category of larceny from a person—constituted around 8 percent of black female crime. In extreme cases badgers could also be convicted of assault and battery, though again the record of prosecutions is haphazard and difficult to pinpoint statistically.[31] Moreover, law enforcement was sporadic and subject to pressures from both reformers seeking to curb urban vice and local ward bosses aiming to protect their financial interests. Most bosses were affiliated with quasi-legal political clubs that doubled as assignation houses.[32] Badger crimes were also underreported since few white men sought prosecutions, fearing the stigma they might incur should their reasons for visiting black women in alleys, courtyards, and seedy rooming houses become public; not to mention the shame of being robbed by a woman.[33] The dishonor white men would suffer if they brought charges made black badgers' crimes that much more ingenious.[34]

Although most badgers seduced their victims into assuming compromising positions before absconding with their cash and valuables, in rare instances black badgers brazenly assaulted and robbed their "johns."[35] Bessie Conway, otherwise known as "Black Bess," would simply muscle her victims into corners, where she would then proceed to relieve them of their money and possessions. Conway, a thirty-one-year-old Philadelphia native, at 5 feet 7 inches and 153 pounds, possessed a formidable stature for the period.[36] According to accounts, Conway merely threw her arms about men and "took money from their pockets."[37] Popular culture and emerging criminologists regarded these feats as evidence of diminished femininity, but badgers' abilities to outwit and, in some cases, outwrangle johns more directly pointed to the women's experiences of social alienation and violence.[38]

Dwelling in the roughest corners of the slums, the more violent badger thieves probably witnessed the horrors of urban poverty and crime firsthand. Fighting, like any physical sport, required conditioning. Few women developed the skill and ferocity to take on their male opponents without having a precise understanding of physical combat as well as knowledge of their own weaknesses and strengths. In this regard, badger thieves expertly assessed the dynamics of power and vulnerability—both physically and culturally. Black badgers did not dissemble their sexuality, and they were not unaware of the rumors of the voracity of black female sexual appetites. Rather, they took up the slurs as armament and transformed the themes contributing to black female victimization into offensive tactical maneuvers. In bringing violence to bear and successfully vanquishing male opponents, badger thieves' actions defied ideological foundations of male prowess and white supremacy.

Perhaps even more than this, the crime, by its very nature, potentially allowed black women to exorcise their demons. In rolling their johns, black badgers may have been lashing out at human effigies of the population most responsible for past slights, insults, and violations. In this sense, the crimes might afford a glimpse into the resentment black women harbored against patriarchy and racist hypocrisy. Mostly nonviolent, badger crimes nonetheless articulate acrimony and frustration as much as they evince cunning and ingenuity.

The badgers who relied more heavily on violent means rather than trickery to swindle johns, moreover, appeared to lead lives permeated by violence. In addition to using it for purposes of badgering, it appears that some relied on violence as a routine way to advance their agendas—this may also be indicative of a larger inner turmoil. Women like Bessie Conway and Josephine Payton, another well-known badger thief, did not, or perhaps could not, confine their aggression to badger crimes.[39] Conway, the bane of penitentiary guards' existence, breeched the prison's policy of silence, ignored the matron's instructions, and incurred extra discipline during her incarceration.[40] Payton violently attacked the female matron at Eastern in 1888. Taking the opportunity to deliver several fierce blows to the woman as she was escorted to bathe, Payton put up quite a struggle before being restrained and forced back into her cell by nearby male overseers.[41]

One of the city's most notorious badger thieves, Sarah Palmer, a mulatto from Delaware, appears to have simmered in a crucible of anger and misery. Palmer, who was twenty-five years old when sentenced to her first term at Eastern, had already served four prior sentences at the county prison. Standing 4 feet, 11 inches and weighing 142 pounds, Palmer bore a scar across her forehead that ran under her right eye to just above her left.[42] Whether Palmer sustained this injury from a fight is uncertain, but her record for forcibly taking money from johns suggests that she may have been an all-around tough customer on the streets.[43] Bearing the signs of hard living, Palmer suffered from episodes of violence and depression, perhaps worsened by her drinking.[44] Yet Palmer's criminal record also indicates that she struggled against the more detrimental aspects of her lifestyle.

Despite her frequent trips to the penitentiary and the warden's characterization of her as "one of the crime class" in 1888, at some point Palmer evidently tried to change. Though she had been in and out of institutions from a relatively early age, after her 1888 arrest, Palmer managed to stay out of the system for five years. Apparently securing legal employment as a servant, she did not serve another sentence at the county prison until 1894.[45] This term would be her last criminal conviction. After an earlier failed attempt, Sarah Palmer succeeded in taking her life on May 19, 1894. Using a strip from her blanket, Palmer hanged herself by her cell bars. The exact reason for Palmer's suicide remains a mystery, but her rough lifestyle, recidivism, and perhaps either her rage or despair over being incarcerated again seem to have been more than she could bear.[46]

Yet as isolating as the badger's lifestyle could be, other cases suggest that badger theft facilitated partnerships and intricate social networks. In 1890, Mary Gillis and her partners, Edward Skinner and Frank Howard, also African American, were arrested and convicted of the theft of a pocketbook, watch, and chain valued at twelve dollars from Peter Larson. Gillis and one of her co-defendants received two-year sentences at Eastern.[47] Johanna Cook of Philadelphia, age twenty-eight, Kate Jones of Berks County, age twenty-two, and Martha Conway of Delaware County, age twenty-three, were all convicted

TRICKING THE TRICKS

together in Philadelphia for "badger pulling."[48] Groups of badgers operating in tandem appeared to make off with larger sums of money, as Lola Green, along with two other African Americans, a man and a woman, was also convicted and sentenced to Eastern for stealing one hundred dollars from Thomas Foy by means of the "badger game."[49]

Badgers might forge unique alliances with women as well as with men who were either spouses or intimate social partners. Husband and wife duos like Annie and Charles Ross were arrested and convicted for robbing Stephen Lane, a white man enticed into their home on Alaska Street. Lane probably was solicited for prostitution, but he testified that he was lured into the Ross home under the pretense of "running the growler," obtaining beer.[50] That married couples engaged in badger theft suggests that both black men and women fashioned notions of gender, marriage, and morality that were neither wholly in opposition to cultural norms nor entirely complicit with broader definitions of propriety.

Philadelphia Vice

Almost as much as sexual exploitation haunted black women, it also functioned as a site where black women sought empowerment or perhaps aimed to redefine sites that typically marked their vulnerability.[51] Just as the numbers of badger thieves are imprecise, so too are the numbers of black female prostitutes in the city, though the city's Commission on Vice suggested that black women accounted for roughly one quarter of the city's 3,748 prostitutes in 1913.[52] Vice in Philadelphia existed in concentrated red light districts as well as in the parlors, tenements, and political clubs that dotted the city's more impoverished neighborhoods. The section in the city referred to as the Tenderloin lay within the Sixth and Eighth police districts—the city's Chinatown section and parts of Northern Liberties (see map, above). But throughout the city there were 372 parlor houses, essentially entire buildings dedicated to prostitution; 127 disorderly houses, places serving liquor and hosting prostitution on the upper floors or in supposed hotels; and close to 500 furnished rooms, massage parlors, seedy employment agencies, and notorious street corners and alleyways that housed the city's vice network.[53]

Though men dominated much of urban vice in 1913, prior to this women appeared to run a substantial number of the city's brothels and sex parlors.[54] Charging from five dollars for sex on down to the smaller fees of the "50-cent" houses, madams and inmates split the cost of the women's services, and inmates received a commission on the number of drinks sold.[55] Individual streetwalkers tended to be poor workingwomen who, after losing gainful employment, temporarily replaced wages by soliciting on street corners or within local disorderly houses.[56] Among black female criminals at Eastern only 3 percent served sentences for such sex crimes as running a bawdy house or brothel, but, given the sporadic nature of policing, it is likely that the actual number of women engaged in sex crimes was much higher.[57]

Albeit highly problematic, sexuality was one of the few areas in their lives in which black women could exert some measure of control. Black prostitutes and vice workers seemed to use sex as a transformative vehicle, possibly embracing the illicit in an attempt to dismantle sex as a potential instrument of violation. Choosing these spaces as a means of survival afforded black women agency and power over those areas that traditionally marked their powerlessness.[58] Rather than being destroyed by rape and sexual battery, black women, by mastering the commodification of their own bodies, might somehow render themselves "unrapeable" in reality, as opposed to the ruinous myth that promoted and pardoned sexual violence.

But prostitution, nonetheless, possessed a dark side. Far from evidencing points of transformation, the litany of assignation houses and sex parlors proved only to reinvent black female sexual subjection. Lisbon Street, for example, was a notorious location for a brothel in 1896. It was crowded with impoverished, "unkempt, miserable looking colored women" selling sexual favors for small sums of money.[59] And while black vice possessed distinct characteristics representative of the women and men engaged in the practices, it was also fairly well integrated in the sense that it catered to broad constituencies, the most lucrative being white men. Moreover, though badgers, prostitutes, and bawdy house proprietors existed on the moral fringes of the black community, this ideological location hardly represented an actual estrangement, spatially or socially.

Political, social, and economic dislocation sometimes made crime a means of survival that was taken up only reluctantly and that often blurred the lines between "criminals" and otherwise "decent" folk.[60] Though most blacks de-

TRICKING THE TRICKS

spised lawbreaking, believing it reflected poorly on the entire community, they were nonetheless well acquainted with the kind of discrimination that sustained it. Because daily racist insults and de facto segregation, though equally unlawful, went on unabated and were ignored by the criminal justice system, African Americans in general viewed the law and the police skeptically. Moreover, many African Americans knew that police tolerated prostitution, gambling, and illegal lotteries in black neighborhoods while safeguarding others.[61]

Within disreputable houses, social networks developed among owners, workers, patrons, and community members.[62] Proprietors in particular were community liaisons of a sort; their informal businesses provided social and financial services within their communities.[63] In some cases this proximity could pose unexpected problems for black female criminals, however. During her trial for selling alcohol without a license, Martha Gibson's sister, Julia Hodge, testified that while living with Gibson she knew her to "sell liquor and keep a disreputable house."[64] The house on 1308 Wood Street and the conduct taking place therein won Gibson a two-year sentence at Eastern and also the apparent disdain of relatives.[65] Yet in spite of disapproving family members and imprisonment, black women returned to their illegal enterprises. One black woman serving time on a bawdy house charge assured the warden that upon her release she intended to continue running her illicit operation.[66]

Though the commercial sale of sex was exploitative, the parlors created spaces for alternative sexual practices, making them paradoxical sites of both humiliation and empowerment for otherwise marginalized communities. This was especially the case for those houses that facilitated nontraditional sexual communities, communities that reformers, sexual psychologists, and upstanding middle-class Christians especially sought to repress. Cross-dressing, same-sex prostitution, and more taboo sexualities took root within this informal economy at the same time that they were localized to black neighborhoods. A rare account published in 1885 in the *National Police Gazette* explained that the "district around Seventh and Lombard streets, Philadelphia, is one of the lowest in the city, being populated almost altogether by negroes and plentifully supplied with grog shops and dance halls." The story reported on a white girl arrested in a black-owned pub for impersonating a man. A prominent Democratic politician in the company of the young woman at the time of her arrest reportedly explained that his young acquaintance "[had] long felt a great curiosity to see the slums of the city and begged that he escort her . . . which he promised to do if she would adopt a disguise." Though the politician assured police that nothing more suspicious than that had transpired, both were detained for questioning. Whether the politician initially knew that his young friend, age sixteen, was a woman or perhaps instead believed he was picking up a young man is unclear. That both went down to the slums to participate in what they considered to be taboo social practices, however, highlights the connection between black vice, white patronage, and white sexual imagination.[67]

But as much as these sites attracted whites hoping to be titillated, they were also periodically targeted by morality campaigns. Reformers intermittently regarded vice districts as dangerous threats to civic morality and particularly cited same-sex intercourse. The Philadelphia Vice Commission noted that "sodomy and other sexual indulgences by unnatural means" constituted an evil "spreading in this city and throughout the country with terrible rapidity."[68] Against this backdrop, police hauled African Americans like Charles France and Mary Bailey out of assignation houses during raids under charges of sodomy. Authorities arrested and convicted black men like Isaac R. Hull, otherwise known as "the Lady" Washington, too, for sodomy in Middle Alley—one of the worst blocks in the Fifth Ward.[69] These convictions display the range of sexual practices springing up in both black and white communities and demonstrate how the rhetoric of domesticity criminalized alternative sexualities.[70]

The Case of Emily Lee and Sexual License

Sexuality existed within an intricate milieu of identity politics and pleasure. Heterosexuality, often the only "privilege" available to black women, was practiced in personal relationships and modeled publicly as a facet of respectability.[71] Modeling notwithstanding, however, sex and sensuality contained complicated layers of struggle for black women. Whether black women embraced pious chastity, wielded sex like a sword, or peddled it on street corners, sex remained a source of pleasure and a means to express desire and love. And expressing desire and romantic love affirmed blacks' humanity. That men and women chose to transgress accepted sexual mores by engaging either in sex outside of marriage or in same-sex relationships marks important challenges to the larger rhetoric of cultural normalcy.

Within the black community, contesting heterosexuality also led to more complicated questions about the widely appropriated aspects of middle-class gender identities, particularly the utility of respectability politics for contesting the racism that affected all African Americans. The arrest and eventual murder conviction of Emily Lee, a young black woman, spotlighted the problematic aspects of uplift ideologies. The strategies selectively chose types of black people worthy of black activism, leaving myriad groups within the black community excluded from antiracist organizing. In 1905, Lee horrified onlookers as she shot and killed her childhood friend Stella Weldon.[72] Born and raised in Scranton, Pennsylvania, both women had attended school and church together and maintained a close relationship until Weldon's marriage.[73]

Press coverage scripted the murder as the result of a love triangle run afoul —Charles Weldon being the object of both of the women's desires.[74] The *Defender*, an independent black newspaper, mercilessly railed against Lee, the unrepentant perpetrator, and charged, "The evil was in her, it possessed her personally."[75] Her church congregation praised Stella Weldon, deemed a saint, for "her good acts, her fidelity to the church, and exemplary life as a faithful wife."[76] But as the details of the case unfolded, a stunned black community discovered that Emily Lee yearned not for Charles's affections but Stella's.

Lee's trial, heralded as "The Sensation of the Hour," shocked and titillated the *Defender*'s readers. Lee's defense attorneys attempted to demonstrate through the testimony of employers, friends, and church members that Lee had been mentally ill long before the murder, thinking of herself as Stella's lover. Witnesses revealed that the two were the best of friends initially, but that over time the friendship appeared to develop into something more.[77] The women walked arm in arm. When they went out, Lee always paid, and she bought Stella expensive clothes. Emily's brother Bert described her as "sort of a tomboy." He testified that after Stella's marriage, his sister acted "just like a man would act whose best girl had rejected him. She told me one night that Stella had been untrue to her. I asked her what she meant by that and she said that Stella had turned her down." Bert Lee further explained, "They would kiss each other just like a boy and a girl."[78]

Church members corroborated Bert Lee's statements, explaining, "They seemed to be a very loving couple. Emily seemed to act toward Stella as if she were a gentleman and Stella her sweetheart." At all the church socials, which they attended together, Lee "always bought refreshments for Stella and the latter never objected when she paid." In response to allegations of an affair between her and Charles Weldon, Lee told her brother, "I love Stella Weldon better than my own life, and I would rather be dead and in heaven with her, than be persecuted down here on earth."[79] After lengthy instructions from the judge, the jury convicted Lee of murder in the second degree. The judge sentenced her to twenty years' solitary confinement at Eastern.

Emily Lee committed a brutal murder. Shooting Stella Weldon four times as the woman wheeled her newborn baby across a city street hardly makes Lee a sympathetic figure. Yet Lee's criminal career had begun long before the murder conviction. It is Lee's sex crime and her apparent openness about her sexuality that make her case especially provocative. Lee's love affair with Weldon evinces her own sexual agency despite laws and social praxis that considered the behavior unnatural and even criminal.[80] Moreover, the relationship between the women forced the black community, on some level, to recognize the possibility of sexualities other than those between men and women and ignited an ideological furor among elite African Americans affiliated with the black press.

Two contributors to the *Defender*, writing under the names Gil Blas and Sancho Panza, engaged in a heated exchange over Emily Lee's crime and the responsibility of the black press as both an advocate for the black community and an instrument of African-American advancement.[81] Blas balked at the growing sympathy for Lee and her apparent heartbreak. He painstakingly guided readers through his experiences on the day of the murder. Blas recorded how he saw Weldon's blood "covering a space of some three feet or more." He reminded his audience that the pool of blood was in fact "the precious blood of a human being." Blas charged that "Lee has no right to demand sympathy and it is absurdity to demand of the people to stand by her." Blas charged that if "Lee possessed those qualities which constitute a perfect womanhood she would be free and happy today. Virtue, chastity, and good morals she ignored; therefore, her calamity."[82] Panza's response, equally critical, was directed primarily at the double standard in criminal justice and the treatment of accused blacks in the press. Panza urged the black community and the black press to lobby for equitable treatment for Lee during the trial regardless of the crime and its circumstances. Panza argued that the same considerations given to accused white women in the press should be given to Lee in the *Defender*.[83]

TRICKING THE TRICKS

The sexual transgressions, initially the love triangle and later the same-sex love affair, together with the heinous nature of the crime, exposed the impossible binaries operating within the uplift ideologies. Blas and Panza, each seeking to promote and protect the race, found themselves unable to reconcile how best to approach Lee and her crimes: whether to disown and denounce Lee for her social trespasses or to advocate for her fair treatment solely on the basis of her race. The binary prevented, critically and ideologically, any discussion of the more complicated aspects of Lee's race and sexuality, her relationship with Weldon, and the larger community's knowledge of the affair. African Americans adopted uplift ideologies to aid and empower the black community, but in this case the ideals barred any genuine understanding or actual acceptance of Lee's sexuality—to label her as biologically deviant might aid racist discourses they sought to contest. Yet embracing Lee might convey the wrong message about the black community's notions of sexual propriety.

Though Lee's and Weldon's relationship apparently received a measure of tolerance from their community, Weldon's ending the affair by marrying implies that perhaps the tolerance lay in the assumption that the relationship was more of a passing fancy than a greater challenge to heterosexuality.[84] The fact that both women participated in the relationship, however, suggests that they envisioned their womanhood and sexuality along more fluid contours, contours more expansive than those advocated publicly. The conflict between Blas and Panza provides insight into the broader impact of black female criminality in contesting customary notions of womanhood, sexuality, and resistance.

Perils and Pitfalls in the Pursuit of Domestic Respectability

For the most part, however, black reformers held steadfastly to more conservative expectations of domesticity and voiced serious concerns about what they considered a laxity in the sexual morality of working-class black women in urban centers. Du Bois himself bemoaned the sizable population of unmarried black women in the city, fearing that these women would likely participate in premarital sex, which would undoubtedly have negative consequences for the entire black community. Du Bois equated the presence of unmarried black women with promiscuity and urban vice and regarded them as threats to the familial paradigm of success. Though he acknowledged employment discrimination and political disenfranchisement, Du Bois harped on "the lack of respect for the marriage bond," arguing that sexual immorality and "adultery and prostitution" punctuated the problems of poor blacks. Moreover, Du Bois attached these transgressions to the masses of single black women, rarely admonishing either black or white men who participated in illicit conduct.[85]

Contrary to popular assumptions, however, black female criminals, like most poor and working-class black women, were keenly aware of the tenets of domesticity. Yet black female crime, particularly violent crime such as assault and battery, murder, and infanticide, discloses blacks' somewhat paradoxical understanding of morality, womanhood, and domesticity. Adhering to the tenets of domesticity was not important to blacks solely as a way of contesting white racism, but on a more personal level it also affirmed them as men and women. Enslavement had denied so many black rights that even the most basic components of African-American masculinity and femininity became politicized. However, because their social reality rarely permitted either of these gender identities to be fully actualized outside of their own communities, internally, gender praxis became a central organizing component in African Americans' social relationships.[86]

Because black women had few avenues for validation, the smallest sign of disrespect could topple a black woman's carefully constructed, though ultimately fragile, notion of womanhood. Ida Howard's 1891 murder conviction perhaps most effectively reveals the overwhelming sense of pride and desperation underscoring black female violence. Howard, a twice-convicted badger thief, stabbed a black man to death in broad daylight. Apparently displeased with the man's unsolicited attentions, Howard profanely inquired, "What in the —— are you looking at?" After the man responded in kind, calling her "out of her name," a scuffle between the two ensued, and Howard stabbed the man, causing his death.[87] Howard's vulnerability could not tolerate even this relatively harmless slight, which apparently, from her vantage, amounted to a grievous offense. This kind of hypersensitivity perhaps speaks to black women's lack of access to standard female protections as well as to their proximity to aggression and violence.[88]

Violence punctuated urban life in general, however, and poverty endangered most racial and ethnic groups in Philadelphia. But African Americans endured the extremities of racial antagonism discursively, economically, and socially. Perhaps given its pervasiveness both in the lives of blacks and in the urban sphere overall—impoverished whites succumbed to this social plague as well—violence functioned as a corrosive agent. Violence subjects all those who witness it to damaging effects, psychologically as well as physically. But most detrimental, violence convinces its victims that its use is the most decisive manifestation of power. Those who are victimized by violence often resort to it in an effort to be powerful. Much of black female violence reflects both experience with brutality and the effort to guard against it. Violence became an instrument of power and vengeance, often supplanting the protection and justice that continued to remain elusive.[89]

Though most crimes against black women garnered few outraged headlines and little compassion from journalists or the justice system, the information available suggests that black women endured extremely violent assaults. Black women in the City of Brotherly Love were beaten, raped, molested, stabbed, shot, and burned. Eastern State Penitentiary scrapbooks contain brief listings, however, of black female victims: women like Grace Jones, who in 1893 was "stabbed in the face with a knife," and Bertha Taylor, who was shot in 1894 by Lewis Weiss, and Mattie Harris, who was "cut in the arm with a knife" by Samuel Sewell.[90]

Domestic violence in particular betrayed the larger pressures of social isolation as well as the profundity of gender strife between black men and women. Violence against women represents the basest level of patriarchy, and crimes of domestic violence did appear in Philadelphia court rosters.[91] But black women often resisted the imposition of male authority by fighting back against their batterers. In some cases these altercations possessed grave outcomes. In 1900, Ella Johnson, a laundress from Virginia, was convicted of murder in the second degree for her attack on James Jackson, another African American. According to witness testimony, Jackson had been in the house drinking and quarreling with Johnson throughout the night, and the argument eventually became physical. During the row, Johnson struck Jackson with a lighted lamp that resulted in his death.[92]

Domestic violence was not confined to black male and female relationships. In another case, Lucinda Johnson, a twenty-two-year-old black woman who lived with Bliss O. Hulburt, a white man, pleaded guilty to manslaughter on July 7, 1902. According to reports, "during a quarrel, Hulburt struck the woman in the face, where upon she hurled a lighted lamp at him."[93] Mamie Johnson accused a friend of becoming too familiar with her husband, an affront that resulted in Johnson's stabbing the woman.[94] Violent and bloody at times, black women did not easily submit to abuse or readily tolerate disrespect. But while certain aspects of domestic violence appeared as acts of self-defense, in other instances the violence was the culmination of furious eruptions that occurred when their attempts to obtain the social accoutrements of womanhood were denied.[95]

Unlike vice criminals, the overwhelming majority of violent black female criminals were first-time offenders. They did not appear to be individuals who were extensively immersed in extralegal activities or practices, but more typically were everyday poor and working-class black women to whom the benefits of domesticity were extremely important. Failure to obtain it often proved devastating—the case of Annie Cutler is a prime example. On April 22, 1885, Cutler shot and killed her ex-lover, William H. Knight. Cutler's case offers unprecedented insight into working-class black women's values and their feelings of turmoil and powerlessness. Born in 1863 in Massachusetts, Annie Cutler was intelligent and fairly well educated. She had seven years of private schooling before ending her education at the age of thirteen. During the summer of 1882, she met Knight and fell in love. He proposed and asked her to migrate with him to Philadelphia. In 1883, at the age of twenty, Cutler left Newport, Rhode Island, where she and her family resided, and followed Knight.[96]

In Philadelphia she found employment as a cook in a concert saloon hall at 835 Race Street, also her residence at the time.[97] Knight, employed as a waiter in a boardinghouse at 1025 Arch Street, lived at 1322 Vine Street.[98] By most accounts, Knight's and Cutler's relationship was a good one. Cutler's employers recalled that Knight often visited, and the two played checkers and dominoes in the kitchen after work. For the next two years the couple worked and continued to date, Knight calling on Cutler at the saloon. Approximately a month before his murder, Knight visited Cutler for the last time. Despite their plans to wed, Knight married another young woman and took up residence with her. Cutler was devastated.[99]

In late March, Cutler wrote two letters, the first to her mother and the second to her employer, Mrs. Mettler. The first letter reveals Cutler's profound grief and despair:

> Philad., March 20, 1885—Dear Mother: I hope when you receive this letter you will not think hard of me or turn your back on me. You have had troubles

and trials in this world, but your constitution permitted you to bear them. I am now in trouble and my constitution is not strong enough to bear anything, that you know.

The deed I am about to commit will surprise you and all of my people. If I could help it I would not do it, but I cannot. I do it for love and revenge. When you receive this letter I will be in hell, for I know that I will not go to heaven.

Please receive my body and bury me in a plain white box. I guess I have got money enough saved to buy one of those. Do not have any ceremony over me whatever. This is my last wish and all that I can ask you to do for me. I have not been a bad girl in this world; that is the reason why I am imposed on.

The bad get along better in this world than the good. Mrs. Metler [*sic*] has been like a mother to me. Ask her all about me. She can tell you whether I have been good or not. I do not consider myself responsible for this that I am about to do.

I cannot write any more for I must write a short note to Mrs. Metler. My hands are too shaky for me to write. I hope God will forgive me and I hope you will. Give my love to all my friends, and tell them for me never to get in love with a man so that they cannot leave him. I will tell you it is hard.

You know how much Henry used to run after me. Well, he has deceived me, for he got some woman in trouble and had to marry her, and that breaks my heart. If I could live and stand it I would, but that is impossible.

I have done everything in this world for him that a woman could do. Nobody but myself and God knows and Henry himself. And now for revenge, for revenge is sweet. Good-bye and may God have mercy on my soul. From your daughter.[100]

An impassioned plea for understanding, Cutler's letter expresses the depth of her sorrow, her feelings about love and marriage, and her sense of powerlessness. She ends by viewing revenge as her only avenue for achieving justice. The letter also points to her isolation. Beyond Knight and her employer, the bulk of her support network appears to be back in Rhode Island. Though more articulate than the average female offender, her hard work, ambition, and goals did not differ from those of most black women in the city. Her sentiment that "the bad get along better in this world than the good" betrays a frustration undoubtedly shared by many black women; yet it also marks the ways in which they struggled within the tight contours of respectable womanhood.[101]

Although their actions clearly breeched the moral standards of middle-class domesticity and their social status generally precluded their participation in its ideological tenets, most black women upheld the value system. Many seemed trapped within a painful dichotomy. Keenly aware of white hypocrisy (most blacks considered whites' racism contrary to the religious and moral values they advocated), violent black female criminals nonetheless seemed to accept that chastity, marriage, and Christian morality was the correct path for "true women."

Because they also understood the difficulties they faced in attempting to follow these ideals, certain practices appeared to be the immoral means that would eventually be justified by the ends. During her trial, Cutler told how Knight had "ruined" her, taken her money, and betrayed her. Having engaged in premarital sex in anticipation of marriage, she felt the loss of her virginity and unmarried status compounded her failure with shame and humiliation.[102] Though unable to adhere to the strictures ordained in the moralistic rhetoric, Cutler never challenged the social belief that assessed the value of her womanhood along a biased double standard.[103]

Far from lacking an understanding of social and civic morality, Cutler clung to domestic ideals to the point that she believed her self-worth was destroyed. Her letter reads like a suicide note, a final epistle from a woman who, in the broader cultural discourse as well as in her own eyes, was unworthy of a respectable funeral ceremony but instead merited no service and a plain white box. The justice system again appears to have shared Cutler's sentiments. Whereas white female criminals usually garnered sympathy as "fallen women," considered as otherwise innocent women led astray by corrupting urban influences, Cutler was sentenced to hang.[104] Subsequent lobbying and an outcry against the death penalty eventually led the court to reconsider the decision, however, and Cutler received an eight-year sentence at Eastern.[105]

Cutler's case is extraordinary in that her schooling enabled her to leave behind a detailed account of her thought processes and of the circumstances of her crime. Cutler's crime also sets her apart from badger thieves and other petty larcenists. Yet she shares an overarching characteristic of black female criminality. Her crime was deeply connected to her concept of womanhood and her perception of the gap that separated what she wanted from what was possible. And by all records, Cutler's disillusionment with her life and her relationships with men was profound. When Alfred Love, a member of the Pennsylvania

Prison Society, sought to meet with her at Eastern, presumably to speak with her about her case, Cutler informed Warden Cassidy that she would not see him or any other man.[106]

The institution of marriage was embedded in the psyches of black women as a legitimizing institution — one previously denied to most blacks. It was tremendously important in their notion of femininity and respectability. Besides the social benefits of being married, however, economic instability also made marriage and motherhood significant elements of survival for working-class women.[107] The Ellen Derry case, from 1885, is an especially potent example. Arrested and convicted of kidnapping, Derry was lambasted in press reports for her apparent gall in trying to pass off a pretty, "light-skinned mulatto child" as her own. Journalists failed to understand the full import of her actions. Destitute and deserted by her husband, a light-complexioned black man, Derry, before her capture, used the child to win a legal suit against her husband for desertion and child support. Far from coveting the child's looks, Derry understood her circumstances all too well and won her initial claim, as the court granted her $1.75 in weekly child support.[108] Moreover, Derry's marriage to a lighter-complexioned black man itself had important ramifications for her economic well-being. The politics of race and skin color, interracially and intraracially, meant that her spouse, being closer to whiteness, could more likely benefit from expanded avenues of social and financial mobility.[109] Derry's kidnapping scheme also highlights the financial, and perhaps social, desperation of poor black women.

The murder conviction of Annie Winson in 1899 showcases how social and financial considerations shaped black female violence. Winson poisoned her husband, believing she would then marry her accomplice, Albert Smith, who promised a better standard of life and financial support. Following the crime, however, Smith starting seeing other women and failed to support Winson. Before her arrest, Winson reportedly threatened Smith, claiming, "Albert, you said you would care for me if I came out here, and that you would marry me and be a father to my children, but you are not doing it."[110] Apparently cognizant of the racial power dynamics operating in the criminal justice system, Winson further advised Smith, "I helped you do the dirty work and I'll put the white man on you."[111] Despite Winson's threats, the white man's justice system proved hardly a viable option for black women. Rather, black female violence often existed as the most expedient avenue, if not for justice, at the very least, for vengeance.[112]

Mary Hannah Tabbs vs. the Justice System

It appears that in a rare case a black woman manipulated justice for her own benefit. She deployed—or rather performed—domesticity in a manner that enabled her to benefit from the kind of chivalry that most white women enjoyed. One of the most interesting and troubling cases revolves around a thirty-two-year-old migrant, Mary Hannah Tabbs, who in 1887 appears to have had a mastery of the social dynamics of the period as well as a firm grasp on violence and brutality (fig. 7). Convicted in the murder of Wakefield Gaines, also black, Mary Hannah Tabbs's crime, extraordinarily brutal, unveiled the extremities of rage, but her well-timed confession and courtroom maneuvering also bear witness to her incisive grasp of the interplay of race, gender, sexuality, and justice.

Born Mary Hannah Shepherd in Virginia in 1855, she most likely was the child of slaves, if she was not enslaved herself, and she may well have witnessed the hardships of enslavement and the carnage of southern brutality. Perhaps these early experiences shaped her relationship with violence as an adult.[113] Though little about her early childhood is recoverable, by 1873 she had married and migrated with her husband, John Tabbs, to Maryland, and the two came to Philadelphia in 1876.[114] Just over a year before she was arrested, William Brock, a wealthy farmer, hired her as a servant for his estate in Cornwells, a suburb just outside Philadelphia.[115] Tabbs worked at the Brocks' residence as a domestic and brought her niece, Annie Richardson, to work there as well.[116]

During her employment at the Brock estate, Tabbs befriended another servant, a young mulatto named Wakefield Gaines. The nature of their relationship at this point is unclear, though rumors of her jealousy over Gaines's interest in her niece suggested that Tabbs wanted more than friendship from Gaines, who was almost ten years younger. According to Gaines's sister, Tabbs "had great influence over young Gaines. He was afraid of her. She followed him wherever he moved."[117] On May 25, 1886, after only a few months at the estate, Richardson vanished without a trace. Many in Cornwells believed that Tabbs had something to do with her sudden disappearance. Authorities would later

FIG. 7. Mary Hannah Tabbs, *Rogues Gallery Books* (1887). Courtesy of the Philadelphia City Archive.

confirm this when Richardson told police and reporters that Tabbs beat her unmercifully if she made the slightest mistake or did anything to upset Gaines. She ran away at the end of May fearing for her safety.[118] Shortly after Richardson's departure both Gaines and Tabbs left the Brock residence as well.[119] Once back in Philadelphia, they remained in close contact.

The two became entangled in an illicit affair, a relationship soon marred by bitter arguments and violent disputes.[120] Gaines's sister told authorities that Tabbs slashed her brother's face after finding him talking to another woman. Tabbs reportedly declared that "she would kill him yet."[121] In another instance, Tabbs sent Gaines a letter telling him "she would catch up to him if it took ten years."[122] Under oath, neighbors of Tabbs and Gaines testified that Tabbs routinely lied about their relationship, often introducing herself as either Mary Shepherd or claiming that Gaines was her nephew or cousin. Despite her attempts to conceal the nature of the relationship, many suspected an affair, as Gaines visited Tabbs daily at her home on 1642 Richard Street, in the Seventh Ward, when John Tabbs went to work.[123] In addition, Mary Tabbs was a frequent visitor at 207 Schell Street, where Gaines rented a room. Gaines's

FIG. 8. George Wilson, *Rogues Gallery Books* (1887). Courtesy of the Philadelphia City Archive.

landlady testified that Tabbs sometimes paid Gaines's rent and did his washing. Other neighbors commented that the two argued every day including Sunday.[124]

Three weeks before the murder, George Wilson, also a former employee of the Brock estate, contacted Tabbs, claiming to have knowledge of her niece's whereabouts (fig. 8).[125] Tabbs offered to pay Wilson two dollars if he brought her niece to her. Some time after, Gaines escorted Wilson to Tabbs's house, where he made another proposition. According to Tabbs, Wilson waited until Gaines left to tell her, "If you send the girl some clothes and money to pay for her fare, Annie will come."[126] Though she said she paid him, Wilson still did not bring her niece. A few days later he left a strange letter at Tabbs's house. The letter, supposedly from Richardson, was addressed to Gaines, though it had no postage stamp or postmark. The letter told of Richardson's difficulty finding work and stated that she was tired and depressed. She thanked Gaines for his concern but asked him to forget about her and warned him not to contact her, as she would be moving soon. Detectives would later conclude that Gaines forged the letter in an effort to dissuade Tabbs from searching for Richardson.[127]

TRICKING THE TRICKS

At their next meeting, Gaines accused Wilson of lying about having knowledge of Richardson's whereabouts. An argument ensued. Before day's end, Tabbs would have a black eye, Gaines would be murdered and dismembered, and Tabbs and Wilson would dispose of Gaines's remains.[128] On February 17, 1887, the torso of Wakefield Gaines, wrapped in a piece of calico, surfaced in a pond just beyond the city limits. Police and medical examiners, after interviewing train conductors, one of whom reported seeing a black woman carrying a large, awkwardly shaped package, and employees at the Brock estate, arrested Tabbs, who eventually confessed to dumping Gaines's remains. However, the events leading to his murder remained cloudy at best.

According to Tabbs's confession, Gaines and Wilson had a violent altercation. Wilson struck Gaines several times on the head with a chair, causing his death. Wilson then dragged the body downstairs to the cellar, removed Gaines's clothing, went out, and returned with a butcher's cleaver. Wilson dismembered the body, wrapped the parts in paper, and used a calico strap for the torso. Wilson disposed of the head, arms, and legs, and Tabbs took Gaines's torso out toward the Brock estate and threw it in the pond.[129] Tabbs also struck a deal with Hattie Armstrong, one of her neighbors, to pawn Gaines's clothes and the cleaver—offering Armstrong twenty-five cents for her trouble.[130]

The authorities, hardly convinced by Tabbs's story, suspected she had played more of an active role, especially considering that witnesses recalled her having a black eye the day after the murder. Upon his arrest, Wilson corroborated Tabbs's story that he was at the house on Richard Street and that Gaines had called him a liar. According to Wilson, he and Gaines fought, and he hit Gaines with a chair, knocking him down. At this point, Wilson ran out of the house, leaving Gaines sitting on the settee. He returned around noon and claimed that Tabbs gave him a package and ordered him to get rid of it, threatening that if he opened it or tried to pawn it "she would kill" him.[131] Wilson admitted that he disposed of the head first and returned later that evening for the rest of Gaines's remains.

During their trial, both prisoners continued to blame each other. There were glaring discrepancies and omissions in each of their testimonies. Wilson's family and employers charged that he was at work for most of the day, save the morning when he was sent on an errand and, presumably, when he took his meals. Tabbs had no alibi and no one to verify whether Gaines was dead when Wilson left her house after the scuffle that morning. To explain her black eye, Tabbs told authorities that she had fallen onto the proverbial doorknob — apparently a timeless culprit in domestic disputes. Evidence of Gaines's blood was found in Tabbs's cellar, on her clothes, and, reportedly, also on Wilson's clothes and personal belongings.[132] Though police had proof of her whereabouts, Annie Richardson did not participate in the trial, and authorities never recovered the head, arms, or legs of Wakefield Gaines.

Trial testimony published in the *Ledger* raised more questions than it answered. The true cause of Tabbs's injury remained a mystery as did any possible motive explaining why either Wilson or Tabbs would help each other dispose of Gaines's body. But beyond the ambiguities, Tabbs and Gaines had the prior stormy relationship, and Tabbs's black eye suggested that she had, perhaps, been involved in a separate altercation with Gaines after Wilson departed — if Wilson's version of events was true. Gaines's sister told police that Gaines was engaged to another woman and soon planned to wed — the authorities speculated that jealousy might have caused some sort of row.[133] Moreover, neighbors and John Tabbs told reporters that his wife had a violent temper, and an anonymous letter surfaced charging that she had killed a man in Richmond, Virginia — though police could not substantiate the charges.[134] Indeed, despite the confusion surrounding the case, the most significant evidence implicated Tabbs as Gaines's murderer. She could have been convicted of murder in the first degree, a charge carrying either a death sentence or lengthy confinement at Eastern.

Tabbs, however, managed to elicit sympathy from the court by packaging herself as a fallen woman. Specifically, Tabbs tailored her conduct with investigators and in the courtroom to associate herself with attributes customarily assigned to white womanhood. She burst into tears during her police interrogation when describing how Wilson savagely beat Gaines. She explained that throughout the entire ordeal, her primary concern was the safe return of her niece, to whom she referred in court as "her little girl." Portraying herself as a bereaved mother, Tabbs openly apologized to her husband, blaming herself for not listening to him and making such a mess of their lives. She also routinely spoke to Wilson during the trial, reaching out to him, asking if he was okay.[135] Publicly deferring to the patriarchal authority of her husband and demonstrating selfless Christian charity in her concern for Wilson, Tabbs distanced herself from her violent past and perhaps the more stereotypical attributes assigned to black women.

When cross-examined about her alleged affair and rocky relationship with Gaines, Tabbs retained her dignity, answering that the others were mistaken: she and Gaines were good friends. Her disposal of Gaines's torso, probable adultery, and history of vitriolic bouts with the victim disappeared behind a façade of contrite womanhood. Remorseful and apologetic, Tabbs represented herself as the embodiment of gentility. Moreover, John Tabbs, her husband, told reporters that because he was so much older than his wife—almost twenty years her senior—and worked such long hours, he initially believed that her friendship with Gaines would be beneficial for his wife, who would otherwise be alone. Isolated and ultimately "led astray," Tabbs, in a rare instance, managed to assume the role of the fallen woman. Tabbs's shrewd maneuvers proved convincing, as she almost eluded punishment entirely. Convicted as an accessory, Tabbs received a two-year sentence, later reduced to sixteen months. Wilson was convicted of murder in the second degree and sentenced to eight years at Eastern. The judge concluded it was more likely that the man was the aggressor—that the two men fought and Tabbs became involved after the murder in attempting to cover up the crime.[136]

The murder of Wakefield Gaines was a complicated ordeal. Mary Hannah Tabbs appears to have lived by her own rules, adhering to female domesticity when it suited her. In switching codes as needed, depending upon her audience, Tabbs was apparently as clever as she was deceitful. Perhaps initiated by a domestic skirmish gone horribly awry, Tabbs's crime hardly reflected the norm as it existed either in crime or outcome among black female offenders. But the complexities of the case reveal a breadth of multilayered, interwoven social relationships that included intimate interactions among family members, spouses, and lovers as well as the interplay of neighbors, landlords, and employers.

The Logic and the Consequences of Black Female Crime

Both illuminating and disturbing, black women's sex crimes and crimes of violence offer potent evidence of surrogate discourses of femininity and make visible proxy responses to social violence. Brazen and wryly clever—even heroic at points—in their schemes to trick the tricks, black women both resisted domestic violence and challenged sexual boundaries. Unfortunately, their crimes also aided and abetted their own exploitation, signaling their acceptance of exclusionary ideals and the objectification of their sexuality.

Perhaps, inescapably, black female criminals too often only recycled and, in appropriating them, validated the instruments of oppression. But whether innovative reformulations of the mechanisms of power or tragic recapitulations, the crimes committed ultimately afforded vengeance in those situations in which justice would have been almost impossible to attain. Black female crime did not constitute collectively organized resistance nor did it create exclusive criminal communities that touted their own discourses of civic morality. Rather, black women's crimes, whether voicing frustration, exhibiting resistance, or responding to dreams deferred, exhibited logic unique to the perpetrators. Neither inherently pathological nor random, the crimes unveil emotional damage and trauma as well as admirable doses of ornery self-determination.

Chapter Four

ROUGHNECK WOMEN, PALE
REPRESENTATIONS, AND DARK CRIMES:
BLACK FEMALE CRIMINALS AND
POPULAR CULTURE

James Denny of Pine st., above 23rd, was held up by two colored Amazons
last night at Juniper and South sts., and robbed of $2. . . . Denny said his
arms were grabbed by a big colored woman while another went through his
pockets and stole his wallet.

— *Philadelphia Evening Bulletin*, April 2, 1909

THE STORY THAT APPEARED IN THE *Philadelphia Evening Bulletin* concerning James Denny's robbery provides a fairly common blend of the fact and
fiction that made press fodder in the early part of the twentieth century. The
robbery that reportedly transpired most likely did take place, but rather than
being overtaken by "two colored Amazons," Denny was more likely a victim
of the badger game. Whereas the justice system might attribute the robbery to
Denny's unseemly solicitation of would-be black prostitutes, popular presses
often either masked or omitted white men's socially unacceptable intentions.
At the same time that news stories erased white male accountability, however,
they invoked exaggerated notions of black female criminals, creating arche-
types and caricatures of urban black femme fatales. The outrageous nicknames
for the caricatures—Colored Amazon being one of the most telling—fit into
a larger social narrative in popular crime reports.[1]

Based on racial bias against black women in general and a bigoted understanding of urban crime and its causes, the caricature affirmed white su-

premacy by embodying physical and social traits contrasting whiteness and white middle-class values. Moreover, press accounts created and deployed the Colored Amazon together with caricatures of white women and black and white men. These caricatures and the folklore assigned to them are important historical artifacts. The depictions demonstrate how popular representations reflected and shaped public perceptions of crime as well as broader notions of race, gender, and sexuality.[2]

The Colored Amazon, along with other stereotypical tropes, shifted public attention away from white male infractions and the broader social barriers that actually contributed to criminal offending. Moreover, notions of the Colored Amazon maligned all black women, not only those arrested or convicted of a crime. The negative images veiled the real urban hazards of poverty, discrimination, and violence that jeopardized the city's inhabitants, promoting instead false notions of the danger that black women posed to whites.

White Farmers vs. Colored Amazons

"Negro Women Rob and Kill Farmer in Den" boldly headlined the *North American* in 1908. Replete with scathing adjectives and incendiary cries for an end to epidemic crime in the city, the feature depicted Mamie Brown and Helen Thomas, two black women accused of the murder of a white man, as unrestrained and sexually rapacious.[3] The article relied on cultural symbols that vilified the alleged perpetrators and manipulated and omitted information to portray black female criminals as direct threats to white male liberty.

According to the *North American*'s version of events, Brown and Thomas "hailed" and "jostled" the victim, Anthony Madden, into their home, where they proceeded to beat him to death with a baseball bat and hatchet.[4] Focusing on the women and their alleged desperate murder of a white farmer, the paper associated Brown and Thomas with disrepute because of their residence in the city's Tenderloin section. The paper conceded that Madden was "not a total stranger to the 'red light' district" but insisted that in this instance he became an unsuspecting victim who in a "half-dazed, semi-drunken condition" fell prey to the Negro abductresses.

Yet even as the paper implied physical coercion, the women's statements, included in the story, indicated otherwise. Brown's statement especially suggested that she had had some prior interaction with Madden. According to her published account, "There were some words . . . and I threatened to throw the man out of the house. Ella heard the row, and came running." Her accomplice, quoted as demanding, "You leave this house, or I'll pitch you out," further supports this notion. The article claimed that after the women ordered Madden to leave, he was "stubbornly drunk" and "braced himself against the casing, refusing to budge."[5] Implicit in the account is that Madden's refusal to leave precipitated the alleged attack. This is a marked difference from the idea that, as the paper alleged, Thomas and Brown abducted Madden against his will and murdered him in cold blood. According to court records, the two women admitted to soliciting Madden for the purposes of prostitution but claimed they ended up having an altercation with him.[6] Ultimately, the motive or precise catalyst of the assault is largely indiscernible, as Brown and Thomas likely made statements minimizing their guilt.

Yet what is discernible is that the reporting of the case invoked a narrative fundamentally out of step with the published facts. The very account that portrayed Brown and Thomas as deliberate, bloodthirsty aggressors included eyewitness statements that pointed to the contrary. How could Brown have been strong enough to "jostle" Madden through her door, yet be unable, even with assistance from Thomas, to remove him? Madden, according to the article, progressed from "half-dazed and semi-drunken" to "stubbornly drunk." How long was Madden in the house? Did he drink with the women? Though the answers to these questions might seem pertinent, in the end the details surrounding the crime proved less important in the piece than the identities of the victim and the perpetrators. The spectacle of black female depravity advanced in the story all but eclipsed Madden's public intoxication and frequent patronage of establishments in the Tenderloin district. Madden, scripted as an "old farmer," is absolved of any impropriety and is cast instead as a martyr in the gruesome "Tenderloin tragedy."[7]

During the course of their arrest, trial, and ultimate conviction, news accounts further ascribed remorselessness, and insanity to Brown and Thomas. The *Philadelphia Record* wrote that Thomas "screamed" about her innocence, threatened suicide, and maniacally "hit her head against the brass railing around the prisoners' dock."[8] This sketch of Thomas as being wild and bereft of control or civility contrasted with depictions of her accomplice. Using incendiary adjectives that connote savagery, accounts reported that Brown, "sat stoically through all of the excitement and remained unmoved, even when the bloody hatchet with which Madden was killed in the negro den . . . was produced."[9]

Despite the story's conclusion that two malefactors brutalized an innocent, unsuspecting citizen, the facts surrounding each of the subjects depict a different scenario. Neither Brown nor Thomas had extensive criminal records. The two young women's educational level, marital status, age, and employment records typified the larger population of black female migrants in Philadelphia. According to Eastern State Penitentiary intake records, Brown and Thomas, each twenty-five years of age, migrated from North Carolina and Washington, D.C., respectively. Both women attended public schools and both worked as domestics in Philadelphia. Like 69 percent of black women imprisoned at Eastern, Mamie Brown was a first-time offender. Helen Thomas had served a prior one-month sentence at the county prison for assault and battery.[10]

Trial testimony also painted a different picture of Brown and Thomas, neither of whom appeared to be the sullen, brooding fiends the press described. Upon her arrest, Thomas did not shriek riotously but was instead, on the oath of Officer George Merriman, "wringing her hands, and crying loudly, and saying repeatedly she did not mean to hurt him."[11] Brown, shaken by the incident and her subsequent arrest, appeared both remorseful and forthcoming with authorities. In fact, she cooperated with investigators despite pleas from Thomas not to "rat" on her. Anthony Madden, too, fell short of the portrait of an innocent farmer. Both women admitted to soliciting Madden for prostitution, but once upstairs Brown claimed that she became uneasy with Madden. When they could not reach an agreement about the particulars of her services, Brown insisted he leave. Madden refused. According to testimony, he stated "he did not give a damn who said so . . . he was going to stay right in bed."[12] After Thomas tried to drag Madden from the bed, a scuffle ensued during which Thomas asked Brown to get a baseball bat. Brown testified that she initially refused, and that it was Madden who declared, "Yes, get the baseball bat, I want to show her how to play ball; she don't know how to play ball."[13]

The altercation became more violent, with Madden and Brown wrestling for the bat, and Thomas getting a hammer. A hatchet was never used in the crime. Madden struck Thomas, and the two exchanged blows, though

Thomas's blows likely inflicted more damage than Madden's fists. The three continued struggling as they moved downstairs, where, according to Thomas, "we both pushed him out of the door. He fell on his back. I then shut the door. I looked out of the window and saw that he was hurt and we both ran away."[14] To further the plausibility of accidental death, medical testimony entered into evidence at both trials suggested that Madden, who died from a fractured skull, could have sustained the fatal injuries from his fall onto the pavement outside Thomas's home.[15] Though described through the eyes of those responsible for his death, the circumstances surrounding the killing seem incompatible with the work of cold, calculating murderers. Whatever the case, neither party was blameless, yet the death that resulted appeared to be far from either Brown's or Thomas's intentions. In the end, Brown received a five-year sentence for involuntary manslaughter, and Thomas was convicted of murder in the second degree and sentenced to ten years.[16]

Despite the outcome of the trials, the inconsistencies in the press coverage cannot be dismissed as the result of simple journalistic error or hyperbole. The attributes assigned to Brown, Thomas, and Madden betray the underpinnings of a larger cultural narrative. Madden's somewhat crude typecasting as an elderly farmer operated as a trope, a cultural icon of traditional white masculinity and the autonomy of the agrarian-based lifestyle. Juxtaposing the farmer trope against the seedy underside of the city subtly played on white men's fears of the broad structural changes caused by industrialization and urbanization. Black women in this cultural landscape signified white men's loss of public and private domination. Madden's violent death, recounted in several papers, positioned customary white manhood in mortal conflict with a modern, urban black female scourge. Black women, in this discourse, were unflinching in their fiendishness, brutal in their attacks, and sexually unrestrained, and they enacted a greed that stripped white men of life and property. As the *North American* decried, "Not even a slip of paper was left on [Madden's] body."[17]

The Supremacist Ideology

White men's prior ownership, control, and uninhibited sexual access to black women had been, at least in theory, subverted in the modern era. As a result, somehow the ultimate submissive was transformed into what whites perceived as a dangerous urban aggressor. Moreover, depicted as large, dark, dangerous, and hypersexual, the Colored Amazon starkly contrasted with mainstream symbols of domesticity.[18] Resting upon stereotypes that supported negative criminal inscription, the caricature chiseled out ideological boundaries of middle-class social and cultural values through its opposition.

Yet Philadelphia's Colored Amazon neither operated within a vacuum nor proved entirely unique to the City of Brotherly Love. Rather, the figure was but one narrative step in a series of both local and national assaults on broadening notions of citizenship and democracy.[19] As supremacist ideologies permeated the body politic, whites positioned themselves as superior not only to blacks in the United States but to all racial others across the globe. Senator Albert J. Beveridge noted in 1900 that the white race, as "trustees under God," were "henceforth to lead in the regeneration of the world."[20] Internationally, this ideology took the form of American imperialism in the Pacific Islands and the Caribbean. Domestically, the rhetoric manifested itself in continued westward expansion, eugenics, and an expansion of prisons and asylums. Pennsylvania established a flurry of institutions such as the State Hospital for the Insane at Norristown in 1880, the State Asylum for the Chronic Insane at Wernersville in Berks County in 1893, and the State Institution for the Feeble Minded of Western Pennsylvania in 1897. The legislature also approved plans for Pennsylvania Village for the Feeble Minded Women in 1913.[21]

White middle-class families existed as both "a constituency and an idea"; their definition of whiteness, masculinity and femininity, and sexuality represented a literal and ideological cornerstone of mainstream American public consciousness.[22] The emerging national identity superimposed a universal order of things that essentialized white dominance, transforming whiteness from a social construct to an American reality. The same rhetoric that promoted imperialism abroad revolved domestically around maintaining stability and social conformity. Physical features, sexual practices, and social mores different from those represented as the cultural norm not only challenged mainstream morality but also represented destabilizing abnormalities.[23]

Crime, intemperance, homosexuality, and violence all testified to social and genetic deficits that endangered the moral fabric of the country. Cultural difference became almost synonymous with pathology and crime. Newly constructed penitentiaries, juvenile detention facilities, workhouses, and reformatories implemented practices designed to protect the public. Administrators measured craniums, facial features, and other atavistic traits to distinguish individuals who could be reformed and reintegrated into society from chronic deviants—those better served by lengthy confinement in prisons and state asylums.[24] Domestic safety, packaged in the language of science, masked the racism underscoring its ideological paradigm. As Senator John T. Morgan explained in 1890, "The inferiority of the negro race, as compared to the white race, is so essentially true, and so obvious that, to assume it in an argument cannot be justly attributed to prejudice."[25]

The Role of Popular Culture and the Press

Popular culture, too, promoted white supremacy by broadcasting images of racial subordination and the purported dangers of deviant sexualities and shifting gender relationships. African-American culture, and blacks in general, made ideal oppositional figures onto which predominant notions of social order could be transplanted.[26] A commercial industry born of economic dispossession, brutality, southern apartheid, and the prevalence of de facto segregation in the North took root. The trading of visual artifacts of black subjugation replaced the literal practice of buying and selling slaves. The American economy—and perhaps the American psyche as well—embarked on a new racialized commercial exchange. Racist depictions of "coons," "mammies," and "sambos" became so entrenched in American life at the turn of the century that industrial factories mass-produced toys, cards, and figurines to meet consumer demand.[27] Blackness, as defined by white nostalgia for the antebellum era, became an especially successful marketing tool. Cartoons of "jungle bunnies," "Aunt Jemimas," and "Uncle Toms" packaged pancake flour, tobacco, and other household items.[28]

Indeed, as everyday household goods flew off the shelves on the promise of providing "A Slave in a Box," equally lucrative were plays, films, and songs mocking the provincial ways of the country's newly freed black masses.[29] Minstrelsy and other early theatrical productions created a profitable lampooning of black culture that gave white audiences, "safe behind the ruthless ridiculing," a vantage point from which they fetishized and projected taboo characteristics onto blacks.[30] By the close of the nineteenth century, however, white

FIG. 9. "Good
Bye My Honey
I'm Gone" (1888).
Courtesy of the Sheet
Music Collection,
Free Library of
Philadelphia.

actors were not the only ones blackening up for the stage. Black entertainers
also toured, performing a variety of "coon songs" and vaudeville acts to packed
theaters and open houses.

Romanticizing plantation life, the performances absolved white guilt while
the raucous buffoonery maintained the white ideology of moral and racial
superiority.[31] Reminiscent of the political cartoonist Edward Clay's damning
series in the 1820s, turn-of-the-century lampoons of black life centered upon
notions of inadequate black women. In 1888, the lyrics of a popular "coon"
song, "Good Bye My Honey I'm Gone," made a mockery of black social relationships (fig. 9). Showcasing black female promiscuity, verses such as "I
thought this girl was the nicest little daisy / Till a dude came along from the
roller rink so crazy / And I hollered for a copper / But he said he couldn't
stop her / Good bye, my honey, I'm gone" intermingled notions of immorality and lawlessness.[32] Whereas white femininity was constructed in alliance
with white masculinity and thus was responsible for morally grounding the

culture—black women's purported inadequacies ultimately bore implications for the entire race.[33]

The popularity of this genre and its performers was not lost on Philadelphians. In 1892, the city's inhabitants eagerly anticipated the "popular plantation melodies" and other "native minstrel treats" promised by the upcoming performance of Sissieretta Jones, otherwise known as the "the Black Patti."[34] Whether on the minstrel stage or in "coon" songs, the theme underscoring popular entertainment was one of wistful yearning for the preceding decades when blacks knew their place. Mainstream newspapers participated in the new trade in blackness by printing stories on everything from diet to dialect. Philadelphia newspapers, like racist southern propaganda, fed an anxious public glorified tales of blacks' prior contentment with plantation life.

Through a plethora of stories and song lyrics like those of "Uncle Isaac's Christmas Song," published in 1892, vignettes obscured the horrors of enslavement, professing that "dem good ole slav'ry Christmusses wus good enough fo' me."[35] In stories such as "The Marvelous and Horrible: Superstitious Lore of the Old Negroes," from 1885, and "Jaspar's Wooing: How the Colored Preacher and 'Sis' Tilda Did Their Brief Courtship," from 1891, Philadelphia exhibited a curious combination of castigation and nostalgia. Ironically, though Pennsylvania was among the first states to pass legislation calling for the gradual abolition of slavery in 1780, local papers frequently reminisced about formerly enslaved black women through figures like "Old Aunt Peggy," described as being "little and old and wrinkled [who] smoked her pipe in the chimney corner and never walked much."[36]

Depictions of carefree, contented blacks effectively regulated by the plantation system stood in stark contrast to representations of chaotic, confused, violent black urban dwellers.[37] Under titles such as "A Raving Maniac," which appeared in 1890, the stories emphasized the recent migration of black women like Emily Chadwick. Chadwick, "after the Emancipation Proclamation," reportedly packed her few clothes, headed north, and "landed in Philadelphia."[38] The "Negro as a Fatalist," published in 1888, charged that fatalism, a morbid affinity for death, was common to "all members of the negro race." Harping on African Americans' "horrible fascination" with scenes of sickness and death, the piece detailed a wild funeral ceremony with black mourners languishing over corpses as long as "circumstance and the police [would] permit."[39] The tales implied that blacks, when left to their own devices, could too easily sink into pathological depravity. The juxtaposing of skewed images of blacks before and after Emancipation validated slavery and justified the need for ongoing white moral supervision. Moreover, more bestial characters soon supplanted the comical watermelon-loving "sambo" and "coon." Representations of urban blacks, especially those of black women, became increasingly tied to immorality and criminal transgression.

In such an atmosphere, crime and an array of caricatured criminal protagonists quickly gained prominence in newspaper reporting. Often portraying a decent white citizenry on the edge of mammoth urban decay, press coverage brought the contours of national middle-class domesticity to the public. Stories cautioning the public against deviance coincided with popular pulp fiction and medical discourses on aberrant social conduct. Epidemic crime and social instability demanded that goodly citizens be vigilant. In addition, the stories aided in that vigilance by compelling whites to conform to strict moral tenets—this while corporate greed quietly rewarded the ruthless avarice of the self-made man.[40] The articles also became a vehicle for white fantasies and taboo desires. While warning of the perils of lawless immorality, the vivid tales facilitated vicarious participation in proscribed behaviors—those assigned to blacks, poor people, or swarthy ethnic immigrants. Far from ruffling mainstream gentility, this sensational coverage fed an insatiable public appetite. Citizens could figuratively participate in a variety of debased activities for the price of a daily, and presses quickly recognized the profit margin for muckraking, yellow journalism, and scandal-revealing exposés.[41]

Reporters, financially rewarded for their outlandish reports of illicit crime, showcased a veritable cornucopia of racial, sexual, and gender transgressions. Crime became a fixed column in a number of dailies, the section typically featuring listings of gruesome offenses, heroic arrests, and stern judicial proceedings. Philadelphia papers, like those in New York, Boston, and New Jersey cities, included lists of convictions handed down in the city's primary criminal court, the Court of Oyer and Terminer.[42] But it was not the dry facts regarding the inner workings of the criminal justice system that captivated readers. Rather, reports of unseemly aspects of the human character grabbed public attention and allowed journalists, predominantly educated whites with ties to those in local government, to inscribe social and civic morality on the public conscience.[43]

ROUGHNECK WOMEN, PALE REPRESENTATIONS

Even more than simply extending an anonymous platform for salacious revelry or championing mainstream mores, crime coverage largely functioned as a forum mediating social change.[44] For a fee, abnormality, deviance, and criminal violence could be laid bare before the public for the just cause of educating citizens about the perils of urbanization and industrialization. The blame for poverty and other pandemics was placed on labor competition from blacks, immigrants, and all women. The breakdown of traditional family values stemmed from the corrupting influence of African Americans and foreigners, who possessed weak social and cultural values. Their role in surveying, dissecting, and reconstituting social praxis to determine good and evil or, in the context of the period, normal and abnormal made newspapers a highly powerful instrument. The press could not only influence, but also shape and project a variety of social and political agendas.[45] In addition, considering the potential for financial gain, white male journalists had little to dissuade them from publishing exaggerated, biased accounts.

African-American women, and blacks in general, were not the only narrative victims: crime reports also employed caricatures of "sexual inverts," "fallen women," and "Chinese white-slavers." But it was African Americans who grounded the gallery of criminal caricatures. The blame for disparaging representations, however, cannot be placed solely on journalists or the press because they, like the criminals they railed against, were products of society. The caricatures evolved within a specific cultural, social, political, and economic context, and it is this context that is reflected in both crime and its representations.

The World of the Colored Amazon

Just as tales of "bad niggers," "desperadoes," and "black rapists" mirrored and justified southern vigilante justice, the image of the Colored Amazon anchored and served a white supremacist agenda in the North and to a lesser extent in certain parts of the urban South.[46] Accounting for less than 2 percent of the penitentiary population and principally imprisoned for larceny, African-American women nonetheless appeared in crime narratives in Philadelphia as being among the most heinous of criminal offenders.[47] Partly because of their rising numbers and partly because poverty forced many to live in the most crime-ridden neighborhoods, urban black women came to embody that which many whites found wholly objectionable about city life. Crowded into tene-ments and often poorly dressed, black female laborers were visually incongru-ous with the developing national identity and emerging dominant culture.

As a central element of popular constructions of crime, race or, to be more specific, color appeared in crime narratives as a social indicator of guilt.[48] Gra-dations of darkness in the case of the aforementioned Mary Hannah Tabbs, a Virginia migrant convicted as an accomplice to murder in 1887, underwent significant changes over the course of her arrest, trial, and conviction.[49] Ini-tially described in the *Inquirer* as a "mulatto, with well-defined African fea-tures, but a sharp clear eye," Tabbs, following her arrest, became "Mary Tabbs, the negress."[50] Shifting her race from one presumably more elite based on a closer proximity to whiteness to one more debased given the attributes asso-ciated with blackness, the descriptions cast shadows on Tabbs's innocence. Ac-counts depicted her captor, a white train conductor, as possessing "big, honest, sharp blue eyes."[51] Honesty and intelligence were assigned to the white con-ductor, but Tabbs's color moves from simply describing her race to impugning its virtue.

Articles made much of the contrast between Tabbs and her victim, Wake-field Gaines, also African-American. According to one account, Gaines was "a remarkably light mulatto, and considerable difficulty would be experienced in distinguishing the difference between him and a white man."[52] Though not nearly as bold or as fully developed as later versions of the narrative, the shifting racial hues and their implications in Tabbs's coverage reveal an early articula-tion of the Colored Amazon's constitutive relationship to whiteness and mas-culinity. Blackness was maligned as criminal and, though honesty and justice shone through blue eyes, the representation just began to hint at the poten-tial threat—Tabbs's victim was *near* white. The heightened danger present in the narrative was not that the victim was black, but that he could easily have been white.

As the number of black female migrants rose, white apprehension about their increased presence intensified, and so did the perceived threat of the Colored Amazon. The image and its narrative evolved to incorporate stigma-tizing notions of violence, sexuality, and morality. As part of a national cultural construction, the figure also marked white anxiety about hiring black women when the number of white women working outside the home began to grow.

FIG. 10. "The Crazy Cook,"
The National Police Gazette
(1885).

Against this backdrop, the Colored Amazon's violence was not confined to the black community but appeared more strongly connected to wage labor in the white community. "A Crazy Cook," published in the *National Police Gazette* in 1885, charged that a rebellious black domestic uttered a "Sioux-like whoop" as she destroyed her employers' home.[53] Reportedly chewing paper off the walls and ripping up the carpet, the cook was depicted as the ultimate example of a Colored Amazon.

The illustration accompanying the account features the faceless, jet-black body of a domestic swinging a chair above a fallen statue of the "Venus de Milo" —a timeless symbol of white female virtue—that lies at her feet (fig. 10).[54] Although not the vessel of disease featured in racist southern propaganda, the "Crazy Cook" was yet another damning social commentary. Full-figured and emitting savage cries like those of a "wild Indian," the cook embodied the antithesis of white womanhood.[55] Her absence of restraint, maturity, and civilized domesticity aided a larger agenda that discouraged white women from abandoning their conventional household duties. At the same time it demonized already exploited black domestics.

The ferocity displayed in both the cook's story and her image points to another aspect taking form in public perceptions of black female wage earners—though not simply as employees but also as coworkers. Popular images, in fact, ridiculed and demonized African-American women's desire for better employment and better wages. Depicting them as unstable and dangerous, press linkages criminalized these aims and further justified white refusals to work with blacks. The manipulation of race and labor could be a particularly divisive tool, as it benefited the established corporate powers in preventing laborers from uniting effectively.

The 1890 assault and battery case of Pearl Smith, a light-complexioned mulatto, is demonstrative of this broader dynamic. Smith, a twenty-one-year-old Virginia native, was convicted of assault and battery with intent to kill for stabbing a white man, Archie Crippen. Two newspapers, the *Inquirer* and the *Times-Philadelphia*, ran stories on the case. Aside from the names and dates, however, there are few similarities between the papers' accounts of what reportedly transpired. The *Inquirer*, identifying Smith as a mulatto, claimed that she knocked a pipe from Crippen's mouth and drew a "large pocket knife" which she "plunged into his back."[56] Recounting only the most vivid details of the assault, the *Inquirer* provided almost no motive for the crime and simply characterized Smith and Crippen as sparring coworkers. Reportedly, "Pearl's temper got the best of her." The *Times-Philadelphia*, on the other hand, believing that Smith was white, charged that Smith "struck [Crippen] in the back with a small knife which she happened to have in her hands."[57] The level of violence associated with the *Inquirer*'s version of Smith spotlights how narratives transposed savagery onto black women accused of crimes. The story also revealed the dangers whites faced in working with blacks; yet the articles also raise questions about Smith's race.[58]

Whiteness in late-nineteenth-century news was perceived as normative; in other words, an individual was typically assumed to be white unless otherwise specified—and usually color was specified only if other parties were not white. The *Times-Philadelphia*'s omission of Smith's and Crippen's race may have resulted from genuine confusion given that Smith was light complexioned. However, it may also have been a deliberate attempt to avoid disclosing an interracial relationship. In the *Times-Philadelphia* coverage, Smith and Crippen appeared to be social partners as well as coworkers. By this account, the altercation was essentially a "drunken quarrel" that transpired after the two had been out drinking "considerable beer" together.[59] The miscegenation implicit in this association challenged customary race relations. Therefore, by obscuring the details of such an affair the newspaper maintained social divisions and avoided promoting social relationships contrary to those proffered as normal by white middle-class morality.

Late-nineteenth-century definitions of womanhood—which highlighted gentility, virtue, domesticity, and motherhood—principally excluded African-American women, describing them instead as anything but feminine, pure, or pious.[60] Rather, depictions of black women in the press emphasized their brute strength, excessive violence, hypersexuality, and utter lack of remorse.[61] Yet these narrative themes also betray a larger sexual fascination that images of dangerous black women engendered. Detailing the number of stab wounds, pools of blood, and rowdy drunken quarrels, press accounts projected illicit elements of sex and violence onto black women. The *Times-Philadelphia*'s 1884 article provided a somewhat explicit scene when it described Carrie Johnson as languishing in blood while "continuing to kiss and fondle [her victim] through his dying moments and was only torn away when arrested by the police."[62] On August 8, 1890, the *Inquirer* printed a jocular account of Annie Davis's attempt to convince a Philadelphia judge that the defendant, another African-American woman, had assaulted her. Quoted as proposing to show the judge "the tooth marks me breast, too," the story ridiculed Davis's virtue at the same time that it provided an eroticized exchange between two black women. By including Davis's offer to reveal her breast ravaged by teeth marks, the article packaged both women as sexual spectacles for mainstream audiences—essentially furnishing a forbidden commodity to the reading public.[63]

That the sexualized aspects of the Colored Amazon replaced white men's unrestrained sexual access to enslaved black women accentuates the crucial role that sex and sexual danger played in the mainstream imagination; yet it demonstrates long-standing notions about black female sexuality. The peculiarities of desire and disdain saturated popular representations of black female criminals, so much so that narratives customarily contained innuendoes of the illicit regardless of whether the offenses were crimes of passion. In the case of Ellen

Derry, a black woman convicted of kidnapping in 1885, the *Inquirer* inserted a thinly veiled accusation of adultery. Reporting that Derry's husband, "returning after an absence, unexpectedly had found evidence which supplied him with the best reason in the world for abandoning his wife," the piece essentially furnished an account of Derry's adulterous sexual exploits.[64] Reports on Bella Beary, a black woman accused of killing a child in 1903, charged that she had "entertained a young colored man" until "five o'clock in the morning," though this was unrelated to her commission of the alleged crime.[65] The preponderance of lasciviousness effaced white male lust and potentially left black women more vulnerable to sexual violation, as it would be harder to prove allegations of sexual assault given widespread assumptions about their immorality.

But mainstream presses were not alone in deploying explicit images of black female criminals; independent black newspapers likewise participated in the cultural construction of Colored Amazons.[66] Before the facts regarding the case of Emily Lee surfaced, black press coverage too printed rather stereotypical pieces about the ordeal. On March 25, 1905, the *Defender*'s front-page story labeled the accused murderess as "cold blooded." It contended that "a jealousy so intense and deep rooted" motivated the attack. Weaving a seamy tale of childhood friendship, betrayal, and adultery, the story described Lee as overwrought with murderous fury when she shot and killed her lover's wife, Stella Weldon, with "four bullets." Depicting Lee as "not in the least remorseful," the *Defender*'s coverage mirrored mainstream news tactics.

The article contextualized the parties involved, describing Mrs. Weldon as being "well-known and highly respected." Lamenting the crime that "sent a good and virtuous woman to a premature death," the *Defender* humanized the victim by describing Weldon's funeral and the sad loss her family and congregation suffered.[67] The *Defender*'s account diverged from the prevailing discourses through its recognition of the black female victim and her virtue—a rare practice in the mainstream press.

In contrast to their accusatory reporting on the sensational atrocities of African-American women's crimes, mainstream narratives adopted a sympathetic view of white female criminals. In 1885, newspapers described Annie Gaskin, a white woman convicted of murdering her ten-week-old infant with a butcher knife, as a "very poor" woman widowed just "five weeks prior." After briefly describing the child's bloody clothes, found hidden in a closet along with a bloody knife, one paper hastened to add that neighbors reported seeing a large cat marked with blood. Gaskin initially claimed that a wild cat had killed the infant. Instead of receiving a prison sentence, Gaskin was sent to the State Asylum in Norristown, Pennsylvania. Whereas bloody rage became symptomatic of black female depravity, it remained a fundamental aberration for whites, especially white women.[68]

For white female criminals, poverty and isolation were dreadful causes of their offenses rather than the stigmatizing characteristics assigned to black women like Ellen Derry, whose attire, according to the press, consisted of "an old dilapidated silk dress . . . of cheap stuff."[69] That Derry was a woman "dependent for her bread upon her daily toil" won her little compassion in news reports or with the authorities.[70] For "unfortunate" white women like Mary Taggart, who was "wearied with her hard work and . . . in a nervous irritable condition and easily excited," stabbing her teenage son to death in 1893 displayed the mournful effects of urban poverty.[71]

News accounts rarely depicted white women as being abnormally strong, evil, or bereft of remorse. On the contrary, the descriptions of their emotional outbursts in courtrooms emphasized their womanhood and often overshadowed their criminality. In 1898, Jennie Rothermel, a white woman convicted of abortion, reportedly "let out a cry of anguish" upon receiving her sentence and "would have fallen to the floor had she not been caught by an officer of the court."[72] Coverage of the assault and battery conviction of Kate Ness in 1905 noted that she received her sentence "without a tremor," but in a letter begged "her parents' forgiveness." Ness's victim, her married paramour, was referred to in accounts as her friend rather than as her lover.[73] By framing Ness's affair as a "friendship," the report avoided portraying Ness as a spurned adulterer. Moreover, Ness's death at Eastern elicited somber sympathy for "frail little" Ness, who, according to the press, fell victim to a bitter matter of the heart after leaving her village "farmhouse" for the big city. This effective parable could potentially deter forays into spheres unknown and wanting in white male authority.[74]

Disallowing white female autonomy, narratives veiled their criminal culpability with the vagaries of feminine vulnerability. According to the cultural logic, white women who lacked proper male guidance could not negotiate the evils of the city. Urban vice endangered white women and potentially tainted their virtue. To further this notion, caricatures of white female criminals relied heavily upon images of white female "sexual-inverts," the period's term for gays and lesbians. Such inverts were cultural anomalies among women—peculiar to the urban landscape—and functioned as an alternative image to that of the fallen women. Female sexual-inverts affirmed white masculinity and heterosexuality, as crime reports scripted them as being unable to compete with white men. Their crimes reflected their unstable responses when the objects of their affections rejected them for men.[75]

The story "Shot Down Woman who Spurned Her," published in 1901, covered the case of Alice Hutchings, a white woman who assaulted her lover, Mrs. Keck, also white. Departing from the customary sensationalism that such a story might elicit, coverage of Hutchings was understated. Papers avoided disclosing her prior sexual relationships with women, choosing instead to depict Hutchings as possessing an "attachment for Mrs. Keck that amounted to infatuation."[76] Quoting a doctor's testimony, Hutchings was portrayed as "insane at the time she made the assault" and "mentally irresponsible for her act."[77] A single woman in the city, Hutchings could not be considered responsible for either her curious infatuation or the resulting crime—at least according to medical testimony and the press spin. Though popular notions of white womanhood reduced Hutchings's responsibility, the legal system did not: she was convicted of assault and battery with intent to kill and sent to Eastern.[78]

Depraved black women and endangered white females were complementary narrative constructions that advanced the emerging social discourse of race and patriarchy. The Colored Amazon exaggerated black female crime and violence and simultaneously promoted traditional white masculinity and female morality. Prevailing narratives highlighted the dangerous outcomes of white women's social and cultural transgressions. Additionally, black and white women's caricatures complemented those defining male lawlessness and social deviance. Indeed, press accounts also made good use of black and white male iconographies. Like the versions deployed in black female crime coverage, black male caricatures exhibited extreme levels of brutality and predatory sexuality and a paucity of principles.[79]

The Black Male Criminal

The most popular depictions of black male lawlessness paralleled those created in the South by focusing on black men's crimes against white women. As portrayals of "bad niggers" surfaced, however, so too did a number of all-too-familiar practices. "Lynched at Midnight" splashed across the *Times-Philadelphia*'s front page in 1886 and chronicled the grisly events of a story headlined "A New Jersey Negro Hanged for Assaulting a Beautiful Girl." The story juxtaposed the white victim's "rosy" face, "Grecian nose," and "pouting mouth and flashing blue eyes" with the "villainous" Negro assailant, Mingo Jack, who was, "apeish in countenance." Vividly describing how "the negro threw himself upon her prostrate body in fiendish fury," the paper meticulously detailed Jack's hanging corpse, whose "mouth and nose were filled with clotted blood." Invoking images of masked avengers with "pistols and weapons that glisten[ed]," the piece recounted the "Negro's pleas" as he cowered at the feet of white men.[80]

Codified through the rhetoric of protection, the stories facilitated voyeuristic participation in rape and murderous violence without the shame associated with being possessed of a weak morality.[81] The narrative situated white women as the exclusive property of white men at the same time that it overshadowed white men's rape and sexual exploitation of black women — such accounts were conspicuously absent in crime reporting. The violent spectacle of lynching publicized white men's ability to mete out justice through extralegal means. By virtue of white men's social and cultural location, their lynching of a black rapist constituted a just response, positing their actions as being above the law.

Though not nearly approaching the scale of lynching that occurred in the South, southern-based lynching narratives worked effectively for the purposes of white supremacy in the North. Even in cases of robbery, theft, or assault and battery, the press invoked the "black male rapist" narrative.[82] "LYNCH HIM! THE CRY" was the *Record*'s 1903 headline for the story of an African-American man accused of robbing a white woman. Along with the bold title appeared a picture of an African-American man, but instead of his name the caption read, "Miss Barr's Assailant."[83] Perhaps this caption tells readers all they needed to know. The literal lynchings in the South enabled Philadelphia judges to enact their own legal "lynchings" with impunity, often handing down unduly harsh sentences to black men convicted of larceny. As one judge stated in sentencing two black men convicted of robbery, he had no choice "for the protection of the community" but to use them "as an example to others [and] to impose the full penalty that the law provides in such a case."[84] In the case of a black man convicted of child molestation, the judge claimed, "This is a crime that members of your race have not infrequently committed, and for which many of them have been hanged in the South without due process of law."[85] The article went on to justify the unusually stiff, fifteen-year sentence the perpetrator received by stating that otherwise, "even in the North there would surely occur the same outbreaks of lynching."[86]

The mainstream press may have considered lynching unlawful, but it seemed to applaud its underlying sentiment. Philadelphians were as concerned with the dangers posed by black masculinity as with the need to protect white womanhood. However, almost as often as accounts castigated the barbaric aspects of black masculinity, narratives inverted racial and gender conventions to deride black manhood. Papers also publicized white women's triumphs over black male assailants.[87] Yet in congratulating white women for defending their honor, the pieces carefully concluded that heroic white men made the final capture of would-be assailants. Narrative battles between white men and black male criminals, also prominent in crime coverage, disclosed the social and economic complexities of the urban landscape.

The matrix of manhood, labor, and blacks' transition from slave to wage laborer became fused and mediated through the public discourse on black male criminality. The image of the farmer surfaced in reports of black male crime as well, but in these instances the farmer engaged in deadly struggles with vicious black field hands bent on extracting unearned wages. Charging that "a murderous negro fatally stabbed a prominent Montgomery County Farmer," an 1899 article told of a "half-crazed" drunken black man determined to quench his "appetite for [his employer's] blood." According to the story, Charles Fortune's dispute with his employer over a quarter led to a heated confrontation. The piece explained that Roberts, the white employer, "struck back, knocking the negro on his back." Despite fighting bravely, the farmer was unfairly matched as Fortune "sprung at Roberts like a tiger, at the same time unsheathing the blade of his knife, which he buried in the young farmer's abdomen."[88] Press narratives like these depicted black laborers as inept, bestial, and violent. Yet the images also fetishized black men's bodies—bodies that leaped like tigers, seemed unquenchable in their thirst for white men's blood, and whose hypersexual masculinity threatened the security of white manhood.[89]

The white farmer metaphor warned an anxious public of urban black female vice and heralded the dangers associated with making blacks wage laborers. No longer enslaved, black field hands doubled as actual and ideological challenges to the country's traditional notion of patriarchal authority. The sensational violence, eroticism, and white heroism obfuscated the exploitation and subsequent exclusion of blacks, both men and women, from the expanding industrial job market. Perhaps this validated white employers' discriminatory hiring policies. But blacks did not exist as the only threats to white hegemony. Before white ethnics' inclusion into the cultural category of whiteness, they, too, found their images and identities criminalized.[90] The pattern of reports of immigrants' crimes bore striking similarities to that used in coverage of black male and female criminals.

Immigrants, Ethnic Representations, and the Racialized White Male Deviant

Although blackness itself marked the epitome of inferiority, the social mantle of whiteness did not immediately incorporate "ethnic others" such as the Irish, Italians, Poles, Jews, and Slavs.[91] As one observer noted, "The best remedy for whatever is amiss in America would be if every Irishman would kill a negro and be hanged for it."[92] Popular discourses filtered all others through a multifaceted racialized lens. Papers deployed the ethnicity of immigrant perpetrators to instantly "other" the subjects, fundamentally distinguishing them from native-born whites. Accounts also inserted irrelevant facts that associated women such as Helen Colefish, an Irish immigrant suspected of poisoning her late husband in 1893, with disrepute. By noting that Colefish, married for ten years, did not have children, the article played on the absence of motherhood to question her domestic virtue. The story also hinted at an adulterous affair with a boarder and added that a prior employer had suspected Colefish of stealing and pawning his belongings.[93]

Coverage of immigrant crimes exaggerated violence at the same time that it affirmed American social and political ideals. Articles detailing the crimes of Balton Bokwick, a Polish immigrant, printed that he "danced with delight and again slashed his young victim" as "blood spurted from the wound."[94] A Philadelphia judge's declaration to a convicted Cuban immigrant in 1899 that "the shooting of American citizens went in Cuba . . . it doesn't go in the United States" disclosed nativist assumptions of citizenship as well as the broader impact of imperialism.[95]

And it is precisely these assumptions—or rather, this production of American nationalism and the oppositional traits its manufacture rested upon—that barred any genuine narrative of white male criminality. Deviance, crime, and immorality, as construed in crime stories, fundamentally precluded their applicability to white men. Criminal caricatures relied on stereotypes that buttressed domestic interpretations of normalcy, principally scripted as white male dominion. The narratives could not readily or ideologically acknowledge a true white male criminal because of the problem it posed for the ideology of white supremacy. To remedy the dilemma, white men's crimes resulted in a public distancing of these men from whiteness. Native-born white male criminals were anomalies in the larger race of white men; they possessed genetic "impurities" that caused their deviance and ideological expulsion from white manhood.

When Philadelphia's own "Ripper" Edward Kane, a white man who brutally slashed three white women, was apprehended, newspapers depicted him as just such a biological anomaly. Echoing theories of crime and atavistic features made popular by Cesare Lombroso, an Italian criminologist, one account insisted that Kane was of "low intellect" and had gray eyes that "were set close together"; the killer's forehead "slant[ed] to the rear at an alarming angle."[96] Newspapers racialized Kane by describing him as being "stolid as an Indian" and a "bloodthirsty fiend." According to the press, Kane's violence resulted from a "sudden mania" and gave "striking indications of the man's probable degeneracy." Depicting Kane as lacking remorse, the report claimed, "When confronted with the evidence of his bloody work, he was as cool as any criminal ever was."[97] The narrative eclipsed Kane's whiteness to position him among the inherently deficient "crime class"—those born criminals endangering civilized society.

Depending upon the volatility of the crime, however, articles occasionally mentioned outside influences such as intoxication or a pitiable degree of poverty for causing white men to be in an "ugly fighting mood." Such characterizations appeared to simultaneously bolster the developing image of the rugged, red-blooded, self-made man and reduce his accountability.[98] The elasticity of the crime narratives in these instances further sketches the contours of whiteness as a social ideology. White male criminals became "othered" by virtue of their offending—their crimes violated the social contract and repealed their white-skin privilege. White men accused of violent crimes existed as degenerates who possessed "dark eyes" and "sandy complexions."[99] To further distinguish normal white men from those lacking in character, press coverage juxtaposed criminal images with those of judges and police—representations of real masculinity that highlighted the important distinctions.[100]

White Justice

The image of white judges in particular acted as a powerful representation of white masculinity. Judges embodied morality and justice in a physical and representational sense, though ultimately the figure played a rather duplicitous role in crime reports. Because of their profession, coverage of judges in press accounts appeared genuine, natural, and somehow incorruptible by muckraking journalism. Taken together with the farmer trope, however, the justice figure promoted white male authority minus any current weaknesses. Whereas the farmer symbolized the traditional freedoms of white masculinity and the urban forces jeopardizing it, the justice figure symbolized the custodial power of the state, imbued with the wisdom, integrity, and force necessary to restore law and social order. The judge promised a return to masculine dominion in the traditional sense, even if the figure could not restore this preeminence in the traditional way. The judge possessed the power to regulate and admonish those challenging white male authority in the urban sphere.

Images of the judge, the farmer, and the Colored Amazon presented a new public relationship between black women and white men—one that erased the inequities of the past, though it surreptitiously reinvented them. The black female caricature effectively subverted the transgressive aspects of black badger crimes. In actuality black badger crimes exposed the hypocrisy of white patriarchy, but press coverage of the crimes effectively reinscribed myths of black female immorality. The figure depicted black women as dangerous and lawbreaking while press accounts largely absolved white male impropriety. In effect, the Colored Amazon perpetuated biases against black women, which helped to validate disparities in the ways that judges responded to crimes against them as opposed to those against white women.

Even as justices handed down lighter sentences for black women's assailants, that judges adjudicated the crimes at all promoted a sanitized, public version of the relationship between black women and white men. White men, traditionally responsible for black female victimization, now appeared as protectors of black women. Judges seemed especially objective given the dangers that Colored Amazons posed for white men. Rewriting the dynamic between the most powerful and, typically, the least, the public relationship between judges and black female victims collapsed the uneven distribution of power and authority. Judges appear as impartial instruments of justice.

Yet in actual cases, as well as in representations, the judge affirmed social hierarchies by issuing degrees of punishment for convicted parties on the basis of their status and that of their victims. Just as they had under legal practices during enslavement, white women benefited from an alliance with white masculinity, and it was expected that judges would sternly punish crimes committed against them.[101] Because hers was an identity constructed jointly with that of white male supremacy, maintaining the primacy of white femininity was of paramount importance. Making white women the ultimate victims, the judge reinforced white male patriarchy that much more and did so to the detriment of black male criminals and black female victims. As one judge proclaimed after sentencing a white woman's attacker, "What in our estimation *is higher* than honor, chastity and purity in woman?"[102] To be sure, this pedestal of honor, chastity, and purity did not support black women.[103]

Consequently, because constructions of the Colored Amazon rested on the black female body and bigoted notions of black femininity, it ultimately stigmatized all black women. Black women's identities became almost indistinguishable from that of the caricature in the public consciousness. This perception made it that much more difficult for black women to benefit from the protections afforded to white citizens and women in general and diminished their ability to obtain impartial justice when victimized. Officers of the court enacted virtual miscarriages of justice by not punishing crimes against black women as severely as crimes committed against white women by either black or white perpetrators.[104]

By blurring distinctions between black women and black female criminals, the trope of the Colored Amazon lessened the responsibility of the justice system toward black female victims. In the 1886 murder trial of William Bush, press coverage, in accord with narratives of black female criminals, cast his wife, the victim, in precarious moral standing. Printing lurid details of how the black woman "rose slightly and fell back dead, the blood rushing from her mouth," the *Ledger* did not denounce Bush for the shooting.[105] Rather, it explained that Bush's wife "had been living with another man while he was in prison and would not acknowledge him anymore."[106] The story characterized Bush, a "tall mulatto," somewhat sympathetically. Reportedly Bush lamented, "I will now, I suppose, have to prepare myself for my doom."[107] The *Ledger* concluded that Bush had killed his wife because she "deserted him after he had been sent to prison on another offense."[108] Bush further benefited from a kind of paternalistic empathy in court. The district attorney stated, "The element of infidelity to him entered into the commission of the crime . . . and operated upon the prisoner's mind. I am, therefore . . . willing to accept a plea of murder in the second degree."[109]

Not every perpetrator avoided public or legal admonition, but the narrative of the Colored Amazon contributed to an erasure of black female victimization. Chronicling the murder of Margaret Alberts in 1908, the *Record* noted that her assailant, Robert Halestock, remarked, "The Alberts woman was much older than [I] and annoyed [me] with her unwelcome attentions." After "meeting with rebuff," Alberts allegedly attacked Halestock, and "being a woman of large physique he resorted to the use of a revolver."[110] Depicting the woman as physically intimidating, scorned, and violent, the descriptions of Alberts resonated profoundly with that of the Colored Amazon.

Furthermore, the article's treatment of the crime readily accepted the notion that Alberts was violent and intimidating enough to warrant being shot to death. Absent from this discussion, and generally from the larger discourse on black female victims, was any recognition of Alberts's humanity. Black women did not register as people or as individuals connected to families or communities that would suffer loss, but rather they were likened to dark, strange things to be secretly lusted after, mocked, or feared.[111] Their alleged immorality made it clear that they only brought misfortune upon themselves: as Sam Skipworth commented after killing his landlady in 1909, "She got what was coming to her, and she deserved it."[112]

The Blessing and the Curse of Press Sources

Crime reporting captured the public imagination and shaped responses to crime and violence as well as shifting notions of race, gender, and sexuality in the urban sphere. Crime caricatures, singly and jointly, broadcasted themes of white supremacy, civic morality, and domesticity. Stigmatized as the "blackest" of criminals, the Colored Amazon's immorality and ruthlessness set her apart from white female and black male criminals and powerfully underscored white masculinity. Like Mammy and Jezebel, the figure ridiculed black women and structured mainstream responses to black female agency.[113]

Reports of black women's crimes presented a false, damning portrait of both black female criminals and black womanhood. The images often muted the victimization of black women—within the justice system and in the eyes of the public. The accounts impugned black victims' morality and recycled and transplanted central themes of the Colored Amazon narrative, hindering black women's abilities to obtain justice. Yet the crime reports, on an elemental level, also testify to the complexities of urban life.[114] Domesticity was the ideal, but evident transgressions convey a variety of experiences that crossed social boundaries. The narrative overlay seems to come almost too late to stem the tide of social and cultural transformation. As definitively as the press surveyed, reconfigured, and deployed images that engendered conformity, the actual crime stories unveiled a collage of bold exchanges and daring liaisons within the panoply of lawbreaking.

Chapter Five

DEVIANT BY DESIGN: RACE, DEGENERACY, AND THE SCIENCE OF PENOLOGY

Crime cannot be prevented or criminality eliminated from the social organism by waiting to cut off the criminal after the crime has been committed. The possible criminal must be caught and rendered harmless before he can act; the constant reinforcement and recruiting of the criminal class must be checked at its source.

—Henry M. Boies, *The Science of Penology: The Defence of Society Against Crime*, 1893

IN 1890, REBECCA WHITELY WAS CONVICTED of murder for stabbing a woman to death during an altercation. When she arrived at Eastern State Penitentiary, the warden dutifully noted the intake of a colored woman. Whitely, who had no prior criminal history, routinely broke the rules at Eastern. Prison guards cited her for disorderly conduct, and she appeared to be on the way to becoming one of the institution's disciplinary problems. After she had served only two years of her sentence, however, the Committee on Lunacy transferred Whitely to the Pennsylvania Insane Asylum. Although an asylum might seem like the second worst place to be confined at the turn of the century (Eastern being the first), in actuality this was hardly the case.[1] Early reform campaigns led by women like Dorothea Dix resulted in clean, orderly mental health facilities. Moreover, hospital administrators encouraged recuperation through rest, proper diet, and positive mental stimulation.[2] Prisoners at Eastern found the therapeutic atmosphere especially appealing, and they frequently feigned illness in the hopes of gaining a transfer to the institutions.

Though members of the lunacy committee believed Whitely's dementia to be genuine, the warden remained skeptical and described Whitely as not insane but "devilish."[3] Warden Cassidy often judged inmates harshly, yet his assessment of Whitely proved more astute than that of the committee. Whitely's maneuvering took her from the penitentiary to the asylum and displayed mental agility far more than insanity. Once at the state hospital, Whitely, apparently a very light complexioned woman, passed as white.[4] She served the bulk of her sentence at the asylum and managed to be "restored" and returned to Eastern just in time for her release.[5]

Two very different sets of records exist on Rebecca Whitely. Prison records describe a violent, disorderly black female prisoner. Asylum records portray a troubled white female patient. The actual identity of Rebecca Whitely may be a different matter entirely, but the two sets of records offer provocative evidence about the nature of crime in turn-of-the-century Philadelphia. Criminality lay largely in the eye of the beholder, and those individuals most likely to be gazing did so through a distorted lens.[6]

At the dawn of the twentieth century, criminologists, police, and prison administrators linked criminality to fixed social and biological attributes, characteristics that could be quickly identified and isolated. They expected to control "the criminal body" by making criminals and potential suspects plainly visible to authorities.[7] Their techniques relied upon and reflected a cultural logic that viewed all aspects outside of white social mores as indicative of innate criminality. By classifying criminals as either occasional or habitual, reformers used scientific methods to justify selective treatment in the rehabilitation of convicts. Habitual criminals—those members of the so-called crime class—were destined to spend years in prisons and penitentiaries; occasional criminals could be rehabilitated and reintegrated into society.

In its turn, policing and prison practice operated as a self-fulfilling prophecy whereby reformers, criminologists, and prison administrators ultimately invented the very crime class they sought to repress. Tracing discourses on criminality and the evolution of surveillance tactics such as mug shot photography marks important transformations in the perception of those who commit crime; it mirrors the shift from emphasizing rehabilitation for all to only recognizing the potential of a few. Moreover, the internal workings of the penitentiary demonstrate the potency of the Colored Amazon as well as the impact of habitual criminality on black women's incarceration.

Penal Philosophy and Praxis

Eastern received its charter legislation in 1822 and opened its doors in 1829. The very first convicts to cross the penitentiary's threshold were African Americans. Charles Williams, a black man imprisoned for larceny, was the first male prisoner, and Amy Rogers, a black woman convicted of manslaughter, was the first female inmate in 1831.[8] Reformers and state legislators believed that the institution would act as an effective deterrent to crime. It would protect society from criminals and mend those who broke the law.[9] Penologists placed their faith in the design of the institution and the practice of solitary confinement. Eastern did not fulfill its promise, however, and, like its predecessor the Walnut Street Jail and Penitentiary House, sank into degradation, corruption, and decay. Yet rather than abandoning the notion of incarceration, reformers upheld the use of prisons and penitentiaries. They dismissed the possibility that imprisonment itself might be fundamentally flawed. Instead they concluded that there existed an unredeemable class of convicts—men and women like Charles Williams and Amy Rogers—that would always pose a threat to society and always require confinement.

The construction of Eastern and the implementation of separate, solitary confinement developed against the backdrop of a national debate over emerging philosophies of punishment, imprisonment, and rehabilitation.[10] Initially, the concept of solitary confinement, an idea gaining in popularity among Europeans, appealed to many jailers in the United States. Based on monastic practices like those of the Carthusian monks, solitary confinement, its proponents asserted, would, through solitude, silence, and hard labor, not only punish the guilty but also redeem their souls.[11] The inmates' sentences would be served in separate cells rather than in public or in disorganized groups warehoused in local prisons. Though the promise of redemption was attractive, the overall philosophy met with mixed reviews.

Early prison reformers in New York argued that such an austere, isolating institution would further traumatize already troubled individuals who at their time of discharge would be ill-prepared for reintegration into society. Alternatively they proposed a system of separate cells with congregate dining and work details. Separate, silent penitence, however, profoundly resonated with Pennsylvanians and the state's Quaker elite. Amid fierce debate over the efficacy of solitary confinement or congregate incarceration, members of the Pennsylvania Prison Society criticized the congregate system because it did little to prevent cohabitation among first-time and repeat offenders.[12]

Through the institution of silent meditation and visitation by members of the Society and the clergy, penal reformers viewed the penitentiary as an important tool for socially engineering moral and legal obedience. According to the rhetoric, theirs was the only "system which secures the convict from the evil association with others of his class," freeing "him to take to the ministration and moral persuasion of those who take an interest in his present condition."[13] Interpreting crime through religious concepts of good and evil, Pennsylvanians envisioned the penitentiary as a site of conversion where criminals, faced with their sins and encouraged by virtuous instructors, would repent. Incarceration in this manner not only protected society but also ignited a rehabilitative catharsis in the inmates.

Constructed to house convicted felons and chronic misdemeanor offenders, Eastern sought to impose the kind of religious and communal surveillance employed to indoctrinate colonists before the country's founding and rapid expansion.[14] Architecturally, the facility embodied the philosophy of both solitary confinement and an all-encompassing notion of surveillance.[15] Structurally, the cellblocks met at an organizational center, like the spokes of a wheel. The hub and prison blocks facilitated the complete separation of inmates while simultaneously maximizing jailers' ability to watch over every ward (fig. 11).[16] The design allowed reformers to create a level of social order inside the penitentiary that seemed unobtainable beyond its walls.

Daily practices at Eastern reflected reformers' commitment to destroy "the vitality of . . . the germs of crime."[17] Steeped in Protestant values of prayer, purity, and hard work, administrators subjected convicts entering the facility to a procedure they hoped would initiate the prisoners' process of conversion. Upon their arrival, prisoners were stripped, washed, and given haircuts; they then received uniforms, and guards led them, in hooded masks, to the registration office. Administrators recorded the prisoner's age, height, weight, complexion, nativity, crime, number of convictions, sentence, and distinguishing marks.[18] Afterward, convicts went into special observation rooms. Separated from one another and the general prison population, the new inmates were interviewed and evaluated by the prison doctor, the moral instructor, and the schoolteacher. In a program lasting anywhere from ten to fourteen days, pris-

DEVIANT BY DESIGN

FIG. 11. Eastern
State Penitentiary
(1872). Courtesy
of Eastern State
Penitentiary Historic
Site, Philadelphia.

oners learned the rules of the institution and were instructed "not to make any unnecessary noise, either by singing, whistling, or in any other manner"; above all, they should, "preserve becoming silence."[19]

Once in their permanent cells, prisoners found a whitewashed room furnished with a bed, a table, a bench, and a stool. Inmates received tin cups, washbasins, victuals pans, and brooms.[20] All cells were eventually equipped with running water and electric light, and their possessions consisted of a flannel shirt and drawers, a jacket, trousers, a waistcoat, shoes, and socks. Women received a blouse, a skirt, a jacket or shawl, and shoes and stockings. The only other possessions allowed to inmates were combs, brushes, and tobacco.[21] The institution prohibited all gifts, including food, as meals were furnished by the facility.[22] Meals and work took place inside the prisoners' cells. Prisoners in the lower cell blocks exercised outside in the tiny yards attached to their cells (see fig. 11). When inmates from upper cellblocks were taken to the main yard for exercise they wore "hood-caps with eye holes" to prevent any communication. This practice lasted until 1904, when "all hoods, except if requested by the prisoner were discontinued."[23] By that time, however, the move to abandon the hoods may have been more a symbolic act on the part of the administration — a last-ditch effort to appear in control.

Eastern failed to accomplish its mission of silent, separate confinement almost from the beginning. Early investigations of the institution in 1834 unveiled a host of charges against the warden, Samuel Wood, a Quaker and a member of the society. Wood and his administration faced a litany of

charges, including the abuse of prisoners, embezzlement, and sexual misconduct. Though Wood managed to retain his position until he resigned in 1840,
the problems plaguing the facility never faltered.[24] The rigid design, meticu-
lous in its aim to control and survey, ultimately contributed to the institution's
failure. Overcrowding alone rendered silent separation almost completely impossible. Originally the prison contained 562 cells roughly seven by twelve in
size, but the growth of the prison population required that the facility be expanded to roughly 740 cells in 7 cell blocks.[25] Administrators contended with
a structure designed for the implementation of one type of system, but the
size of the population forced them to operate under another. When the population reached as many as 1,400 inmates occupying 740 cells, prisoners were
routinely doubled up and in extreme cases tripled and quadrupled.[26]

Staff shortages also posed a serious problem for the institution. In 1887, the
facility employed only 49 overseers to guard the 1,096 inmates, while its sister institution, Western State Penitentiary, had 59 overseers for 686 inmates.[27]
Much of the growth took place in the male prison population, but by 1883
Warden Cassidy noted that the female ward had become so overcrowded that
it would soon need an extension.[28] The ward employed 1 matron, whose re-
sponsibilities included managing all operations in the female department in
addition to supervising some 30 female inmates.[29] Ultimately, prisoners were
hardly solitary and few were silent. Conditions meant that the administration
could never maintain the kind of control for which Eastern was designed. In
1894, to alleviate overcrowding, the prison expanded to 11 cell blocks, and between 1908 and 1911, block number 12 was erected.[30]

Early advocates naively envisioned an institution shrouded in silent meditation. Little concerned with the mundane problems of overcrowding and corruption, early reformers considered Eastern a divinely inspired instrument.
Criminals were maladjusted individuals, and the penitentiary machine would
fix them. They would somehow emerge from confinement as replicas of their
former selves, now made better in an image conceived by the Society and penologists. But most prisoners did not leave Eastern restored, and crime endured. Moreover, by the beginning of the twentieth century, overcrowding,
corruption, and routine scandals made Eastern a disappointment—and sometimes an embarrassment.[31] The Society changed its position from that of Eastern's staunchest advocate to being among its harshest detractors. Soaring in-

mate population, funding problems, and management blunders replicated the breeding ground of vice within the penitentiary that reformers and legislators had erected Eastern to destroy.

Yet reformers, legislators, and most penologists could not relinquish the notion of incarceration. The penitentiary, with its high walls and stern over-seers, became a fixture in society and the public consciousness—it symbolized stability and control as well as law and social order. Rather than abandoning the massive structures, penal reformers fixed their gaze upon the masses of men and women confined within them.[32]

Mastering the Crime Class

Discourses on crime developed alongside a growing enthusiasm for racist he-redity science.[33] Greatly influenced by social Darwinism and the work of Cesare Lombroso, turn-of-the-century reformers largely understood crimi-nals as falling into one of two categories: occasional or habitual.[34] Most crime stemmed from poverty, poor environment, and poor moral training, typi-cal motivating factors for occasional criminality. Habitual criminals, however, were biologically deficient and morally bankrupt individuals. Criminal an-thropologists like Lombroso believed that habitual criminals possessed com-mon atavistic traits—physical and mental characteristics that distinguished them from otherwise normal human beings.[35] European theories of heredi-tary criminality were easily assimilated into emerging American discourses. The idea of occasional and habitual criminals possessed a fluidity that comple-mented the country's racial caste system and the rhetoric of civil morality.[36]

According to the theories, defective heredity spawned a latent type of criminal that posed dangerous threats to society. Proponents asserted that low morals—sexual impurity, alcoholism, and other debilitating conduct—resulted in degenerate heredity. This stock passed down through genera-tions and, if unchecked, could give rise to hordes of genetic inferiors. The ideology ultimately accented social Darwinism, which heralded a struggle be-tween primitive and complex organisms.[37] Theorists envisioned civilized white heterosexual society in a perilous battle not simply to maintain social, politi-cal, and moral authority, but also to preserve their gene pool and the sanctity of whiteness.

Race underscored these theories, and fears of blackness as a disease abounded. One report, in 1880, claimed that an otherwise healthy white baby's once fine brown hair "grew stiff and jet black, and [his] eyes grew darker, so that the line between the pupils and the iris could not be distinguished." In spite of medical treatment the boy grew worse, "all the time the color of his skin deepening. At last he became as black as a full-blooded negro."[38] And to become a "full-blooded negro" was to be the lowest of the low. African-American women in particular embodied degenerative stock.

Blacks had always been perceived as less evolved than whites, and the rising notions of defective heredity naturalized blacks' low status and possessed profound implications for linkages between morality and crime. In his treatise *The Female Offender*, Lombroso argued that female crime stemmed from precocity and a minor "degree of differentiation from the male." In other words, the lack of a clear divide between men and women played a key factor in female criminality. Likening them to savages, Lombroso used images of black women to stress the uncivilized nature of the race, particularly noting that the women were nearly indistinguishable from the men: "so huge are their jaws and cheekbones, so hard and coarse their features. And the same is often the case in their crania and brains."[39] Lombroso's characterization of black women as mannish, unsophisticated, and prone to criminality did not differ terribly from those sentiments uttered by social reformers—especially those who charged that the presence of single black women would negatively impact crime and vice in urban centers.[40] Furthermore, in linking born or habitual criminality to physical traits, mainstream whites could take comfort in the fact that these degenerates could be easily identified.[41]

Notions of habitual criminality encompassed a range of negative attributes that matched stereotypes of blacks and ethnic immigrants, thereby buttressing ideologies of white supremacy. In his discussion of crime and pauperism, Henry Boies, in 1893, defined criminality as inherently abnormal—he held that each member of the crime class "diverges in some respects from the normal type of mankind." Implicit in this statement, as Nicole Hahn Rafter points out, is the notion that individuals who are physically normal cannot in actuality be criminals.[42] At the same time, Boies characterized blacks as having "strong animalism by nature and cultivation." This primitive heredity resulted in a lack of "virtue and little moral restraint . . . sexual sins, with all their deplor-

DEVIANT BY DESIGN

able consequences, become common."[43] Boies's observation of the black lower classes contained little more than recycled stereotypes that haunted blacks almost from the nation's founding, but connected to this larger rhetoric of biological criminality, he ultimately positions blacks as abnormal and thus criminal.

Poor native-born whites could also be classified as habitual criminals, though their characterization as such distanced them from whiteness in its true sense. White habitual criminals contained genetic defects or abnormalities that made them different from normal whites. A classic example was the Jukes, a rural family that became the focal point of Richard Dugdale's work on crime, pauperism, and heredity in 1877. According to Dugdale's research, over several degenerate and inbred generations, the Jukes produced a small army of beggars, thieves, prostitutes, and murderers. Dugdale's work, for many of his contemporaries, proved that "habitual criminals spring almost exclusively from degenerating stocks."[44]

In Pennsylvania, organizations such as the Association of Medical Officers of American Institutions for Idiotic and Feeble-Minded Persons powerfully contributed to genetic theories of criminality. Medical officers combined theories of feeblemindedness, or mental retardation, with budding eugenics theories to suggest that innate immorality or "moral imbecility" was linked to and most likely the cause of crime and vice. In 1895, Martin Barr asserted that the "moral imbecile" was "born not made." In doing so, Barr attempted to prove that "authority over [moral imbeciles] should be shifted from lawyers to physicians." More than anything else, however, the association's members, perhaps unwittingly, helped canonize biological criminality in mainstream consciousness.[45] Ultimately, all of the theories—moral imbecility and that of the born criminal—served to confirm the existence of habitual criminals and the threat they posed to civilized society.

The construct of the habitual criminal, defective, unfit, poor, bestial, Negro, dusky, and foreign, allowed all kinds of racial and ethnic others to be lumped into a group that had been *scientifically* proven to possess dangerous criminal characteristics.[46] The discourses enabled white middle-class reformers, police, and prison workers to engage in racist practices in the criminal justice system under the guise of scientific neutrality.[47] Frances Kellor, in her examination of criminal anthropology and jurisprudence, noted, "The negro element of the population, which presents such a large class of citizens out of harmony with the advanced civilization existing in the greater part of the United States, is responsible for no small degree of criminality." Kellor further explained that black criminality "has given the United States the preeminence which it enjoys as the exponent of the lynch law."[48] Dismissing studies by Ida B. Wells-Barnett that exposed lynching as racist mob violence, Kellor deployed the rhetoric of habitual criminality to blame black victims and exonerate the white men responsible for the murders.[49] Crime theories padded racism and validated sentiments like those expressed by William Freeman, a white juror, in 1908. Freeman, a potential juror in the case of Mame Johnson, a black woman accused of murder, stated that blacks' "morals are not as good as those of white people. I have a natural prejudice against them."[50] Indeed, "natural prejudice" underscored a host of emerging practices in the criminal justice system.

Tracking the criminal body assumed the utmost importance, and a number of technologies emerged. In 1882, Alphonse Bertillon, a French detective, created an identification system that featured a complicated series of measurements. Employing unique "calipers, gauges and rulers," the Bertillon system required eleven "anthropometric measurements" by trained specialists. In addition to measuring such body parts as the cranium, wrists, and ears, the system recorded detailed physical descriptions of prisoners using Bertillon's own "morphological vocabulary."[51] Though Bertillon endeavored to create a language that precisely described inmates, notions of normalcy and abnormality influenced officers' descriptions of prisoners. Listings of blacks and ethnic immigrants contrasted native-born whites, who were typically characterized as fair-skinned, versus blacks, Irish, and Italians, who were almost always described as black, ruddy, and dark.[52]

In 1899, the Pennsylvania state legislature passed an Act for the Identification of Habitual Criminals. The act reorganized the practices of district attorneys, police, and prison administrators and in so doing essentially birthed the class of criminals these agencies feared.[53] Containing six sections, the legislation instructed prison wardens to maintain detailed records and photographs of all felons, ordered district attorneys to provide wardens with copies of inmates' criminal histories, and mandated that the records be used to help police and citizens identify persons accused of crimes. The statute further stipulated that wardens and officers of the law were to adopt the Bertillon system and that copies of the registers were to be furnished upon request to officers from any state in the country and to the city's own Bureau of Police.[54]

Apparently before the 1899 act codified the tracking of habitual criminals into law, several branches of justice had already begun implementing similar tactics. Administrators at Eastern maintained *Bertillon Hand Books* starting in 1895, and detectives in Philadelphia developed a criminal registry that listed prisoners' names, addresses, aliases, race, crime, and detailed physical descriptions as early as 1892.[55] However, the act called for the implementation of a comprehensive intradepartmental strategy for gathering and sharing information about habitual criminals.

The 1899 act marks the institutionalized transformation of notions of crime and also points to how these notions modified policing, specifically with respect to mug shot photography. Police began using photography to identify criminals in the 1850s, but they rarely employed the large collections of often cumbersome archived photographs to apprehend criminals. By the 1890s, however, rogues' gallery books enjoyed a renewed significance. New York City Inspector Thomas Byrne's publication *Professional Criminals in America* (1886) popularized the technology and put images of forfeiters and confidence men in the hands and minds of the general public.[56] Making otherwise invisible swindlers, pickpockets, and con men visible created a sense of empowerment among citizens, and it powerfully transformed ideas about criminals. Like the effect that Lombroso's theories created, the images comforted an anxious public by promising that the criminals could be readily identified.[57]

By stipulating the institutionalization of photographs, the act unwittingly provides a visual map of the ideological transformation underscoring the rhetoric of habitual criminality. The changes in how mug shots were taken before and after the act traces the shift in thinking about people who committed crimes to tracking those members of the crime class. In their early versions, pictures of prisoners largely resembled portrait photographs. Men and women appeared in the pictures wearing hats, jewelry, scarves, and coats. Indeed, the early photographs of criminals were indistinguishable from typical photographic portraits. But as the technology evolved and in accord with theories of occasional and habitual criminality, how prisoners were photographed contributed to a not so subtle branding that distinguished normal citizens from those who were criminal.[58]

Although photography existed as an "objective reproduction of reality," by staging front and side shots and eventually adding criminal registry numbers, officials used the photographs to aid authorities and citizens in identifying criminals and potential suspects; but in addition, the medium itself informed the viewer's gaze — looking at a mug shot meant one was looking at a criminal, not at a citizen accused of a crime or even an individual convicted of a crime (figs. 12a–f).[59] Criminality became the subject's primary identity. The staging in mug shot photography parallels a more rigid cultural consciousness about criminality, one driven largely by fears of the habitual criminal community. Black skin had long been regarded as indicative of criminality, but the shifts in mug shot photography criminalized all those who were arrested, regardless of whether they received convictions. Moreover, in paralleling criminological theories, the mug shots further chiseled out the boundaries of mainstream hegemony — the images contrasted those of "normal," middle-class society.[60]

The invention of the crime class and habitual criminals doubled as a discourse on social transitions. The theories about criminals and the new methods used to track them convey the thoughts and fears of mainstream urban dwellers ill at ease with the changes occurring in society. The theories allowed mainstream whites and white middle-class reformers to participate in a variety of racist discourses while safely shrouded in the idea of scientific objectivity. In addition, the ideas and bigotry behind the postulates did not just influence how authorities tracked or categorized prisoners, but also contributed to inequitable treatment in the penal system. The experiences of black and white prisoners at Eastern demonstrate that controlling the crime classes was as much about maintaining white cultural hegemony as it was about eradicating crime.

On the Inside of Eastern

After a series of temporary wardens, Eastern came under the direction of its first professional warden, Michael Cassidy, in 1881. Cassidy, an overseer at the institution since 1861, rose through the ranks to assume the position of warden and ran Eastern for nearly twenty years, from 1881 to 1900. Under his stewardship all of the players involved in confinement become visible and so too do the blurred lines of power and submission.[61] Power in the facility, still stacked heavily on the side of the administration, was nonetheless far from absolute.

12A.

12B.

12C.

12D.

12E.

12F.

FIG. 12A–12F. Evolution of mug
shot photography, *Rogues Gallery
Books* (c. 1880–1920). Courtesy of
the Philadelphia City Archive.

FIG. 12A. Johanna Twiggs (c. 1880)
FIG. 12B. Lizzie Reese (c. 1880)
FIG. 12C. Annie alias Clara Davis
(1st picture, c. 1890)
FIG. 12D. Annie alias Clara Davis
(2nd picture, c. 1890)
FIG. 12E. Wilmina Johnson (c. 1900)
FIG. 12F. John Hodge (c. 1920). *Rogues
Gallery Books*, courtesy of the
Philadelphia City Archive.

Yet administrators established a hierarchy of confinement and rehabilitation predicated upon race, gender, and sexuality.

Economic status also powerfully shaped prisoners' incarceration: other than one former "bank president" almost all of the inmates at Eastern were either poor or working class.[62] Of the top fifteen occupations held by convicts prior to their imprisonment at Eastern, the largest categories consisted of unskilled laborers at roughly 30 percent and thieves at 6 percent; 9 percent were unemployed.[63] The crimes of prisoners largely reflected poverty and financial hardship—larceny, burglary, robbery, and receiving stolen property accounted for nearly 61 percent with another 8 percent representing fraud and embezzlement charges.[64] But while the population lacked economic diversity, who and where prisoners hailed from afforded a little more variety. Women comprised about 3 percent of the penitentiary population—black women accounted for nearly 40 percent of women. White men accounted for about 79 percent, and black men represented the remaining 19 percent—though this amount included a small number of Chinese prisoners.[65] The bulk of convicts were from Pennsylvania, 32 percent from surrounding counties and 21 percent born in Philadelphia. Twenty percent, however, were foreign born, coming from places like Germany, England, Ireland, and Italy. Another 2 percent represented countries such as Canada, China, Mexico, and Barbados.[66] The inmates' origins reflected demographic shifts in Philadelphia as well as the heightened surveillance of communities thought to be responsible for breeding habitual criminals.

When these varied masses entered the penitentiary, Warden Cassidy and his successors screened them in an effort to "find that man that is not a crime class man."[67] Although all time at Eastern was difficult, the distinctions made among prisoners translated into special privileges for some, to the detriment of others. Those inmates considered salvageable were assigned work when it was available and were encouraged to improve themselves while at Eastern, for example, by taking advantage of the reading materials in the penitentiary's library of one thousand volumes.[68] Overseers also doled out work assignments and special privileges such as the right to play instruments to those prisoners they believed could be rehabilitated or those perceived as powerful enough to keep other inmates in line. These inmates were regarded as trustworthy enough to aid guards with daily tasks.[69]

DEVIANT BY DESIGN

A prisoner's status likewise affected his or her physical placement within the institution. One's placement could mean the difference between hard time and the more serious consequences of imprisonment, such as illness, abuse, and even death. Overcrowding not only obliterated the institution's ideological philosophy, but also affected the physical state of its buildings. The lower cells were almost always cold and damp and never received sun because of Eastern's high exterior walls.[70] Dilapidated conditions magnified sickness, and typhoid, dropsy, and tuberculosis ravaged the institution and resulted in a number of inmates' deaths.[71]

African-American prisoners were packed together and likely received the least desirable cells—this dynamic probably contributed to their illness and high mortality rates. Prison reports noted dozens of cases like that of Cornelia Crapper, a thirty-two-year-old black woman and Philadelphia native convicted of larceny. In 1884, Crapper battled "consumption for several months, was not expected to live to the end of her term."[72] Although Crapper survived to be escorted home "by her mother and sister," other ailing black women were not so fortunate.[73] Laura Williams, a black woman in her early twenties convicted in 1887, died of tuberculosis one month before her sentence ended.[74] Blacks died at almost three times the rate of white inmates. In 1897, of the sixteen deaths at Eastern, ten were African American, nine men and one woman.[75] But not all of the deaths stemmed from illness. Irene Archey, an African American from Chester County age nineteen, attempted to hang herself four days after arriving at Eastern in 1905.[76] Illness claimed many lives at Eastern, but the severity of confinement weighed heavily on the minds of many prisoners— nervous breakdowns, paranoia, and dementia were especially common.[77]

Although criminal sentences might stipulate hard labor, in 1897 there were only sixty jobs at the institution.[78] Following an industrial depression in 1893, shoemakers, carpet makers, and representatives of other industries complained that convict labor sharply affected their markets. As a result, in 1897 legislators passed the Muelbronner Act, which prohibited the state from employing more than 5 percent of prison inmates in the manufacture of brooms and brushes and 10 percent in the production of goods that might be manufactured elsewhere in the state by free labor.[79] Although justices attached hard labor to sentences as a punitive measure, it often was the only constructive outlet for alleviating the mind-numbing miseries of confinement. Ultimately, the Muelbronner Act left the majority of inmates to suffer in crowded cells with precious few diversions.

The social status of inmates on the outside perhaps most profoundly influenced how they were treated on the inside. The same stereotypes that haunted all black women followed black female criminals inside prison, leaving them especially vulnerable to harsh treatment and exploitation.[80] Parallel to broader assumptions about black female criminality, prison workers often regarded African-American female convicts with suspicion and loathing. Warden Cassidy routinely characterized black female inmates as he did Jennie Hogan, whom he considered "a dangerous negro among others." Hogan was convicted of assault and battery. Ida Howard, convicted of murder in the second degree, was described by Warden Cassidy as a "Black Negress twenty four years of age desparate and dangerous."[81] The uncharitable judgment contrasted with the compassion Cassidy extended to white women such as Catherine Burns, who murdered a child in 1883. According to the warden, Burns received "much sympathy and consideration . . . because of her general character for honest and correct behavior. She pleaded guilty to the charge. Which was shooting a little girl 6 years old who amongst other children were plagueing her."[82]

Cassidy's characterizations typified the racial and gendered notions of domesticity—white female inmates, scripted as fallen women, benefited from chivalry. Matilda Pierson, a white woman convicted of murder in 1882, violently destroyed the furniture in her cell. Rather than the harsh condemnation and swift punishment other prisoners received for similar conduct, the warden simply noted, "She is not of sound mind and is not entirely responsible."[83] Mary Ann Sells, also convicted of murder in the second degree, was characterized as, "a poor miserable creature broken down by hard work and abuse by a worthless man."[84] Mary Taggart, found guilty of stabbing her son to death, also garnered compassion and concern from prison administrators. Warden Cassidy noted upon her arrival, "She killed her son a lad of 19 years of age during an altercation, murder or killing was not intended. This is a sad case."[85] Harriet Burrows, a white woman convicted for the murder of her husband, was characterized as "frail and small and does not look as if she would live long under any conditions."[86]

Occasionally white female inmates found themselves subject to prison administrators' hostilities—this typically depended upon their criminal status and ethnicity as well as the gender of the prison workers. Warden Cassidy often wrote contemptuously of white women who were documented as "professional shoplifters," though many of these were foreign-born whites.[87] In 1893, however, the warden reported on the unusual motivation behind a doctor seeking to visit Josephine Smith, a white woman convicted of murder. According to his journal, a female doctor from the county prison wanted to visit Smith, who apparently gave the doctor a hard time. The physician hoped to "look at her behind bars as a sort of satisfaction." Though he may have sympathized with a fellow prison worker, the warden spared Smith this humiliation, as "the Doctor was not permitted to do so."[88] That the physician made the trip to Eastern in an effort to humiliate Smith provides a glimpse into the intensity of animosities between jailers and inmates.

Although the female matron primarily supervised female inmates, the women nonetheless remained vulnerable to rape and sexual exploitation. The warden routinely commented on the looks of male and female inmates, noting whether they were attractive, strong, or healthy in appearance, but his descriptions of black female inmates sometimes crossed the line. On March 3, 1885, Warden Cassidy described Sarah Scott, a black woman convicted of larceny, as "a young muscular finely developed woman weighing 218 lbs 5 ft 8 inches in height clean and straight without superfulers of flesh." Scott, a badger thief, was, in his estimation, "well adopted to that business."[89] The marginal social status of black women permitted Warden Cassidy to make such observations about Scott. Apparently Scott was alluring enough to attract johns and big enough to rob them. Scott, being "well adopted to" the crime business, deserved to be in Eastern, unlike white women such as Mary Taggart and Mary Ann Sells. Moreover, Scott could be admired and desired as a sexual object.

Warden Cassidy appears only to have expressed an attraction to certain black female prisoners, but prison records suggest that other overseers at Eastern acted on their sexual impulses. Despite the vehement denials of charges of sexual misconduct noted in an 1897 investigation, the facility was once again engulfed in controversy when, at the beginning of the twentieth century, a long-confined black woman appeared to be pregnant. The trouble seems to have started when the lunacy committee transferred Susan Watson from Eastern to the Pennsylvania Insane Asylum.[90] According to her patient file, Watson told psychiatrists that "there were people waiting at her cell door, wanting to take her out," and that "this was stopped . . . when she reported it to the warden." Asylum psychiatrists also noted that Watson was "getting fat. Appetite very good."[91] Though Watson seemed delusional, her claim probably contained more substance than the doctors realized. It would have been unlikely for guards to visit Watson's front cell door, but it was possible for guards to enter female cells through the tiny exercise yards adjacent to the cells on the female block (see fig. 11). Moreover, similar allegations had surfaced in the 1897 investigation of the penitentiary.[92]

After a five-month respite, Watson returned to Eastern, where she quickly became the subject of much speculation. The warden suspected her of being "advanced in pregnancy." When confronted, Watson claimed she had had intercourse at the asylum but declined to name the father, though she did state that the child would be a mulatto. But where she conceived could not be proven until she delivered, and prison administrators feared another scandal if it occurred at Eastern. The matron accused Watson of "feigning illness" again. The warden ordered a series of examinations by the prison doctor and two outside physicians. After several examinations, the doctors concluded that Watson was not pregnant. After this entry, Watson's case is no longer discussed.[93]

Although it is impossible to state with any certainty whether Watson was delusional or indeed pregnant and aborted by one of the physicians, her statements at the asylum suggest that something untoward occurred in her cell at Eastern. Moreover, subsequent reports indicated that the sexual abuse of female inmates was hardly a rarity in Pennsylvania's prison system. Mamie Pinzer, a white prostitute in Philadelphia, charged that the nighttime-keepers at the Central Station in City Hall removed her from a rat-infested cell "only after I permitted one of the men, who seemed to be in charge at the time, to take all sorts of liberties with me."[94] Given the almost absolute powerlessness of women inmates, sex may have been the only means for prisoners to access the few privileges available at Eastern. Discipline tended to be so severe that some women may have even sought out relationships with guards to escape otherwise brutal prison practices.[95]

Punishment at Eastern included handcuffing, stripping, and isolation, and misconduct investigations show that guards also used the unofficially sanctioned practices of beating, torture, and starvation. Initially, separate confinement made the punishing of disobedient prisoners relatively simple, as they were located in dark cells and either meals or work could be withheld. In the wake of severe overcrowding, however, overseers stripped inmates, bound them naked in cold, dank cells, and doused them with icy water. Some inmates became deathly ill from the treatment, and despite investigations and official statements admonishing against the practice, guards routinely implemented this form of punishment.[96] Prisoners were also gagged with an iron bar. The gag was fastened around their heads and connected to handcuffs behind their backs. This tactic caused excruciating neck and back muscle spasms in addition to dizziness and fainting. In 1885, an inmate smuggled a letter detailing inmate abuse to local presses. Printed in a number of newspapers, the letter charged that "all sorts of abuse [was] being perpetrated by Officers of the prison on the inmates."[97]

Charges of cruelty, neglect, inmate suicide, and increasing cases of insanity prompted a senatorial investigation of the facility. Spearheaded by a prominent Philadelphia judge, the 1897 investigation of the prison's practices disclosed horrific instances of abuse. Several inmates made allegations of starvation and physical brutality, as did one African-American man who was tied to heating pipes and severely burned as a result. Investigators found inmates locked in cells naked, bound, starved, and forced to lay in their excrement. One extreme case involved a man who was discovered bound on the floor of his cell; he weighed only 95 pounds, although his normal weight was between 140 and 150 pounds. This inmate's sister helped initiate the investigation by begging authorities to save her brother's life, as she feared he would soon die from the treatment. Other inmates told of stabbings and reported broken limbs caused by their jailers.[98] In the end, investigators concluded that the problems of abuse stemmed from the fact that mentally disturbed inmates were improperly confined at the prison, where guards were ill-prepared to effectively oversee them.

Brutality appears to have been the modus operandi at Eastern, however; whether prisoners were neglected or subject to attempts to "restore" them, violence and exploitation dominated interaction between inmates and jailers. Yet inmates used and manipulated the basest aspects of abusive confinement to resist overseers' authority. Contesting the heightened surveillance, prisoners rebounded from the loss of privacy by reformulating the private sphere—that is, by making all behaviors public. By masturbating publicly and, as the warden decried, "shamelessly," inmates subverted the punitive goals of panopticism. Prisoners boldly masturbated, defecated, and urinated on cell floors to the chagrin of the warden, guards, and medical staff. As the warden noted, one inmate "smear[ed] his person all over with excrement and watche[d] for every opertunity to throw filth on the attendants."[99] Black female prisoners routinely tested the boundaries of authority by talking loudly, swearing, and in some cases attacking prison staff when the opportunity presented itself.[100]

By repeatedly confronting administrators with their sexually and socially transgressive behaviors, inmates compelled administrators to recognize, investigate, and mediate acts that were supposed to be entirely forbidden.[101] Moreover, the eliciting of punitive responses from overseers fundamentally forced the administration to participate in an exchange with prisoners—by their actions, disorderly convicts controlled the controllers. When prison workers witnessed the acts and attempted to regulate them, they became a part of the events—inmates turned them into voyeurs and often provoked sadistic responses. In many ways, they implicated the jailers in their misconduct and exposed criminal conduct on the part of the overseers.[102] Each time guards brutalized inmates to compel submission they simultaneously and inevitably marked their own loss of control and humanity.

Controlling Sodomites and the Restoration of White Masculinity

Power and control at the penitentiary were intimately connected to social order in society. Whereas most degenerates and shameless masturbators were chalked off as members of the crime class, administrators at Eastern found white men convicted of sodomy particularly disturbing—essentially an unacceptable waste of white manhood. They carefully tracked the young men and devoted extraordinary measures to try to both control and correct their behavior. Prison workers also theorized about why some men committed the crime. In 1890, Eastern's warden suggested that an absence of proper patriarchal authority led to a sodomy conviction for John Henry McDowell, a white seventeen-year-old at Eastern. McDowell, "a nice looking boy," unfortunately displayed "all the general peculiarities of people who do what he was convicted for." In reviewing his family history, Warden Cassidy speculated that his father's death when the boy was at an early age probably initiated his inversion—that and McDowell's having been in the House of Refuge and Saint John's Orphans Asylum.[103] Whereas most deviance was linked to racial or ethnic others, Cassidy reported that sodomy was an "unnatural crime on the increase" and one "not confined to any class of people." Yet administrators concentrated their reform efforts on young white men.[104]

The warden especially appeared to be fanatical in his efforts; he and the guards at Eastern left few tactics unexplored. In one instance, a young white man earmarked as "salvageable" turned out to be a "sexual invert." Initially noticing the prisoner's talent for drawing and mechanics, Cassidy placed the young man in the charge of Engineer McGarry in the hope of providing him with an employable skill upon his release. However, the young man "showed signs of being a sodomite." Cassidy locked the boy up for a month but after releasing him and giving him another job, the warden noted that "[at] every opportunity he would slip away from the wash house to the dynamo room for the purpose of carrying on his filthy habit." In an effort to "break him of his dirty habit," Cassidy moved him around from place to place, "cleaning bricks, wheeling stone, but to no purpose, every opportunity that presented itself he would slip away to the dynamo room." As a last resort, Cassidy placed the youth "under charge of Overseer Redmond who as a former officer of the House of Refuge knows how to handle boys."[105] Apparently Redmond "handled" the boy's problem, as Cassidy no longer complained about his actions.

Whereas every attempt seems to have been made to save this youth from his "filthy habits," other white inmates did not fare nearly as well. And black male sodomites were regarded as loathsome and degenerate and, though subject to scorn, perhaps luckily did not concern administrators to the same extent.[106] Ironically, neglect in this instance probably worked to their advantage, as persuasive methods often descended to unrelenting forms of coercion. In spite of extreme overcrowding, administrators isolated unrepentant white male sodomites. Locked away in dank, dark cells for long periods of time, one prisoner grew so despondent that authorities placed him on suicide watch. Cassidy insisted, however, "from the nature of his offence it is necessary that he should not have a cellmate."[107]

Although the warden meticulously policed white male sodomites, his treatment of women convicted of sodomy was less consistent, yet his vacillation on their treatment diagrams how sexuality often collided with race and gender. The experiences of Alice Hutchings, a white female inmate convicted in 1902 of assault and battery with intent to kill, reveal the dynamics of such a collision. Described by the warden as "exceeding[ly] vulgar and depraved," Hutchings apparently made no secret of her fondness for "cohabitating" with other women.[108] Though her sexual proclivities concerned prison administrators, the warden took no direct action until he learned that Hutchings was housed with an African-American female convict; this even though, as he later discovered, "there were cells containing white women" where Hutchings could have been placed. He "ordered an immediate removal" despite the matron's claim of overcrowding.[109] The cell reassignment makes visible the conflicting concerns of the warden and the matron as well as the double standards pertaining to both white female and black female sexuality.

The warden, in spite of his contempt for Hutchings, appears to have been more attached to the primacy of racial segregation than to restricting sexual intimacy between women. It is unclear whether segregated cell blocks existed, but prisoners of the same race were usually paired in cells. Although disgusted by Hutchings's sexual predilections, he made no demands that she be housed separately, as he frequently did with white male sodomites. Whether the matron believed that Hutchings and the black woman were well suited as cellmates or that isolating Hutchings would "protect" other white female inmates is unclear. Yet what seems certain is that both administrators acted in what they believed was the best interests of white female convicts. The protection of black female inmates was never a concern.

Public Containment vs. Erased Confinement

The emphasis on restoring young white male sodomites perhaps more powerfully unveils the ultimate motive of penal reform: the protection of white middle-class society. Eastern's administrators worked tirelessly to restore these young men above all others because they saw them as the embodiment of those destined to be at society's helm. The administrators' actions also demonstrate the slippery aspects of habitual criminality and the centrality of race in determining this categorization. It further points to where criminal praxis diverged from public representation. In press accounts, these young white male sodomites most likely would be identified as abnormal—somehow "othered" from normal whiteness. However, once inside, where these notions held true for black women, the reasoning broke down when the future of young men was at stake.

Designed as a place for solemn penitence, Eastern descended into a fortress of putridity. Additional allegations of abuse surfaced in 1903, but Eastern and its administration endured. The penitentiary remained open until the Commonwealth closed the facility in 1971. In 1913, legislators cemented plans for a female reformatory in Muncy, Pennsylvania.[110] Before the removal of female prisoners, however, black women served sentences punctuated by exploitation and neglect. Though their negative representations figured centrally in popular and institutionalized discourses of urban and penal reform, once imprisoned black female inmates were largely invisible—warehoused at Eastern as irredeemable members of the crime class.[111]

Conclusion

"SHE WAS BORN IN THIS PRISON":
BLACK FEMALE CRIME, PAST AND PRESENT

*A 56 colored female died at 4 pm "she was Born in this prison" was 27 years
of age the body was taken by her friends.*

— Michael Cassidy, Eastern State Penitentiary, Warden's Journals, May 27, 1882

THE ROOTS OF THE COLORED AMAZON sink deep into the social and cultural foundation of America and its legal system.[1] Warden Cassidy's notation about the black female prisoner born at Eastern aptly summarized the origins of black female criminality and, ultimately, broader notions of black womanhood. Public perceptions of both found their origins in the justice system—metaphorically appropriate, a prison. Race and gender bias helped justify unequal treatment beginning with enslavement and the use of separate Negro Courts.[2] These biases later metamorphosed to validate the social exclusion of African-American women after abolition. In the late nineteenth and early twentieth centuries, the caricature fully emerged and promoted exaggerated notions of black female criminality. It also projected a representation of black femininity fundamentally incongruous with prevailing definitions of domesticity.

Significant social transformation in the post-Reconstruction era further complicated matters. Black women perhaps more than ever before expected to enjoy the rights of citizenship as well as the benefits that domesticity afforded. The realities of enduring social and economic exclusion touched off a profound sense of disappointment, frustration, and anger. Adding to their disillusionment were ongoing assaults on their virtue. The rise of the Colored Amazon vilified black women in popular discourses and figured centrally in campaigns for urban and penal reform. It embodied the barriers that contributed to both black female crime and racist stereotypes about black female criminality. Most African-American women countered this alienation by forming uplift organizations. Others lobbied their cause through independent black periodicals and literary magazines.[3] Working within these parameters was not always a viable option, however, and for others it simply may not have been enough.

Crime reflected the desperation of many impoverished black women. But a cadre of women used crime to obtain financial and social autonomy. Not an organized means of resistance, these crimes encompassed the perpetrators' desires to lash out at the system at the same time that they sought to wield agency within it. Some crimes articulated women's breaking points, while others demonstrated that black women often fought the most intense battles inside of their own homes and communities. In this sense, crime provides a new language for, or context of understanding, histories of otherwise marginalized black women. Additionally, black female crime and its representation speak of the society in which they offend.

The Colored Amazon not only operated as a ruinous characterization of black female crime and femininity, but also supported white fantasies about black female sexuality. Simultaneously, the image warned white men against acting on those desires. Lawmakers, policemen, and reformers, too, made use of the Colored Amazon in the sense that fears of her existence propelled their agendas and reconfigured notions of white supremacy.[4] Under the guise of scientific neutrality, ideologies of habitual criminality mandated increased surveillance and more stringent police tactics. As a by-product, higher rates of conviction and longer prison sentences typified black women's experience in the justice system. But beyond these, the caricature ultimately marks the failures of the period. It can be likened to the first black criminal discussed in this book, Alice Clifton, in that it represented two worlds. The concept driving the image spanned the earliest days of enslavement through the institution's demise. At the same time, the Colored Amazon reflected the limits of black women's freedom, citizenship, and residency in the urban sphere.[5]

Sykes, Levin, and the Legacy of the Colored Amazon

Despite racist barriers, however, African Americans advanced their cause for social and political equality, and many decried the inequities of criminal justice. Blacks refuted negative representations often by attempting to present alternative transcripts. Presenting images of black victims in addition to denouncing black criminals in their presses, African Americans also carefully staged their own photographs and family portraits. These images directly contrasted reports of pathological urban blacks and promoted *respectable* images of black womanhood.[6] Activists like Ida B. Wells-Barnett helped found the National Association for the Advancement of Colored People in 1909, and greater numbers of blacks surpassed exclusionary obstacles. Black Philadelphians like Sadie Tanner Mossell Alexander, for example, would defy the odds: in 1918, Alexander became the first black woman to obtain a Ph.D. Not long afterward, in 1927, she became the first African-American woman admitted to the Philadelphia bar.[7]

Although the dynamics of race, gender, and sexuality had undergone further changes by the 1940s, traces of earlier criminal caricatures surfaced in that decade in two infamous cases that rocked the City of Brotherly Love. The crimes of Corrine Sykes and Seymour Levin sketch the more durable aspects of turn-of-the-century cultural narratives. In 1945, Philadelphia was still the third largest city in the country. Though it lacked the cultural capital of New York and the political clout of Washington, D.C., the city nonetheless existed as a "preeminent urban center."[8] Like most cities throughout the period, it experienced increased tensions surrounding shifting social boundaries. The World War Two era would lay the groundwork for radical transformations in race relations, gender praxis, and sexual identities that would occur in the 1950s and 1960s.[9]

The Sykes and Levin murder cases touched off a storm of social anxiety because the cases involved, respectively, interracial violence and homosexuality. Corrine Sykes, a twenty-year-old black female domestic, brutally robbed and murdered her employer, Freeda Wodlinger, a white woman, in 1944. Sykes stole one hundred dollars, jewelry, and a fur. She also stabbed the woman to death in the bathroom of her Oak Lane home. Seymour Levin, a white sixteen-year-old just two weeks shy of his seventeenth birthday, viciously raped and murdered a twelve-year-old white boy, Ellis Simons, in 1949. Information gathered during the two investigations reveals a number of common circumstances. Both assailants had prior criminal convictions. Sykes had served an eleven-month sentence at the county prison for theft. Levin had been convicted as a juvenile for kidnapping a small boy. Psychiatrists testified in both cases, finding that both Sykes and Levin were "constitutional psychopathic inferiors," Sykes because of an IQ of 63 and Levin because of his sexual proclivities and history of antisocial behavior. Each crime horrified the public and became the focal point of a barrage of sensational media coverage.[10]

Despite the overarching similarities of the two cases, however, Sykes and Levin received patently different treatment in the criminal justice system. The district attorney successfully challenged and preempted all potential African-American jurors in the Sykes trial, and, though questions about her competency dogged the proceedings, Sykes was tried and convicted of murder in the first degree. Sentenced to death, Sykes was executed on October 14, 1946. Her execution marked the last time a woman was put to death in the state of Pennsylvania.[11] Levin pleaded guilty and received a life sentence that was later commuted to twenty-eight years. He received parole in 1975. Aside from the outcomes, there are other differences in the cases. Sykes was a poor, uneducated domestic from North Philadelphia, a black ghetto. Levin was the son of middle-class whites in Wynnefield, a West Philadelphia suburb.[12]

Yet both of their victims were white, wrongfully murdered, and mourned by many in their respective communities — each came from groups associated with power and status according to the overarching social and racial hierarchy. Moreover, both of the perpetrators committed particularly vicious, taboo crimes. For Sykes the interracial nature of her crime undoubtedly raised the stakes. For Levin the same-sex nature of his crime made him particularly loathsome in the eyes of the public as well as the justice system.[13] In fact, the legislature proposed a bill to give judges, with the aid of a panel of psychiatrists, the ability to identify and confine indeterminately all "constitutional psychopathic inferiors" that fit Levin's profile.[14] Yet the justice system condemned Sykes and spared Levin. Levin's age and class factored heavily into the outcome, but his race also likely influenced the decision.

In Sykes's case, black female criminality had a long history in the court of public opinion as well as in Philadelphia criminal courts. This is not to say that public sentiment leaned toward leniency for Levin, however. Rather, in anticipation of public outrage over Levin's sentence of life imprisonment rather than the electric chair, the *Evening Bulletin* argued that Levin's sentence was in accord with a long-standing legal precedent for convicts of his age. Moreover, the paper asserted that even older, more vicious criminals had been spared execution.[15]

Although the press noted that criminals more violent than Levin, who stabbed his victim over fifty times, had received life sentences, the need for stern justice in Sykes's case apparently proved more pressing.[16] In the 1940s, the majority of working black women still labored as domestics in white households, and the protection of this populace was of the utmost importance. In the same month Sykes was arrested, a Philadelphia judge sentenced Catherine Scott, another black domestic, to twenty-two to forty-four years in prison for larceny. Scott stole close to ten thousand dollars' worth of merchandise from employers over a two-year period. According to the judge, he wanted to "set an example to other women who may be entertaining similar intentions."[17] The sentence served to warn black domestics about their conduct in white homes, but it may also have been a broader comment about shifting racial boundaries, as both Scott's and Sykes's crimes occurred at a moment when more social upheaval loomed on the country's horizon.

During World War Two, blacks battled oppression on two fronts, using the country's war for democracy abroad as means to battle racial segregation and discrimination at home.[18] Sykes's case, in some ways, thus took on broader significance. She symbolized the potential danger not only of all black domestics, but also of larger dangers if the roles of race and gender in the society changed.[19] Sykes's punishment signaled to black domestics the severe consequences of committing crimes against white employers. At the same time, it unearthed larger white fears about the potential dangers of all black domestics in white homes.

In some ways, the justice system and the public alike were not too far off the mark in the sense that Sykes's employment and economic status typified those of most single working black women in the city and across the nation.[20] But on a fundamental level, Corrine Sykes and her crime remained exceptional. She was slow mentally, she had a prior criminal conviction, and she committed the violent murder of a white woman during a robbery. Despite being overrepresented for their crimes, black female criminals represented only a fraction of the total population of working black women in the city.[21] The overwhelming majority of black women did not commit crimes, yet the image of the Colored Amazon cast long shadows.

At the time of Syke's death, black women accounted for 40 percent of all women executed in the United States.[22] From the Walnut Street Jail and Penitentiary House in 1790 to Eastern State Penitentiary at the beginning of the twentieth century to the State Correctional Institution at Muncy in 2003, black women have been consistently overrepresented in the criminal justice system.[23] Currently, 42 percent of the women imprisoned in Pennsylvania are African American. The pattern of disproportionate representation is a national one, as recent surveys have found that black women account for 48 percent of female inmates in state prisons.[24] Poverty, unemployment, racism, and gender bias in the legal system remain central factors underscoring black female criminality, which was primarily defined as crimes committed against property and illegal narcotics (the reigning crime-control theme).[25] Moreover, strong evidence suggests that sexual and physical abuse plays a significant role in female crime—perhaps lending credibility to the notion that psychological trauma factored into black badger crimes and crimes of violence in the nineteenth century.[26]

Yet discrimination does not wholly account for black female criminality, and it does not absolve the perpetrators. Crime and criminal offending germinate from both the perpetrators and the society in which they live. The criminal acts bespeak a range of motivating factors, as African-American women's decisions to break the law open a window on their desires, rage, and values (or lack thereof). The crimes, too, delineate the limits of the perpetrators' autonomy as well as the scope of the obstacles they face. Arguably the current rate of black female crime and incarceration may be seen as evidencing more of the same, their goals and values as well as the obstacles they face. Whether cities bemoan the increasing hordes of Colored Amazons, Welfare Queens, or Crack Fiends, the images and the realities surrounding black female criminals point to a web of profoundly entrenched social inequalities and social anxieties.[27]

On Studying Black Female Criminals

Colored Amazons pays homage to the legacy of black scholarship by investigating the history of a social problem currently facing African Americans.[28]

However, it also diverges from that legacy by choosing subjects and subject matter largely ignored and regarded as taboo.[29] *Colored Amazons* is not only about black female criminals. Rather it embodies one of the fundamental lessons these women offer. Often black female criminals manipulated social bias and broke laws to cleave out autonomy where none existed. In much the same way, this book exploits the dearth of firsthand accounts by using crime itself to push past evidentiary limitations. This work recognizes the necessity of both formal and extralegal means to transcend enduring social inequalities — inequalities that left black women with limited options as well as an inability to leave behind richer source materials about their experiences. Undoubtedly there are consequences to this approach, but also there are rewards.

Unearthing black women's crimes provides a more substantial historical context for understanding the current incarceration of black women. Specifically, it points to a number of factors that contributed to their crimes in the past, and in doing so it offers clues about tackling the problem in our time. Based on the findings, there can be little doubt that systemic biases — in the courts, in policing practices, and in the minds of everyday citizens — play a fundamental role in disproportionate rates of arrest and criminal conviction. Yet equally important are the ways that the women regarded themselves, both as individuals and as black women in America. What they believe they are entitled to as well as their ability to access those things is equally significant. Black women today may not be trapped between starvation and crime; yet black women's continued economic and social disenfranchisement as well as their unequal access to education operate as de facto barriers to better employment, housing, and overall social stability.[30]

Ultimately, black female criminals of old demonstrate that crime is a multi-faceted issue stemming from the perpetrators' relationship to the justice system and the political economy as well as to their avenues for social mobility. Potential remedies for the disproportionate rate of black female incarceration might consider an approach that is at least as expansive as the problem, perhaps not solely seeking to capture and punish criminals but also to rectify the relationship between social inequities, crime, and justice.[31] *Colored Amazons* is one investigation, but the subject of black female criminality merits much more scholarly attention from historians as well as policymakers.

APPENDIX

Data Set I: 158 cases, total number of black female prisoners, ESP 1880–1910. Source: *Eastern State Penitentiary Convict Descriptive Registers*, 1829–1903 (CDR) and *Convict Reception Registers*, 1842–1929 (CRR).

Data Set II: 386 cases, total number of female prisoners, ESP 1880–1910. Source: CDR, CRR.

Data Set III: 700 cases, collected randomly at five-year intervals between 1880 and 1910. Source: CDR, CRR.

Data Set IV: 3,226 cases, total number of female prisoners, PCP 1885–1910. Source: *Philadelphia County Prisoners for Trial Docket* (PTD).

Data Set V: 648 cases, randomly collected at five-year intervals, PCP 1885–1910. Source: PTD.

TABLE I. *Black Female Recidivism at Eastern State Penitentiary, 1880–1910*

Number of Convictions[a]	Percent
1	69.3
2	18.0
3+	12.8

Source: Data Set I
[a]Data are missing for 8 of 158 black female inmates.

TABLE 2. *Employment Data for Black Female Criminals, 1880–1910*

Occupations	Percent
Servant[a]	52.5
Housekeeper[b]	15.2
Thief	12.7
Idle	5.7
Dressmaker	3.8
Laundress	3.2
Waitress	2.5
Actress	1.3
Cook	1.3
Bawdy House—Owner/Inmate	0.6
Bookkeeper	0.6
Laborer	0.6

Source: Data Set I
[a]Includes 9 cases listed as "housework."
[b]Includes 1 maid.

TABLE 3. *Average Age of Prisoners at Eastern State Penitentiary, 1880–1910*

Prisoner	Age
White Women	32
White Men	31
Black Women	28
Black Men	29

Source: Data Set III

TABLE 4. *Women's Marital Status at Eastern State Penitentiary, 1880–1910*

Prisoner	Single/Widowed (%)	Married (%)
Black Women[a]	55.2	44.8
White Women[b]	51.8	48.2

Source: Data Set II
[a] Data are missing in 15 cases for black women.
[b] Data are missing in 31 cases for white women.

TABLE 5. *Black Female Crime at Eastern State Penitentiary, 1880–1910*

Crime	Percent
Larceny	51.3
Assault and Battery, Aggravated and Intent to Kill	9.5
Larceny from a Person	7.6
Murder	6.9
Manslaughter, Voluntary and Involuntary	3.8
Receiving Stolen Property	3.8
Robbery, Attempted Robbery	3.8
Bawdy House—Owner and/or Inmate	2.5
Perjury	2.5
Fraud—Pension and Mail	1.9
Accomplice to Murder, Attempted Murder	1.3
Arson	1.3
Abduction	0.6
Attempted Poisoning	0.6
Bigamy	0.6
Burglary	0.6
Liquor: Sale without License and/or Sale on Sunday	0.6
Abortion	0.6
Sodomy	0.6

Source: Data Set I

TABLE 6. *Birthplace of Black Female Criminals, 1880–1910*

Birthplace	Percent
Pennsylvania	29.7
Virginia	16.5
Philadelphia	15.8
Maryland	9.5
Delaware	7.0
District of Columbia	5.1
New Jersey	3.8
West Virginia	1.9
Canada	1.3
North Carolina	1.3
Nova Scotia	1.3
Ohio	1.3
West Indies[a]	1.3
Cuba	0.6
Florida	0.6
Georgia	0.6
Illinois	0.6
Massachusetts	0.6
South Carolina	0.6
Unlisted	0.6

Source: Data Set I
[a]Includes 1 case listed as "East Indies."

TABLE 7. *Crime and the Origins of Black Female Criminals*

	Birthplace		
Crime	Pennsylvania[a] (%)	Virginia (%)	Maryland (%)
Larceny	46.9	13.6	12.3
Assault and Battery[b]	37.5	25.0	12.5
Larceny from a Person	25.0	16.7	8.3

Source: Data Set I
[a]Includes those born in Philadelphia.
[b]Includes assault and battery with intent to kill.

TABLE 8. *Race and Gender of Philadelphia County Prisoners, 1885–1910*

Crime Categories	White Men (%)	Black Men (%)	White Women (%)	Black Women (%)
Assault and Battery[a]	18.2	6.2	1.9	1.1
Larceny	30.7	7.1	4.5	2.0
Murder	0.6	0.2	0.5	0.2
Miscellaneous Misconduct[b]	12.5	1.2	1.9	0.2
Vice[c]	4.8	1.4	4.2	0.9
Total	66.8	16.1	13.0	4.4

Source: Data Set V
[a]Includes assault and battery with intent to kill.
[b]Encompasses a variety of minor charges, most frequently disorderly conduct and common scolds.
[c]Vice includes prostitution, bigamy, rape, attempted rape, and sodomy.

TABLE 9. *Race and Gender of Prisoners at Eastern State Penitentiary, 1880–1910*

Inmates	Percent of ESP Population
White Men	78.8
Black Men[a]	18.5
White Women	1.7
Black Women	1.1

Sources: Data Set III combined with data collected from *Pennsylvania State Board of Charities Annual Report*, for the years 1879, 1884, 1889, 1894, 1899, 1904, 1909
[a] Black Men includes 1 Asian male convict.

TABLE 10. *Women at Eastern State Penitentiary and the Philadelphia County Prison*

Institution	Number of Black Women	Number of White Women
Philadelphia County	855.0	2,371.0
Percentage of Total	26.5	73.5
Eastern State	158.0	228.0
Percentage of Total	40.9	59.1

Source: Data Set IV

TABLE II. *Occupations of Eastern State Penitentiary Inmates*

Occupation	Percentage of Total
Laborer	29.7
Idle	8.6
Thief	5.5
Painter	2.3
Driver	2.1
Barber	2.0
Brakeman	1.4
Miner	1.9
Shoemaker	1.7
Teamster	1.6
Waiter	1.4
Fireman	1.3
Huckster	1.1
Cook	1.0
Machinist	1.0

Source: Data Set III

TABLE 12. *Crime at Eastern State Penitentiary*

Crime	Percentage
Larceny	26.6
Burglary	13.3
Assault and Battery[a]	10.0
Sexual Misconduct[b]	8.0
Receiving Stolen Property	7.9
Fraud	7.4
Robbery	5.0
Felonious Assault	4.0
Larceny and Receiving	3.9
Murder	2.7

Source: Data Set III
[a] Includes assault and battery with intent to kill.
[b] Includes prostitution, bigamy, rape, attempted rape, and sodomy.

TABLE 13. *Nativity of Prisoners at Eastern State Penitentiary*

Nativity	Percentage	Nativity	Percentage
Pennsylvania	32.2	Barbados	0.3
Philadelphia	21.1	California	0.3
New York	6.6	Florida	0.3
Virginia	4.7	France	0.3
Germany	3.7	Greece	0.3
England	3.4	Hungary	0.3
Ireland	3.1	Kentucky	0.3
Italy	2.7	Lithuania	0.3
New Jersey	2.6	Mississippi	0.3
Delaware	1.7	Poland	0.3
Austria	1.3	Prussia	0.3
Massachusetts	1.1	Rhode Island	0.3
Ohio	1.1	Austria	0.1
District of Columbia	1.0	Colorado	0.1
Russia	1.0	Cuba	0.1
Illinois	0.9	Denmark	0.1
Scotland	0.7	Indiana	0.1
Canada	0.6	Iowa	0.1
China	0.6	Louisiana	0.1
Connecticut	0.6	Maine	0.1
Georgia	0.4	Mexico	0.1
North Carolina	0.4	Missouri	0.1

Source: Data Set III

ABBREVIATIONS AND NOTES ON SOURCES

Records and Institutions

Eastern State Penitentiary (ESP)

Bertillon Hand Books (BHB)
Convict Description Register (CDR)
Convict Reception Register (CRR)
Discharge Descriptive Docket (DDD)
Scrapbook, Vol. 1, 1884–93 (SB1)
Scrapbook, Vol. 2, 1908–25 (SB2)
Warden's Journals (WJ)
House of Refuge (HR)

Philadelphia County Prison (PCP)

Prison Diary, Female (PDF)
Prisoners for Trial Docket (PTD)

Pennsylvania Insane Asylum (PIA) (pseudonym)

Admissions Register, Female Patients

Pennsylvania Prison Society Minutes (PPSM)
Pennsylvania State Board of Charities (PSBC)
William Dorsey Collection (WDC)

Newspapers

National Police Gazette (NPG)
Philadelphia Daily News (PDN)
Philadelphia Evening Bulletin (EB)

Philadelphia Evening Item (PEI)
Philadelphia Evening Telegraph (PET)
Philadelphia Inquirer (PI)
Philadelphia Press (PP)
Philadelphia Public Ledger (PL)
Philadelphia Record (RC)
Philadelphia Tribune (PT)
Times-Philadelphia (TP)
Scranton Defender (SD)
Voice of the Negro (VN)

Archives and Historical Societies

Free Library of Philadelphia, Central Branch (FL)
Historical Society of Pennsylvania (HSP)
Library Company of Philadelphia (LCP)
Pennsylvania Historical and Museum Commission (PHMC)
Pennsylvania State Library (PSL)
Philadelphia City Archive (PCA)
Schomburg Center for Research in Black Culture (SCH)
Temple University Urban Archives (TUA)
Van Pelt Library, University of Pennsylvania (VP)

Journals

American Quarterly (AQ)
Pennsylvania Magazine of History and Biography (PMHB)
William and Mary Quarterly (WMQ)

Frequently newspaper clippings in scrapbooks lack titles and dates—those abbreviations are as follows:

Missing paper title (MPT)
Missing story title (MST)
Missing date (MD)

About Sources and Citations

I have endeavored to cite my sources as clearly and as precisely as possible. However, in certain instances, especially with regard to articles contained in the Eastern State Penitentiary scrapbooks this task has been a difficult one. The scrapbooks are loosely dated, and sometimes the clippings lack titles and dates. I approximated dates in these instances by cross-referencing the inmates in the stories with the prison intake records.

Statistics are used to sketch the prison population and the general nature of crime in Philadelphia. I use information from the Philadelphia County Prison in a limited fashion because the institution held prisoners awaiting trial as well as prisoners tried and convicted and awaiting transportation to Eastern. The county prison also held convicted prisoners serving light sentences. Often prisoners appeared two or three times in the *Prisoners for Trial Docket* before their cases were decided. Because they had common names like Charles, William, Thomas, Annie, Catherine, and Mary and last names such as Smith, Williams, and Johnson, pinpointing specific prisoners often amounted to a statistical nightmare. Creating databases for Eastern State Penitentiary proved a more manageable task, though even here there are points when the ink on the records faded in the *Convict Reception Register* and *Convict Description Register*. Because much of the information in these registers overlaps, sometimes a faded case in one register could be documented because it appeared in the other. However, in some instances the data were unrecoverable. To account for these irregularities I combined data from the penitentiary records with information available in the *Annual Reports* from the Pennsylvania State Board of Public Charities. However, the *Annual Reports* contain raw numbers of the prison population rather than detailed accounts of specific inmates and are likely to possess errors as well.

Also, in the prison dockets crimes were sometimes listed plainly as burglary or larceny and at other points the crime might appear as "servant-theft." I grouped crimes and listed criminal categories in a manner that would remain true to the nature of offenses but also in a manner that allowed the data to be analyzed effectively—these decisions are documented throughout the book and are noted in the statistical tables.

NOTES

Introduction

1. EB 4/9/1909 (TUA).

2. This percentage refers to the demographics of that particular class; in the general population at SCI-Muncy black women's numbers are just over 40 percent. *Pennsylvania Department of Corrections: Female Offenders* (Report published by the Pennsylvania Department of Corrections, February 2003), 1.

3. Examples include *David Walker's Appeal: To the Coloured Citizens of the World, but in particular, and very expressly, to those of the United States of America* (1830; reprint, with an introduction by James Turner, Baltimore: Black Classic, 1993); *Maria W. Stewart, America's First Black Woman Political Writer: Essays and Speeches*, ed. and introduced by Marilyn Richardson (Bloomington, Ind.: University of Indiana Press, 1987); Malcolm X, *The Autobiography of Malcolm X*, With the Assistance of Alex Haley, Introduction by M. S. Handler (New York: Grove Press, 1965). For examinations of the emotional and psychological impact of racism, see Frantz Fanon, *Black Skin, White Masks*, trans. Charles Lam Markmann (New York: Grove Press, 1967), and *The Wretched of the Earth*, Preface by Jean-Paul Sartre, trans. Constance Farrington (New York: Grove Press, 1968); Aime Cesaire, *Discourse on Colonialism*, trans. Joan Pinkham (New York: Monthly Review Press, 1972).

4. Ida B. Wells-Barnett, *Southern Horrors and Other Writings: The Anti-lynching Campaign of Ida B. Wells, 1892–1900*, ed. with an introduction by Jacqueline Jones Royster (Boston: Bedford Books, 1997), and *The Reason Why the Colored American is not in the World's Columbian Exposition: The Afro-American's Contribution to Columbian literature*, ed. Robert W. Rydell (Urbana: University of Illinois Press, 1999); W. E. B. Du Bois, *The Souls of Black Folk: Essays and Sketches*, 2nd ed. (Chicago: A. C. McClurg, 1903); Anna Julia Cooper, *A Voice from the South* (1892; reprint, New York: Oxford University Press, 1988); Carter G. Woodson, *The Mis-Education of the Negro* (Washington, D.C.: The Associated Publishers, Inc., 1933).

5. Evelyn Brooks-Higginbotham, *Righteous Discontent: The Women's Movement in the Black Baptist Church*, 1880–1920 (Cambridge, Mass: Harvard University Press, 1993), 186–87, 193; Kevin Gaines, *Uplifting the Race: Black Leadership, Politics, and Culture in the Twentieth Century* (Chapel Hill and London: University of North Carolina Press, 1996), 5; Kali N. Gross, "Examining the Politics of Respectability in African American Studies," *University of Pennsylvania Almanac* 43, no. 28 (April 1, 1997).

6. Evelyn Brooks-Higginbotham, "Beyond the Sound of Silence: Afro-American Women in History," *Gender and History* 1 (1989): 50–67; Michele Mitchell, "Silences Broken, Silences Kept: Gender and Sexuality in African-American History," *Gender and History* 11, no. 3 (November 1999): 433–44; Gaines, *Uplifting the Race*, 5.

7. I am not suggesting that gays and lesbians are deviant, but rather that the histories of gays and lesbians, especially within African-American history, have been largely ignored. However, works that address this gap include George Chauncey, *Gay New York: Gender, Urban Culture, and the Making of the Gay Male World, 1890–1940* (New York: Basic Books, 1994); Eric Garber, "A Spectacle in Color: The Lesbian and Gay Subculture of Jazz Age Harlem," in *Hidden from History*, ed. Martin Bauml Duberman, Martha Vicinus, and George Chauncey (New York: Meridian, 1989); Gloria T. Hull, " 'Lines She Did Not Dare': Angelina Weld Grimké, Harlem Renaissance Poet," in *The Lesbian and Gay Studies Reader*, ed. Henry Abelove, Michèle Aina Barale, David M. Halperin (New York: Routledge, 1993); Cheryl Clarke, "Lesbianism: An Act of Resistance," in *Words of Fire: An Anthology of African-American Feminist Thought*, ed. Beverly Guy-Sheftall (New York: New York Press, 1995); *Beloved Sisters and Loving Friends: Letters from Rebecca Primus of Royal Oak, Maryland, and Addie Brown of Hartford, Connecticut, 1854–1868*, ed. Farah Jasmine Griffin (New York: Knopf, 1999).

8. For pioneering books, see E. P. Thompson, *The Making of the English Working-Class*, (New York: Vintage Books, 1963); Robin D. G. Kelley, *Hammer and Hoe: Alabama Communists During the Great Depression* (Chapel Hill: University of North Carolina Press, 1990), and *Race Rebels: Culture, Politics, and the Black Working Class* (New York: Free Press, 1994); Nell Painter, *Exodusters: Black Migration to Kansas After Reconstruction* (New York: Knopf, 1976) and *The Narrative of Hosea Hudson, His Life as a Negro Communist in the South* (Cambridge, Mass: Harvard University Press, 1979); Joe Trotter, *Black Milwaukee: The Making of an Industrial Proletariat, 1915–45* (Urbana: University of Illinois Press, 1985).

9. For historicizing race and the ways in which blackness and whiteness are mutually constitutive, see Barbara J. Fields, "Ideology and Race in American History," in *Region, Race, and Reconstructing: Essays on C. Vann Woodward*, ed. J. Morgan Kousser and James McPherson (New York: Oxford University Press, 1982), 143–77; Evelyn Brooks-Higginbotham, "African American Women's History and the Metalanguage of Race," *Signs* 17, no. 21 (1992): 251–77; Toni Morrison, *Playing in the Dark: White-*

ness and the Literary Imagination (Cambridge, Mass: Harvard University Press, 1992), 12; David Roediger, *The Wages of Whiteness: Race and the Making of the American Working Class* (Cambridge, Mass: Harvard University Press, 1991), 30; Kim F. Hall, *Things of Darkness: Economies of Race and Gender in Early Modern England* (Ithaca: Cornell University Press, 1995), 255. For works that examine gender and sexuality, see Joan Wallach, "Gender: A Useful Category of Historical Analyses," in *Feminism and History*, ed. Joan Scott Walllach (New York: Oxford University Press, 1996), 167; Judith Butler, *Gender Trouble: Feminism and the Subversion of Identity* (New York: Routledge, 1990), 140; Robert Padgug, "Sexual Matters: On Conceptualizing Sexuality in History," in *Passion and Power: Sexuality in History*, ed. Kathy Peiss and Christina Simmons (Philadelphia: Temple University Press, 1989), 22; Barbara Melosh, ed., "Introduction," *Gender and American History Since 1890* (London and New York: Routledge, 1993), 1–7; Gayle Rubin, "Thinking Sex: Notes for a Radical Theory of the Politics of Sexuality," in *Pleasure and Danger: Exploring Female Sexuality*, ed. Carol S. Vance (London: Pandora Press, 1989), 309; Maurice Berger, ed., "Introduction," *Constructing Masculinity*, ed. Brian Walls and Simon Watson (New York: Routledge, 1995), 2; Michel Foucault, *The History of Sexuality: An Introduction*, vol. 1, trans. Robert Hurley (New York: Vintage Books, 1990), 1–13, 53–57, 92–102. Also see Cornel West, "The New Cultural Politics of Difference," in *Out There: Marginalization and Contemporary Cultures*, ed. Russell Ferguson, Martha Gever, Trinh T. Min-ha, and Cornel West (Cambridge, Mass: MIT Press, 1990), 19–38; Nancy Hartsock, "Foucault on Power: A Theory for Women?" in *Feminism/Postmodernism*, ed. Linda Nicolson (New York: Routledge, 1990), 158–63.

10. James W. Messerschmidt, *Crime as Structured Action: Gender, Race, Class, and Crime in the Making* (Thousand Oaks, London, New Delhi: Sage Publications, 1997), 3–4; Lawrence M. Friedman, *Crime and Punishment in American History* (New York: Basic Books, 1993), 1–5; Beth E. Richie, *Compelled to Crime: The Gender Entrapment of Battered Black Women* (New York: Routledge, 1996), "Introduction."

11. Anna Julia Cooper's argument about the centrality of black women's liberation in ending racial oppression significantly shaped my thinking about the importance of black women's experiences in the justice system. See *A Voice from the South*, 31; Mae G. Henderson, "Toni Morrison's *Beloved*: Re-membering the Body as Historical Text," in *Discourses of Sexuality: From Aristotle to AIDS*, ed. Domna C. Stanton (Ann Arbor: University of Michigan Press, 1992), 322; Patricia Hill Collins, *Black Feminist Thought: Knowledge, Consciousness, and the Politics of Empowerment* (Boston: Unwin Hyman, 1990), 221–38; Paula Giddings, *When and Where I Enter: The Impact of Black Women on Race and Sex in America* (New York: Bantam Books, 1988), 5–8; Messerschmidt, *Crime as Structured Action*, 10–12.

12. bell hooks critiques the concentration on the heroic aspects of black history—she charges that doing so ultimately dehumanizes blacks by negating their trauma. See

Talking Back: thinking feminist, thinking black (Boston: South End Press, 1989), 178. Patricia Scott Bell also calls attention to these biases in black women's history: see "Debunking Sapphire: Towards a Non-Racist and Non-Sexist Social Science," in *All the Women are White, All the Blacks are Men, But Some of Us are Brave: Black Women's Studies*, ed. Gloria T. Hull and Barbara Smith (Old Westbury, N.Y.: Feminist Press, 1982), 87.

13. U.S. Department of Justice, Office of Justice Programs, Bureau of Justice Statistics, *Women Offenders*, rev. 10/03, NCJ 175688; U.S. Department of Justice, Office of Justice, Bureau of Justice Statistics, *Prisoners in 2002*, 07/03 NCJ 200248.

14. Although several works explore the experiences of blacks and women in the justice system, only a few concentrate on black women or include significant discussions about their history: Leslie Patrick-Stamp, "Numbers That Are Not New: African Americans in the Country's First Prison, 1790–1835," *PMHB* 119 (1995): 95–128; G. S. Rowe, "Women's Crime and Criminal Administration in Pennsylvania, 1763–1790," *PMHB* 109 (1985): 335–68; Roger Lane, *The Roots of Violence in Black Philadelphia, 1860–1900* (Cambridge, Mass: Harvard University Press, 1986); Nicole Hahn Rafter, *Partial Justice: Women, Prisons, and Social Control* (New Brunswick: Transaction Publishers, 1990); Anne Butler, *Gendered Justice in the American West: Women Prisoners in Men's Penitentiaries* (Urbana: University of Illinois Press, 1997); L. Mara Dodge, *"Whores and Thieves of the Worst Kind": A Study of Women, Crime, and Prisons, 1835–2000* (Dekalb: Northern Illinois University Press, 2002).

15. There are a number of excellent histories on race and the criminal justice system—particularly in the post-Reconstruction South—but they include limited treatment of the experiences of black women. Among these works are Edward Ayers, *Vengeance and Justice, Crime and Justice in the 19th Century South* (New York: Oxford University Press, 1984), 200, 243–44; David M. Oshinsky, *"Worse Than Slavery": Parchman Farm and the Ordeal of Jim Crow Justice* (New York: Free Press Paperbacks, 1996), 157–77.

16. Hazel V. Carby, "Policing the Black Woman's Body in an Urban Context," *Critical Inquiry* 18, no. 4 (Summer 1992): 738–55. Wahneema Lubiano argues that racism, sexism, capitalism, and homophobia create a distorted prism that allows elite whites to imagine themselves functioning in morally just ways, while ignoring their widespread violence against blacks and all other poor and marginalized members of society. She explains that this distorted vision, or analytical prism, depicts poverty and crime through racist images of blacks. See Wahneema Lubiano, ed., "Introduction," *The House that Race Built: Black Americans, U.S. Terrain* (New York: Pantheon Books, 1997), vii. For historical evidence of this in earlier periods, see G. S. Rowe, "Black Offenders, Criminal Courts, and Philadelphia Society in the Late Eighteenth-Century," *Journal of Social History* 22 (Summer 1989): 704; Patrick-Stamp, "Numbers That Are Not New," 98.

17. The work of such scholars as Tera Hunter, Robin D. G. Kelley, Earl Lewis, Nell Irvin Painter, and Joe Trotter are among the most notable exceptions.

18. David R. Johnson, *Policing the Urban Underworld: The Impact of Crime on the Development of the American Police, 1800–1887* (Philadelphia: Temple University Press, 1979), 4 and "Conclusion."

19. Messerschmidt, *Crime as Structured Action*, 67–86.

20. Shane White comments on these difficulties and also explores how studies of blacks and crime help to combat absences in the historical record; see "The Death of James Johnson," *AQ* 51, no. 4 (1999): 753–95 at 754.

21. I used the *Eastern State Penitentiary Convict Descriptive Register, 1829–1903* and the *ESP Convict Reception Register, 1842–1929* (PHMC), to create two statistical databases. The first database, comprised of 386 cases, includes all of the women who appear in ESP records between 1880 and 1910; the second is a random sample of the inmate population for the same period—it consists of 700 cases based on 100 cases collected at five-year intervals. I also created a database of 3,226 cases of women who passed through the city's justice system as they appear in the *Philadelphia County Prisoners for Trial Docket, 1790–1948* (PCA).

22. Press sources primarily consist of the following newspapers: *Philadelphia Inquirer*, *Philadelphia Evening Bulletin*, *Philadelphia Press*, *Philadelphia Public Ledger*, which later merged with the *North American*, *Times-Philadelphia*, and *Philadelphia Record*. Five of these papers were generally Republican in their politics, and the latter two tended to be more Democratic or Independent. The *Philadelphia Public Ledger and Transcript* (*Ledger*) was edited conservatively and with less offense to the "respectable." Printing substantial coverage of crime and criminal trials, the *Ledger* is among the most reliable of the papers. The *Philadelphia Inquirer*, a more popular and economically successful newspaper, by the 1890s claimed to be the largest Republican paper in the city. The *Times-Philadelphia*, however, founded by Alexander K. McClure in 1871, was among the more sensational of the papers and was second in readership only to the *Ledger*. For more on the papers, see Roger Lane, *William Dorsey's Philadelphia and Ours: On the Past and Future of the Black City in America* (New York: Oxford University Press, 1991), 10–11, and *Roots of Violence*, 181–82; Frank Luther Mott, *American Journalism: A History of Newspapers in the United States Through 1690–1950*, rev. ed. (New York: Macmillan, 1950), 239–40.

23. I am borrowing from Jennifer DeVere Brody, who uses written texts as "cultural artifacts" and as texts that express "popular anxieties about race, gender, sexuality, class and nationalism." See *Impossible Purities: Blackness, Femininity, and Victorian Culture* (Durham and London: Duke University Press, 1998), 9. Judith Walkowitz's work also shaped my analysis—particularly the process of using popular narratives as a means to understand the social context of its subjects and also to understand the narratives as a mainstream means to both represent and understand society; see *City of Dreadful*

Delight: Narratives of Sexual Danger in Late-Victorian London (Chicago: University of Chicago Press, 1992), 7, 8–10.

24. Many scholars have written about racial and sexual violence in American history, but for my purposes I have been particularly interested in multilayered ways to read and interpret that violence. A few works have been especially helpful in this respect: Saidiya Hartman, *Scenes of Subjection: Terror, Slavery, and Self-Making in Nineteenth-Century America* (New York: Oxford University Press, 1997), 79–112; Nell Painter, "Soul Murder and Slavery: Toward a Fully Loaded Cost Accounting," in *U.S. History as Women's History: New Feminist Essays*, ed. Linda K. Kerber, Alice Kessler-Harris, and Kathryn Kish Sklar (Chapel Hill: University of North Carolina Press, 1995), 125–27; Wells-Barnett, *Southern Horrors and Other Writings*.

25. Michele Mitchell argues that not only have silences around black women's history remained, but that she suspects historians are avoiding subjects or topics that "have been deemed either dangerous or damaging." I agree and argue that part of the problem lies in historians' shying away from the more murky depths of race, rage, and violence. See Mitchell's "Silences Broken, Silences Kept," 433–44, and Brooks-Higginbotham, "Beyond the Sound of Silence," 50–67. Tera Hunter's incisive method of making the most of limited source material also provided an important model for my research. See Hunter's "Preface" in *"To 'Joy My Freedom": Southern Black Women's Lives and Labors After the Civil War* (Cambridge, Mass: Havard University Press, 1997).

26. I aim to create a more "fully loaded cost accounting" of black women's experiences, particularly those of trauma and emotional damage. See Painter, "Soul Murder and Slavery," 125–27; Toni Morrison, "Unspeakable Things Unspoken: The African American Presence in American Literature," *Michigan Quarterly Review* 28, no. 1 (Winter 1989): 1–34.

27. Darlene Clark Hine, "Rape and the Inner Lives of Black Women in the Middle West: Preliminary Thoughts on the Culture of Dissemblance," in *Words of Fire*, ed. Guy-Sheftall, 383–85.

28. David Cohen, "Social Injustice, Sexual Violence, Spiritual Transcendence: Constructions of Interracial Rape in Early American Crime Literature, 1767–1817," *WMQ*, 3rd ser., 56, no. 3 (July 1999): 481–526, esp. 486–88; Mitchell, "Silences Broken, Silences Kept," Brooks-Higginbotham, "Beyond the Sound of Silence," and Hunter, "Preface."

29. W. E. B. Du Bois, *The Philadelphia Negro: A Social Study* (1896; reprint, Philadelphia: University of Pennsylvania Press, 1996); Gary B. Nash, *First City: Philadelphia and the Forging of Historical Memory* (Philadelphia: University of Pennsylvania Press, 2002), and *Forging Freedom: The Formation of Philadelphia's Black Community, 1720–1840* (Cambridge, Mass: Harvard University Press, 1988); Emma Lapsansky, " 'Since They Got Those Separate Churches': Afro-Americans and Racism in Jacksonian Philadel-

phia," in *African Americans in Pennsylvania: Shifting Historical Perspectives*, ed. Joe William Trotter, Jr. and Eric Ledell Smith (Harrisburg: Pennsylvania Historical and Museum Commission; University Park: Pennsylvania State University Press, 1997).

30. Harry Elmer Barnes and Negley K. Teeters, *New Horizons in Criminology: The American Crime Problem* (New York: Prentice-Hall, 1946), 446–92; Henry Boies, *The Science of Penology: The Defense of Society Against Crime* (New York and London: G. P. Putnam's Sons, 1901); Ayers, *Vengeance and Justice*, 35–40.

31. David Rothman, *The Discovery of the Asylum: Social Order and Disorder in the New Republic* (Boston: Little, Brown and Company, 1971), chapter 4, "The Invention of the Penitentiary"; Nicole Hahn Rafter, *Creating Born Criminals* (Urbana: University of Illinois, 1997), 56–69, 123–25.

32. Michel Foucault's works are seminal texts, especially *Discipline and Punish: The Birth of the Prison*, 2nd ed., trans. Alan Sheridan (New York: Vintage Books, 1995). Also see Rothman, *The Discovery of the Asylum*, and Michael Meranze, *Laboratories of Virtue: Punishment, Revolution, and Authority in Philadelphia, 1760–1835* (Chapel Hill: University of North Carolina Press, 1996), 19–54, 132–36.

33. Harry Elmer Barnes, *The Repression of Crime: Studies in Historical Penology* (New York: George H. Duran, 1926), 233.

34. Jacqueline Jones, *The Dispossessed: America's Underclasses from the Civil War to the Present* (New York: Basic Books, 1992); Michael S. Kimmel, *Manhood in America: A Cultural History* (New York: Free Press, 1996), 83–89; Gail Bederman, *Manliness and Civilization: A Cultural History of Gender and Race in the United States, 1880–1917* (Chicago: University of Chicago Press, 1995), 11–15.

35. Chauncey, *Gay New York*, 12–13; Kathy Peiss, *Cheap Amusements: Working Women and Leisure in New York City, 1880–1920* (Philadelphia: Temple University Press, 1986), 3, 34–45; Kevin Mumford, *Interzones: Black/White Sex Districts in Chicago and New York in the Early-Twentieth Century* (New York: Columbia University Press, 1997), xii–xiv.

36. Rafter, *Creating Born Criminals*, 56–69, 86–89; Rothman, *The Discovery of the Asylum*; Foucault, *Discipline and Punish*; Simon Cole, *Suspect Identities: A History of Fingerprinting and Criminal Identification* (Cambridge, Mass: Harvard University Press, 2001), 2–4.

37. Peter McCaffery, *When Bosses Ruled Philadelphia: The Emergence of the Republican Machine, 1867–1933* (University Park: Pennsylvania State University Press, 1993); James A. Kehl, *Boss Rule in the Gilded Age: Matt Quay of Pennsylvania* (Pittsburgh: University of Pittsburgh Press, 1981).

38. Edmund Morgan's discussion framed my thinking, though his work does not concentrate on Philadelphia specifically; see "Slavery and Freedom: The American Paradox," in *Journal of American History* 59, no. 1 (June 1972): 5–29. Barbara Savage touches on this dynamic as well in her work on blacks in the 1940s; see *Broadcasting*

Freedom: Radio, War, and the Politics of Race, 1938–1948 (Chapel Hill and London: University of North Carolina Press, 1999), 63–64.

39. *Elite* is used to discuss a privileged class of African Americans. This privilege is not solely based on economic standing, but rather *elite* is defined in conjunction with, though not limited to, African Americans who possessed an increased access to education, better employment, and overall social standing in community organizations —benefit societies, churches, etc. This improved status typically stemmed from certain advantages they may have gained because of a mulatto heritage or ancestry.

40. Carby, "Policing the Black Woman's Body," 39.

41. I am building on Darlene Clark Hine's examination of the culture of dissemblance— in the sense that I want to reposition black female violence as evidence of those traumas that black women could not dissemble. See Hine, "Rape and the Inner Lives of Black Women," 380–82. I am also trying to employ an interpretive historical analysis of female violence similar to Melton McLaurin's examination of a young female slave who killed her master in 1851. See *Celia, A Slave: A True Story* (New York: Avon Books, 1991), 36–37. For a broader reading of violence, representation, and language, see Teresa DeLauretis, *Technologies of Gender: Essays, Theory, Film, and Fiction* (Bloomington: Indiana University Press, 1987), 33. In terms of rethinking and expanding how black women demanded and sometimes actualized elements of respectability, see Hazel Carby, *Reconstructing Womanhood: The Emergence of the Afro-American Woman Novelist* (New York: Oxford University Press, 1987), 7, 17, and Claudia Tate, *Domestic Allegories of Political Desire: The Black Heroine's Text at the Turn of the Century* (New York: Oxford University Press, 1992), 88.

42. Like Walkowitz in her work on narratives of sex and danger in late-Victorian London, I want to examine the construction of the "Colored Amazon" as evidence of social and cultural anxieties about race, gender, sexuality, and crime in late nineteenth-century Philadelphia—see *City of Dreadful Delight*, 5–7; David E. Ruth argues that the twentieth-century gangster was a media invention, and as such less an accurate reflection of reality and more a projection created from various Americans' beliefs, concerns, and ideas about crime and media profits. See *Inventing the Public Enemy: The Gangster in American Culture, 1918–1934* (Chicago: University of Chicago Press, 1996), 1–3. I use a modified version of Ruth's argument, asserting that media images also reflect widespread beliefs held about race, gender, and sexuality.

43. Although this term appears in some Philadelphia press accounts as well as in news accounts in the South, I am using it to refer to a press construction of a general black femme fatale. bell hooks discusses the prevalence of such characterizations of black women in the nineteenth century; see *Ain't I a Woman?: Black Women and Feminism* (Boston: South End Press, 1981), 81–82.

44. A. Leon Higginbotham, Jr., *In the Matter of Color, Race and the American Legal Process: The Colonial Period* (Oxford: Oxford University Press, 1978), 268.

1. Of Law and Virtue

1. I am using the term *unfree* in much the same way that Peter Kolchin does in his work — to encompass lifelong slaves as well as indentured servants. For discussions about these types of labor along with an exploration of serfdom, see *Unfree Labor: American Slavery and Russian Serfdom* (Cambridge, Mass: Harvard University Press, 1987).

2. Gary B. Nash and Jean Soderlund, *Freedom by Degrees: Emancipation in Pennsylvania and Its Aftermath* (New York: Oxford University Press, 1991), 9–11; Nash, *Forging Freedom*, 62–63; Sharon V. Salinger, *To Serve Well and Faithfully: Labor and Indentured Servants in Pennsylvania, 1682–1800* (Bowie, Md: Heritage Books, 2000), 3, 15–17.

3. Gary B. Nash, "Slaves and Slave Owners in Colonial Philadelphia," in *African Americans in Pennsylvania*, ed. Trotter and Smith, 43–44; Patrick-Stamp, "Numbers that Are Not New," 100–101.

4. Susan E. Klepp, "Seasoning and Society: Racial Differences in Mortality in Eighteenth-Century Philadelphia," *WMQ*, 3rd. ser., 51, no. 3, Mid-Atlantic Perspectives (July 1994): 473–506, at 474–78, 481.

5. For more about runaways in Pennsylvania, see Billy G. Smith and Richard Wojtowicz, *Blacks Who Stole Themselves: Advertisements for Runaways in the Pennsylvania Gazette, 1728–1790* (Philadelphia: University of Pennsylvania Press, 1989). On the impact of Independence, see Nash and Soderlund, *Freedom by Degrees*, 75–78; Nash, *Forging Freedom*, 38; Du Bois, *The Philadelphia Negro*, 16. Also see Morgan, "Slavery and Freedom, 5–29.

6. *The Trial of Alice Clifton for the Murder of her Bastard-Child, At the Court of Oyer and Terminer and General Gaol Delivery, held at Philadelphia, on Wednesday the 18th of April 1787*, 3 (LCP).

7. Jean R. Soderlund, "Black Women in Colonial Pennsylvania," in *African Americans in Pennsylvania*, ed. Trotter and Smith, 81–82.

8. *Trial of Alice Clifton*, 1–2, 4.

9. This defense is introduced in Doctor Jones's testimony. See "Doctor Jones Sworn" in *Trial of Alice Clifton*, 6–7. It is revisited again throughout the hearing but is perhaps most directly summed up by the judge in pages 12–13.

10. "Mr. Bartholomew Sworn," *Trial of Alice Clifton*, 11.

11. Soderlund, "Black Women in Colonial Pennsylvania," 82.

12. C. W. Larison, *Silvia Dubois, A Biografy of the Slav Who Whipt Her Mistress and Gand Her Freedom*, ed. Jared C. Lodbell (1883; reprint, New York: Oxford University Press, 1988), 78–79, 54–55, 66; Klepp, "Seasoning and Society," 483.

13. Stephanie Camp's discussion of spatial mobility and resistance is particularly salient and can be applied to the actions of slave women in the North. See *Closer to Freedom: Enslaved Women and Everyday Resistance in the Plantation South* (Chapel Hill: Uni-

versity of North Carolina Press, 2004), 60–62; Billy G. Smith, "Black Family Life in Philadelphia from Slavery to Freedom," in *Shaping a National Culture: The Philadelphia Experience, 1750–1800*, ed. Catherine E. Hutchins (Winterthur, Del.: Henry Francis du Pont Winterthur Museum, 1994), 78.

14. "Dr. Foulke Sworn," *Trial of Alice Clifton*, 7–10.

15. Ibid., 9.

16. "Mrs. Bartholomew Sworn," *Trial of Alice Clifton*, 2–4.

17. Apparently, Mrs. Bartholomew's sister-in-law was also named Mary—see "Miss Mary Bartholomew Sworn," *Trial of Alice Clifton*, 4–5.

18. Two houseboys initially removed the razor but later returned it for the investigation; see "Samuel Bullfinch Sworn," *Trial of Alice Clifton*, 5–6.

19. Ibid., "Mrs. Mary Bartholomew Sworn."

20. "Dr. Jones Sworn" and "Dr. Foulke Sworn," *Trial of Alice Clifton*, 5–7, 7–10.

21. "Dr. Foulke Sworn," *Trial of Alice Clifton*, 9.

22. "Nathaniel Norgrave Sworn," 10.

23. Charge to the jury by his Honor Chief Justice, *Trial of Alice Clifton*, 12.

24. *Trial of Alice Clifton*, 14.

25. Ibid.

26. This abrupt end is perplexing. Perhaps in an effort to avoid compensating the Bartholomews for the value of their slave, the justice worked out an alternative punishment. A. Leon Higginbotham discusses the compensation of masters in his work—see *In The Matter of Color*, 283.

27. Quoted in Peter Wood, " 'Impatient of Oppression': Black Freedom Struggles on the Eve of White Independence," *Southern Exposure* 12, no. 6 (1984): 10; Nash, *Forging Freedom*, 39.

28. Many authors explore this evolution, although Deborah Gray White's work is among the most compelling; for her discussion, see *Ar'n't I a Woman?: Female Slaves in the Plantation South* (New York and London: W. W. Norton, 1999), 30–33; hooks, *Ain't I a Woman?*, 52–54.

29. Brown, *Good Wives, Nasty Wenches, and Anxious Patriarchs*, 5–6; Higginbotham, *In The Matter of Color*, 269–71.

30. Henry Flanders and James T. Mitchell, *Statutes at Large of Pennsylvania: From 1682 to 1801* (hereafter *Statutes at Large*), 18 vols. (Harrisburg: 1896–1915), 11:78; Higginbotham, *In The Matter of Color*, 270.

31. Quoted in Higginbotham, *In The Matter of Color*, 271; Du Bois also notes William Penn's hypocrisy in *The Philadelphia Negro*, 11.

32. Nash, *First City*, 39; Negley K. Teeters, *The Cradle of the Penitentiary: The Walnut Street Jail at Philadelphia, 1773–1835* (Philadelphia: Temple University Press, 1955), 3. For a detailed examination of the social characteristics of Philadelphia's wealthy elite, including affluent Quakers, see Robert J. Gough, "The Philadelphia Economic Elite at the End of the Eighteenth Century," in *Shaping a National Culture*, 17–28.

33. Penn's negotiations with the Lenni Lenape are often lauded, yet Thomas Sugrue demonstrates that his participation in the dislocation of remaining Lenape should not be overlooked; see "The Peopling and Depeopling of Early Pennsylvania: Indians and Colonists, 1680–1720," *PMHB* 106 (1992): 3–31.

34. Brown, *Good Wives, Nasty Wenches, and Anxious Patriarchs*, 112–14; Roediger, *The Wages of Whiteness*, 21–27.

35. Brown, *Good Wives, Nasty Wenches, and Anxious Patriarchs*, 116–20; White, *Ar'n't I a Woman?*, 30–32.

36. Brown, *Good Wives, Nasty Wenches, and Anxious Patriarchs*, 185–86.

37. Ibid., 114.

38. Brown, *Good Wives, Nasty Wenches, and Anxious Patriarchs*, 39–40; White, *Ar'n't I a Woman?*, 30–31. Meranze, *Laboratories of Virtue*, 19–21. For a brief discussion of the English justice system, see Lawrence M. Friedman, *A History of American Law* (New York: Touchstone Book, 1985), 19–29; Winthrop Jordan, *White Over Black: American Attitudes Towards the Negro, 1550–1812* (Baltimore: Penguin Books, 1969); Jennifer Morgan, " 'Some Could Suckle Over Their Shoulder': Male Travelers, Female Bodies, and the Gendering of Racial Ideology, 1500–1770," *WMQ*, 3rd ser., 54, no. 1 (January 1997): 167–92.

39. Winthrop D. Jordan, *The White Man's Burden: Historical Origins of Racism in the United States* (Oxford: Oxford University Press, 1974), 10–15, 18–22, 50–54.

40. Brown, *Good Wives, Nasty Wenches, and Anxious Patriarchs*, 108.

41. Higginbotham, *In The Matter of Color*, 275.

42. Camp, *Closer to Freedom*, 16–28.

43. Leslie Harris, *In the Shadow of Slavery: African Americans in New York City, 1626–1863* (Chicago: University of Chicago Press, 2003), 43; Peter Thompson, *Rum Punch and Revolution: Taverngoing and Public Life in Eighteenth-Century Philadelphia* (Philadelphia: University of Pennsylvania Press, 1999), 7–9, 21–23.

44. Higginbotham, *In The Matter of Color*, 270; *Statutes at Large*, 11:78.

45. C. Dallett Hemphill, *Bowing to Necessities: A History of Manners in America, 1620–1860* (New York: Oxford University Press, 1999), 54–55.

46. Brown, *Good Wives, Nasty Wenches, and Anxious Patriarchs*, 115, 116–20, 136.

47. The constable in Mulberry Ward received instructions in 1722 that if they came upon debauched persons or servants said parties should be searched and committed to the "Gaol in order to be brought before some magistrate next morning"—Howard O. Sprogle, *The Philadelphia Police: Past and Present* (Philadelphia, 1887), 40 (LCP).

48. *Statutes at Large*, "An Act for the Trial of Negroes" (1700), 2:77–79, and "An Act for the Trial of Negroes" (1705), 2:23–36; Du Bois, *The Philadelphia Negro*, 13; Higginbotham, *In The Matter of Color*, 281–82; Patrick-Stamp, "Numbers That Are Not New," 98–99.

49. Rowe, "Black Offenders, Criminal Courts," 686; Edward R. Turner, *The Negro in Pennsylvania, Slavery—Servitude—Freedom* (Washington: American Historical As-

sociation, 1911), 26–31; Richard Wright, Jr., *The Negro in Pennsylvania: A Study in Economic History* (New York: Arno Press, 1969), 11; Higginbotham, *In The Matter of Color*, 281–82.

50. Higginbotham, *In The Matter of Color*, 282, 285. For more acts that contain punishments specific to black people, see *Statutes at Large*, "An Act for Preventing Accidents That May Happen By Fire" (1722), 3:252–54; "An Act for the More Effectual Preventing Accidents Which May Happen By Fire and for Suppressing Idleness, Drunkenness and Other Debaucheries" (1750), 5:108–11; "An Act for the Better Regulating of the Nightly Watch Within the City of Philadelphia" (1750), 5:111–28. Patrick-Stamp has done excellent work in this area and provides richer sources in her article; see "Numbers That Are Not New," 99, n7.

51. Higginbotham, *In The Matter of Color*, 285; Turner, *The Negro in Pennsylvania*, 29.

52. Higginbotham, *In The Matter of Color*, 282.

53. In the case of a slave girl tried for murdering the master who raped her, the court finds that the slave did not have the right to defend herself. See McLaurin, *Celia, A Slave*, 107–14. Also, in 1859, a Mississippi judge reversed the conviction of an enslaved black man who had been found guilty of raping a ten-year-old slave girl— White, *Ar'n't I a Woman?*, 152; Higginbotham, *In The Matter of Color*, 282.

54. White, *Ar'n't I a Woman?*, 30–38; hooks, *Ain't I a Woman?*, 52–54.

55. See the charge to the jury by his Honor Chief Justice, *Trial of Alice Clifton*, 12.

56. Barnes and Teeters, *New Horizons in Criminology*, 469; John D'Emilio and Estelle B. Freedman, *Intimate Matters: A History of Sexuality in America* (New York: Harper and Row, 1988), 4–6, 10–13.

57. D'Emilio and Freedman, *Intimate Matters*, 31–32, 44; Lawrence Friedman also notes that early rape laws "really protected only 'respectable' white women (and their menfolk). Women who were not 'respectable,' or who were black, or Native American, were effectively outside the circle of protection"; see Lawrence Friedman, *Crime and Punishment in American History* (New York: Basic Books, 1993), 215.

58. While Sprogle notes that women were whipped for having illegitimate children, he makes no mention of this punishment being routine for the fathers involved; see Sprogle, *The Philadelphia Police*, 31, 59–60; Barnes and Teeters, *New Horizons in Criminology*, 411.

59. Punishing women in this manner exemplifies how policing female autonomy factors into the creation and maintenance of gendered hierarchies. See Gayle Rubin, "The Traffic in Women: Notes on the 'Political Economy' of Sex," in *Feminism and History*, ed. Joan Wallach Scott (New York: Oxford University Press, 1996), and "Thinking Sex: Notes for a Radical Theory of the Politics of Sexuality," in *Pleasure and Danger: Exploring Female Sexuality*, ed. Carol S. Vance (London: Pandora Press, 1989), 309.

60. In 1761 young men from wealthy families terrorized the city by slashing women's clothes and breaking public property. Rather than being prosecuted or receiving pub-

lic punishment, the families paid their bail and made financial restitution to the victims. See John F. Watson, *Annals of Philadelphia: Being a Collection of Memoirs, Anecdotes, and Incidents of the City and Its Inhabitants from the Days of the Pilgrim Founders* (Philadelphia: 1830), 260 (LCP). Also see Higginbotham, *In The Matter of Color*, 279, and D'Emilio and Freedman, *Intimate Matters*, 28.

61. Higginbotham, *In The Matter of Color*, 279.

62. Ibid., 291.

63. Meranze, *Laboratories of Virtue*, 21–24. Early justice conditioned blacks and whites and is itself a profound testament to pervasive white power and supremacy; see Higginbotham, *In The Matter of Color*, 280–84.

64. In some ways I am building on Saidiya Hartman's discussion of how men and women are both subject to sexual violation; however, for my purposes I refer to the ways in which the lack of distinction between the two impacted black femininity. See Hartman, *Scenes of Subjection*, 101.

65. Higginbotham, *In The Matter of Color*, 283–85, 286–87; Du Bois, *The Philadelphia Negro*, 13–15; Soderlund, "Black Women in Colonial Pennsylvania," 74.

66. Du Bois, *The Philadelphia Negro*, 12–13; Nash, *Freedom by Degrees*, 52–55.

67. Nash, *Forging Freedom*, 45–50, 61; Du Bois, *The Philadelphia Negro*, 12–13; 14–15.

68. Du Bois, Appendix B, "Legislation, Etc., of Pennsylvania in Regard to the Negro," 415.

69. Soderlund uses the experiences of two enslaved black women in colonial Pennsylvania to discuss the heightened value of freedom toward the latter part of the eighteenth century. See Soderlund, "Black Women in Colonial Pennsylvania," 74.

70. *Statutes at Large* (1780), 10:70; Du Bois, *The Philadelphia Negro*, 415; Patrick-Stamp, "Numbers That Are Not New," 99.

71. Higginbotham, *In The Matter of Color*, 282.

72. In 1790 Pennsylvania housed 10,274 blacks, 6,540 of whom were free; Du Bois, *The Philadelphia Negro*, 13–24; Rowe, "Black Offenders, Criminal Courts," 696.

73. Du Bois, *The Philadelphia Negro*, 17, 25; Nash and Soderlund, *Freedom by Degrees*, 27; Billy G. Smith, *The "Lower Sort," Philadelphia's Laboring Peoples, 1750–1800* (Ithaca: Cornell University Press, 1990), 18–19.

74. Du Bois, *The Philadelphia Negro*, 17.

75. Nash, *First City*, 125–27.

76. Nash, *Forging Freedom*, 96; Du Bois, *The Philadelphia Negro*, 17–24. Also see Fredric Miller et al., *Still Philadelphia: A Photographic History, 1890–1940* (Philadelphia: Temple University Press, 1983), 4, 228–30.

77. Lapsansky, "'Since They Got Those Separate Churches,'" 92–96; Watson, *Annals of Philadelphia*, 485; Nash, *Forging Freedom*, 38.

78. Richard Allen described the ordeal in his memoirs; see Dorothy Sterling, ed., *Speak Out in Thunder Tones: Letters and Other Writings by Black Northerners, 1787–1865*

(New York: Da Capo Press, 1998), 29–30; Du Bois, *The Philadelphia Negro*, 18–19, 21–22.

79. Nash, *Forging Freedom*, 78–79; Erica Armstrong, "Negro Wenches, Washer Women, and Literate Ladies: The Transforming Identities of African American Women in Philadelphia, 1780–1854" (Ph.D. diss., Columbia University, 2000).

80. Du Bois, *The Philadelphia Negro*, 32–39.

81. Julie Winch, ed., *The Elite of Our People: Joseph Willson's Sketches of Black Upper-Class Life in Antebellum Philadelphia* (University Park: Pennsylvania State University Press, 2000), 11–13; Charles L. Blockson, *Philadelphia: 1639–2000* (Charleston, S.C.: Arcadia Press, 2000), 24; Nash, *Forging Freedom*, 74–79; Armstrong, "Negro Wenches, Washer Women, and Literate Ladies," 46.

82. Blockson, *Philadelphia: 1639–2000*, 28; Soderlund, "Black Women in Colonial Pennsylvania," 86; Armstrong, "Negro Wenches, Washer Women, and Literate Ladies," 46.

83. Rowe, "Black Offenders, Criminal Courts," 688; Winch, *Philadelphia's Black Elite*, 18.

84. Blockson, *Philadelphia: 1639–2000*, 20; Nash, *First City*, 127.

85. *A Narrative of the Proceedings of Black People, During the Late, Awful Calamity in Philadelphia*, (1794) (LCP); Nash, *First City*, 127.

86. Du Bois, *The Philadelphia Negro*, 22. Initially the Pennsylvania Constitution did not limit the franchise to free white men; however, in 1838 the constitution was amended to limit the vote to whites. See A. Leon Higginbotham, Jr., *Shades of Freedom: Racial Politics and Presumptions of the American Legal Process* (New York: Oxford University Press, 1996), 171.

87. Armstrong, "Negro Wenches, Washer Women, and Literate Ladies," 49. In 1832 there were proposals to limit black migration into the city. For an example of black responses to this legislation, see *To the Honourable the Senate and House of Representatives of the Commonwealth of Pennsylvania, in General Assembly Met: The Memorial of the Subscribers, free people of colour, residing in the County of Philadelphia* (1832) (LCP).

88. Winch, *Philadelphia's Black Elite*, 18–20.

89. James Forten, *Series of Letters by a Man of Colour, 1813*, in *Pamphlets of Protest: An Anthology of Early African American Protest Literature, 1790–1860*, ed. Richard Newman, Patrick Rael, and Phillip Lapsansky (New York: Routledge, 2001), 72.

90. Rothman, *The Discovery of the Asylum*, 78; Michael Ignatieff, *A Just Measure of Pain: The Penitentiary in the Industrial Revolution, 1750–1850* (New York: Columbia University Press, 1980).

91. Rothman, *The Discovery of the Asylum*, 69–70; Rowe, "Black Offenders, Criminal Courts," 686–88, 698–99, 701.

92. Cesare Beccaria, *On Crimes and Punishments, and Other Writings*, ed. Richard Bellamy, trans. Richard Davies, Virginia Cox, and Richard Bellamy (Cambridge: Cambridge University Press, 1995), 49–60; Benjamin Rush, *Enquiry into the Effects of Public Punishments upon Criminals, and upon Society; Read in the Society for Promoting*

Political Enquiries, Convened at the House of His Excellency Benjamin Franklin, Esquire, in Philadelphia, March 9th, 1787 (Philadelphia, 1787) (LCP); Foucault, *Discipline and Punish*, 73–74, 104–10; Eric Foner, *Tom Paine and Revolutionary America* (New York: Oxford University Press, 1976), 28–45, 107–44; Meranze, *Laboratories of Virtue*, 61–65, 131–137; Friedman, *Crime and Punishment*, 77–82; Barnes and Teeters, *New Horizons in Criminology*, 686–89; Cole, *Suspect Identities*, 13–14.

93. Barnes and Teeters, *New Horizons in Criminology*, 689.

94. Ayers, *Vengeance and Justice*, 37–39; Michael S. Hindus, *Prison and Plantation: Crime, Justice and Authority in Massachusetts and South Carolina, 1767–1878* (Chapel Hill: University of North Carolina Press, 1980).

95. Negley K. Teeters, *They Were In Prison: A History of the Pennsylvania Prison Society 1787–1937* (Philadelphia: John C. Winston, 1937), 448–51, and *The Cradle of the Penitentiary*; Negley K. Teeters and John D. Shearer, *The Prison at Philadelphia, Cherry Hill: The Separate System of Penal Discipline, 1829–1913* (New York: Columbia University Press, 1957), 8–11; Harry Elmer Barnes, *The Evolution of Penology in Pennsylvania: A Study in American Social History* (Indianapolis: Bobbs-Merrill, 1927), 70; Sprogle, *The Philadelphia Police*, 62–65; Allen Steinberg, *The Transformation of Criminal Justice: Philadelphia, 1800–1880* (Chapel Hill: University of North Carolina Press, 1989), 96–97.

96. Teeters, *They Were In Prison*, 448–51. For a sense of the optimism and expectations for the reforms, see Robert Turnbull, *A Visit to the Philadelphia Prison: Being an Accurate and Particular Account of the Wise and Humane Administration Adopted in Every Part of That Building* (1796) (LCP).

97. For examples of the early problems, see *A Just and True Account of the Prison of the City and County of Philadelphia; Accompanied with the Rules, Regulations, Manners, Customs, and Treatment of the Untried Prisoners, Who Have the Misfortune of Being Committed to This Place For Trial* (1820) (LCP). For a list of the prison breaks and violent escapes made by inmates, see Sprogle, *The Philadelphia Police*, 62–65.

98. Patrick-Stamp, "Numbers That Are Not New," 98.

99. David R. Johnson, "Crime Patterns in Philadelphia, 1840–70," in *The Peoples of Philadelphia: A History of Ethnic Groups and Lower-Class Life, 1790–1940*, ed. Allen F. Davis and Mark Haller (Philadelphia: University of Pennsylvania Press, 1998), 98–101; Sprogle, *The Philadelphia Police*, 89–90.

100. New York in many ways parallels Philadelphia in its social developments; for a detailed description of vice and the bawdy houses in the city, see Christine Stansell, *City of Women: Sex and Class in New York, 1789–1860* (Urbana: University of Illinois Press, 1987), 14–15.

101. *A Guide to the Stranger, or Pocket Companion for the Fancy, Containing a List of the Gay Houses and Ladies of Pleasure in the City of Brotherly Love and Sisterly Affection* (Philadelphia, c. 1849), 17 (LCP). Marcia Carlisle also provides a wonderful discussion

of early vice in Philadelphia. See "Disorderly City, Disorderly Women: Prostitution in Ante-Bellum Philadelphia," *PMHB* 110, no. 1 (October 1986): 549–69.

102. Rowe, "Black Offenders, Criminal Courts," 697–98.

103. Steinberg, *The Transformation of Criminal Justice*, 129.

104. Stansell aptly describes the intermingled texture of the city that so disturbed mainstream elites and the white middle-class; see Stansell, *City of Women*, 42.

105. Du Bois demonstrates that black arrest rates fluctuated before and after the Civil War; see Du Bois, *The Philadelphia Negro*, 242.

106. Patrick-Stamp, "Numbers That Are Not New," 101–02.

107. Ibid., 111.

108. Steinberg, *The Transformation of Criminal Justice*, 43; Dodge, *"Whores and Thieves of the Worst Kind,"* 123–24; Rafter, *Partial Justice*, 154–55; Butler, *Gendered Justice in the American West*, 91–93.

109. Rowe, "Black Offenders, Criminal Courts," 704; Patrick-Stamp, "Numbers That Are Not New," 98; Steinberg, *The Transformation of Criminal Justice*, 43.

110. Steinberg uses this example to stress the corruption in Philadelphia courts and to demonstrate how more "well-heeled defendants escaped prosecution"; this case also is a poignant example of how black women were often on the fast track to conviction and incarceration. See Steinberg, *The Transformation of Criminal Justice*, 108.

111. Leslie Harris explains that whites excluded black women from "the best of women's roles in the new republic"; enslavement and servitude barred them for the roles of republican wives and mothers. See Harris, *In the Shadow of Slavery*, 98–99. Karen List also provides a thorough discussion of republican motherhood; see "The Post-Revolutionary Woman Idealized: Philadelphia Media's Republican Motherhood," *Journalism Quarterly* 66, no. 1 (Spring 1989): 65–75, at 67–68.

112. Nash, *First City*, 200–202; Armstrong, "Negro Wenches, Washer Women, and Literate Ladies," 181–85; Stansell, *City of Women*, 12. Sherri Broder explains that in 1848 George G. Foster's series "Philadelphia Slices" relied on stereotypes that conflated disease, poverty, and immorality in a manner that implicated the working classes, particularly the city's free black community; see Broder, *Tramps, Unfit Mothers, and Neglected Children: Negotiating the Family in Late Nineteenth-Century Philadelphia* (Philadelphia: University of Pennsylvania, 2002), 61.

113. Rafter, *Partial Justice*, 155; Patrick-Stamp, "Numbers That Are Not New," 101–03. For examples of inconsistent sentencing, see Lane, *Roots of Violence*, 108. Carlisle's exploration of vice also contains some examples of harsher penalties for black prostitutes — see "Disorderly City, Disorderly Women," 563–64.

114. Armstrong, "Negro Wenches, Washer Women, and Literate Ladies," 46–47. Letters between Rebecca Primus and Addie Brown spotlight working-class black women's economic hardships. See Griffin, ed., *Beloved Sisters and Loving Friends*, 35–36, 39, 67–68.

115. Quoted in Lapsansky, " 'Since They Got Those Separate Churches,' " 103; Watson, *Annals of Philadelphia*, 485.

116. Armstrong, "Negro Wenches, Washer Women, and Literate Ladies," 180; Winch, *Black Elite*, 130–31. Mifflin Gibbs described the impact of Nat Turner's rebellion in Philadelphia among blacks in his book *Shadow and Light* (Washington, 1902) — this selection is quoted in Sterling, *Speak Out in Thunder Tones*, 161–62.

117. Armstrong "Negro Wenches, Washer Women, and Literate Ladies," 180.

118. Nash, *First City*, 167–68.

119. Amstrong, "Negro Wenches, Washer Women, and Literate Ladies," 49; *To The Honourable the Senate and House of Representatives of the Commonwealth of Pennsylvania*, 1–12; Steinberg, *The Transformation of Criminal Justice*, 136; Du Bois, *The Philadelphia Negro*, 26–30, 45n. For an excellent investigation into one of Pennsylvania's infamous race riots, see Thomas P. Slaughter, *Bloody Dawn: The Christiana Riot and Racial Violence in the Antebellum North* (New York: Oxford University Press, 1991).

120. Mary Frances Berry, *Black Resistance, White Law: A History of Constitutional Racism*, 2nd ed. (New York: Penguin Books, 1994), 54; Du Bois, *The Philadelphia Negro*, 416. For black Philadelphians' attempts to combat disfranchisement, see Robert Purvis, *Appeal of Forty Thousand Citizens Threatened with Disfranchisement, to the People of Pennsylvania*, (1837) (LCP); Roediger, *The Wages of Whiteness*, 59–60.

121. Sarah Douglass lamented segregated seating in Quaker meetinghouses in Philadelphia in December 1837; see Sterling, *Speak Out in Thunder Tones*, 96–97; Lapsansky, " 'Since They Got Those Separate Churches,' " 99–100.

122. Nash, *First City*, 169–70; Sprogle also described another infamous race riot that occurred on St. Mary Street in 1849; see *The Philadelphia Police*, 89–93.

123. Steinberg, *The Transformation of Criminal Justice*, 177–78, 187–88.

124. *The Liberator*, April 23, 1858, in Sterling, *Speak Out in Thunder Tones*, 131.

2. Service Savors of Slavery

1. Thomas Holt makes a similar point about the long-term impact of racial and economic exclusion in *The Problem of Race in the 21st Century*, (Cambridge, Mass: Harvard University Press, 2000), 59–60.

2. *The Trial of Alice Clifton*.

3. Hine, "Rape and the Inner Lives of Black Women," 381–82. Earl Lewis, *In Their Own Interest: Race, Class, and Power in Twentieth-Century Norfolk, Virginia* (Berkeley: University of California Press, 1991), 5, 23.

4. Du Bois, *The Philadelphia Negro*, 323; Isabel Eaton, *Special Report on Negro Domestic Service in the Seventh Ward, Philadelphia*, in *The Philadelphia Negro*, 428; Theodore Hershberg, ed., "Free Blacks in Antebellum Philadelphia: A Study of Ex-Slaves, Freeborn, and Socioeconomic Decline," in *Philadelphia: Work, Space, Family, and Group*

Experience in the Nineteenth Century, Essays Toward an Interdisciplinary History of the City (Oxford: Oxford University Press, 1981), 375; Lane, *William Dorsey's Philadelphia*, 70–71, 76–77.

5. Eaton, *Special Report on Negro Domestic Service*, 467; Hunter, *"To 'Joy My Freedom,"* 4–19, 21–22.

6. Lucy M. Salmon, *Domestic Service* (London: Macmillan, 1897), 139–41, 146–52; Victoria Wolcott explains that many black women sought to escape domestic service altogether; see *Remaking Respectability: African American Women in Inter-war Detroit* (Chapel Hill: University of North Carolina Press, 2001), 27–31; Holt, *The Problem of Race*, 102.

7. I use *decided* rather than *chose* in order to hold the women accountable for their crimes but also to call attention to the circumstances that often made crime their only viable financial alternative to low-paying, exploitative domestic service work. African-American women accounted for 4.4 percent of prisoners at the Philadelphia County Prison, but this number includes those sentenced as well as those awaiting trial. I use this statistic as a rough indicator of the percentage of black women who were in some ways involved in criminal activity; see appendix, table 8.

8. Fannie Smiley, #A5053, CDR, 1889 (PHMC).

9. PL 1/5/1887, SBI.

10. For a detailed explanation of Pennsylvania's commutation law, see Barnes and Teeters, *New Horizons in Criminology*, 816.

11. WJ, vol. 6, 2/2/1889 (PHMC).

12. MPT, 9/20/1889, SBI; Smiley, #A5053, CDR, 1889.

13. Ibid.

14. I verified Barber's address in *Gopsill's Philadelphia City Directory, for 1900* (PCA). L. L. Prince was not listed in the directory, but his address appears in the article covering Smiley's crime; see MPT, 9/20/1889, SBI.

15. PP, 1/7/1900, WDC #15:125. Smiley's fence, William Lessner, worked as a jeweler and resided at 742 South St.; see *Gopsill's Philadelphia City Directory, for 1900* (PCA).

16. Under the alias of Lizzie Smith, Fannie Smiley was again incarcerated at ESP on May 15, 1908, #B4241; WJ, vol. 10, 5/5/1909.

17. Appendix, table 1.

18. Appendix, table 2.

19. "Thieving Negress Goes to Prison," MPT, c. 1902, SB2; Sadie Shotwell, alias Smith, #B1609, CDR, 1902; Johanna Twiggs, #A4277, CDR (PHMC), 1888, #A6126, CDR, 1891, #A8018, CDR, 1895; mt., c. 1895, SBI.

20. The Pennsylvania state legislature passed an Act for the Identification of Habitual Criminals, which instructed wardens to provide detailed descriptions of repeat offenders, and it stipulated that the district attorney furnish arrest histories to the wardens. See *Laws of the General Assembly of the State of Pennsylvania (Penns. Laws)*, (1889), no. 109 (PHMC).

21. My ideas have been greatly influenced by Robin Kelley and other scholars committed to recovering the histories of poor and working-class blacks. I am not arguing that servant-thieves enacted organized resistance—rather, that their crimes betray a logic unique to the women's experience. See Robin D. G. Kelley, *Race Rebels: Culture, Politics, and the Black Working Class* (New York: Free Press, 1994), 5–9, 43; Kenneth W. Goings and Gerald Smith, " 'Unhidden Transcripts': Memphis and African American Agency, 1862–1920," in *The New African American Urban History*, ed. Kenneth W. Goings and Raymond A. Mohl (Thousand Oaks: Sage Press, 1996), 147–48; Brooks-Higginbotham, *Righteous Discontent*, chapter 7.

22. "What it Means to Be Colored in the Capital of the United States," *The Independent*, vol. 62, no. 3014 (January 7, 1907), in Gerder Lerner, ed., *Black Women in White America: A Documentary History* (New York: Vintage Books Edition, 1992), 181–86.

23. Appendix, tables 3, 4.

24. Appendix, table 5.

25. Appendix, table 6.

26. Du Bois, *The Philadelphia Negro*, 47, 56; Richard Hofstadter, *The Age of Reform* (New York: Vintage Books, 1995), 8–9, 137; Jacqueline Jones, *Labor of Love, Labor of Sorrow: Black Women, Work, and the Family from Slavery to the Present* (New York: Basic Books, 1985), 156.

27. Darlene Clark Hine, "Black Migration to the Urban Midwest: The Gender Dimension, 1915–1945," in *The Great Migration in Historical Perspective: New Dimensions of Race, Class, and Gender*, ed., Joe William Trotter, Jr. (Bloomington: Indiana University Press, 1991), 127, 130–31; Carby, *Reconstructing Womanhood*, 39; Hine, "Rape and the Inner Lives of Black Women," 380.

28. White, *Ar'n't I a Woman?*, 30–34; Hunter, *"To 'Joy My Freedom,"* 26–27; hooks, *Ain't I a Woman?*, 55.

29. Hine, "Rape and the Inner Lives of Black Women," 382; Hannah Rosen, " 'Not That Sort of Women': Race, Gender and Sexual Violence," in *Sex, Love, Race: Crossing Boundaries in North American History*, ed. Martha Hodes (New York: New York University Press, 1999), 267–69.

30. "More Slavery at the South," by a Negro Nurse, *The Independent*, vol. 72, no. 3295 (January 25, 1912), in *Black Women in White America*, 197–200.

31. Ibid., 198; Hunter, *"To 'Joy My Freedom,"* 106–07.

32. Hine, "Rape and the Inner Lives of Black Women," 382; Rosen, " 'Not That Sort of Women,' " 268.

33. Fannie Barrier Williams, "A Northern Negro's Autobiography," *The Independent*, vol. 57, no. 2902 (July 4, 1904), in *Black Women in White America*, 165; hooks, *Ain't I a Woman?*, 55–57.

34. *Annual Report of the National League for the Protection of Colored Women* (New York, 1910) (SCH), 3; Frances Kellor, "Southern Colored Girls in the North: The Problem of Their Protection," *Charities*, vol. 15 (March 18, 1905): 585 (SCH).

35. Hine argues that racism and sexual exploitation caused black women to "quit the South"; see Hine, "Rape and the Inner Lives of Black Women," 380–82; Williams, in *Black Women in White America*, 165.

36. Wright, *The Negro in Pennsylvania*, 56.

37. Hine, "Rape and the Inner Lives of Black Women," 381, and "Black Migration to the Urban West," 127–28.

38. Eaton, *Special Report on Negro Domestic Service*, 467; Salmon, *Domestic Service*, 152–53.

39. Deborah McDowell, " 'The Changing Same': Generation Connections and Black Women Novelists," in *Reading Black, Reading Feminist*, ed. Henry Louis Gates, Jr. (New York: Meridian Press, 1990).

40. Hershberg, ed., "Free Blacks in Antebellum Philadelphia," 375; Nathaniel Burt and Wallace E. Davies, "The Iron Age, 1876–1095," in *Philadelphia: A 300 Year History*, ed. Russell F. Weigley (New York: W. W. Norton, 1982), 488–98; Lewis, *In Their Own Interest*, 6.

41. Du Bois, *The Philadelphia Negro*, 328; Lane, *Roots of Violence*, 37.

42. TP, 18/8/1890; PEI, 18/8/1890, WDC #8:73.

43. Carby, "Policing the Black Woman's Body," 738–55.

44. Ibid., PEI 8/18/1890. For more examples of labor clashes, see "Riot at the Reservoir," MPT, 7/15/1894, and "A gang of Slav strikers attacked some imported Virginia negroes," MPT, 1894, WDC #10:86; Tera Hunter, "The 'Brotherly Love' for Which This City Is Proverbial Should Extend to All: The Everyday Lives of Working-Class Women in Philadelphia and Atlanta in the 1890s," in *W. E. B. Du Bois, Race and the City*: The Philadelphia Negro *and Its Legacy*, ed. Michael B. Katz and Thomas J. Sugrue (Philadelphia: University of Pennsylvania Press, 1998), 131.

45. Du Bois, *The Philadelphia Negro*, 111; Eaton, *Special Report on Negro Domestic Service*, 446, 452; Nancy F. Cott, *The Grounding of Modern Feminism* (New Haven and London: Yale University Press, 1987), 132–33.

46. Du Bois, *The Philadelphia Negro*, 109; Dennis Clark, Caroline Golab, and Richard Varvero each demonstrated the hardships ethnic immigrants faced as well as the immigrants' abilities to move beyond employment discrimination as opposed to African Americans, particularly African-American women, who in addition to being confined to low-wage work as servants were also more likely to be in single-headed households. See *The Peoples of Philadelphia*, ed. Davis and Haller, 203–30, 255–76.

47. TP, 1/10/1898.

48. Angela Y. Davis, *Women, Race and Class* (New York: Random House, 1981), 90–98; Venus Green discusses sexual division of labor and job segregation in the phone company; see *Race on the Line: Gender, Labor and Technology in the Bell System, 1880–1980* (Durham: Duke University Press, 2001), 53–55, 87–88.

49. Kellor, "Southern Colored Girls in the North," 585. Du Bois also lists an example of a family that "left their work in Virginia through the misrepresentations of an Arch

NOTES TO CHAPTER TWO

Street employment bureau"; see *The Philadelphia Negro*, 276; Lane, *William Dorsey's Philadelphia*, 87.

50. *Penns. Laws*, 1887, 130–31; *Penns. Laws*, 1895, 432. Also see Charles B. McMichael, ed., *The Municipal Law of Philadelphia: A Digest of the Charters, Acts of Assembly, Ordinances, and Judicial Decisions Relating Thereto, from 1701 to 1887* (Philadelphia: J. M. Power Wallace, 1887).

51. Du Bois, *The Philadelphia Negro*, 324.

52. Two African-American men, William Warner and Agustine Campbell, lost claims against proprietors that violated the Equal Rights law. See "They Want Equal Rights," *Pittsburgh Commercial Gazette*, 7/11/1889, and an African-American man was refused treatment at Pennsylvania Hospital; see "He Was Turned Out," MPT, 5/18/1895, WDC #7:71; Lane, *Roots of Violence*, 6, 19, 29; Du Bois, *The Philadelphia Negro*, 322–52.

53. *Annual Report of the National League for the Protection of Colored Women* (New York, 1910), 3–5 (SCH); Kellor, "Southern Colored Girls in the North," 585.

54. Eaton, *Special Report on Negro Domestic Service*, 436–65.

55. Kellor, "Southern Colored Girls in the North"; Eaton, *Special Report on Negro Domestic Service*, 450–51; Broder, *Tramps, Unfit Mothers, and Neglected Children*, 13; depressions also plagued the 1890s and had devastating effects on black lives; see Nell Painter, *Standing at Armageddon: The United States, 1877–1919* (New York: W. W. Norton, 1987), 110–40.

56. Irish immigrants obtained employment as contractors and bricklayers in addition to jobs in the police and fire departments. Germans, as skilled laborers, became independent entrepreneurs—gunsmiths, watchmakers, bakers, and brewers. Italians, a population that increased from three hundred to roughly eighteen thousand between 1870 and 1890, occupied construction and public works positions. A small group of Russian Jews dominated smaller industries, becoming the primary laborers for handcrafts in the cigar and garment trades. See Burt and Davies, "The Iron Age, 1876–1095," 488–98; Hunter, "The 'Brotherly Love,'" 131; Jacqueline Jones, "'Lifework' and Its Limits: The Problem of Labor in *The Philadelphia Negro*," in *W. E. B. Du Bois, Race and the City*, ed. Katz and Sugrue, 105.

57. Du Bois, *The Philadelphia Negro*, 322–30, 466; Hunter, "*To 'Joy My Freedom*," 60–66, 132–33; Kellor, "Southern Colored Girls in the North," 585.

58. Hunter, "*To 'Joy My Freedom*," 28, 60–61, 132–33 and, "The 'Brotherly Love,'" in *W. E. B. Du Bois, Race and the City*, ed. Katz and Sugrue, 136–37.

59. Eaton, *Special Report on Negro Domestic Service*, 445–46, 481.

60. Salmon, *Domestic Service*, 109–10.

61. Hunter, "*To 'Joy My Freedom*," 106; Lane, *William Dorsey's Philadelphia*, 79.

62. Eaton, *Special Report on Negro Domestic Service*, 467, 447, table VII.

63. Hunter, "*To 'Joy My Freedom*," 56–57, and "The 'Brotherly Love,'" 134–36.

64. Hunter, "*To 'Joy My Freedom*," 78–79, 152.

65. Eaton, *Special Report on Negro Domestic Service*, 445; Hunter, *"To 'Joy My Freedom,"* 55–56.

66. PT, 9/29/1888, WDC #3:23; Lane, *William Dorsey's Philadelphia*, 80; Eaton, *Special Report on Negro Domestic Service*, 444–45.

67. Housekeepers performed domestic tasks but also oversaw all household duties. Servants received their orders from either housekeepers or their employers. See Martha Louise Rayne, *What a Woman Can Do* (Detroit: F. B. Dickerson, 1883), 20, 230 (LCP); Salmon, *Domestic Service*, 114.

68. Eaton, *Special Report on Negro Domestic Service*, 444.

69. Ibid.

70. Ibid., 448–52.

71. Ibid., 454.

72. Du Bois, *The Philadelphia Negro*, 328, 58, 287–90.

73. John F. Sutherland, whose work I rely on heavily in this chapter, explains that in spite of blacks' past residency, the influx of Russian immigrants into the Fourth and Fifth wards of the city resulted in a decrease in the number of black residents. Moreover, while the largest group of the city's blacks lived in the Seventh Ward, significant black communities developed in the Twenty-Sixth and Thirty-Sixth wards. This discussion on housing conditions in Philadelphia, in particular, owes a debt of gratitude to the Sutherland's work. See his "Housing the Poor in the City of Houses," in *The Peoples of Philadelphia*, ed. Davis and Haller, 181; *U.S. Bureau of the Census, Thirteenth Census, 1910, Population*, 111, 604–08.

74. Lane, *Roots of Violence*, 22–23.

75. Hunter, "The 'Brotherly Love,' " 129; Lane, *Roots of Violence*, 109.

76. Du Bois, *The Philadelphia Negro*, 60–61, 61fn, 311; Alaska was in the Fourth Ward, Minster in the Seventh Ward, and Middle Alley in the Fifth Ward running west from 334 South 6th Street to 333 South 7th Street; see *Gopsill's Philadelphia City Directory, for 1885* (PCA).

77. Du Bois, *The Philadelphia Negro*, 60.

78. Lane, *Roots of Violence*, 12.

79. Sutherland, "Housing the Poor in the City of Houses," 186–94.

80. Ibid.

81. Ibid, 176–80.

82. Ibid.

83. Ibid,183–85.

84. Because boarders took shelter in every room, their clothing and nearby debris would easily be ignited by coal or stove cinders. See "Woman and Child Fatally Burned," PI, 11/15/1897 (FL).

85. Du Bois, *The Philadelphia Negro*, 60; Hunter, "The 'Brotherly Love,' " 129; Lane, *Roots of Violence*, 109.

86. "An Open Verdict Given," MPT, 8/5/1898, WDC #7:101; "Carbolic Acid as a Cure for Heartache," MPT, 5/17/1898, WDC #7:104; "Drank Laudanum on the Street," TP, 1/21/1898; "Poison Proved Fatal," PET, 2/7/1903, WDC #15:127; Du Bois, *The Philadelphia Negro*, 267; Lane, *William Dorsey's Philadelphia*, 88. Data are limited, but the available evidence suggests that black suicide rates steadily increased, though actual numbers are fairly small. Between 1870 and 1900 only twenty-one black suicides were documented; see Roger Lane, *Violent Death in the City: Suicide, Accident, and Murder in Nineteenth-Century Philadelphia* (Columbus: Ohio State University Press, 1999), 28–29.

87. "New Home for Fallen Women," MPT, 1888, WDC #65:18. Elisabeth Lasch-Quinn explains that most settlement houses during the progressive era excluded African Americans; see *Black Neighbors: Race and the Limits of Reform in the American Settlement House Movement, 1890–1945* (Chapel Hill: University of North Carolina Press, 1993), 3.

88. Robert Gregg, *Sparks from the Anvil of Oppression: Philadelphia's African Methodists and Southern Migrants, 1890–1940* (Philadelphia: Temple University Press, 1993) 60. Elizabeth Ralls organized the Sarah Allen Mission and Faith Home to provide Christmas dinners for poor blacks and to house poor elderly blacks who could not gain admission to white almshouses. See Gertrude N. F. Mossell, *The Work of the Afro-American Woman*, 2nd ed. (1908; reprint, New York: Oxford University Press, 1988), 29.

89. Appendix, table 2.

90. Quoted in Hunter, *"To 'Joy My Freedom,"* 133.

91. *Philadelphia Prisoners for Trial Docket* (PCA); Hunter, *"To 'Joy My Freedom,"* 60–61, 67, 132–33.

92. "Ida Washington Pleads Guilty," Carlisle, Pennsylvania *Evening Sentinel*, 11/12/1900.

93. Louisa Brooke or Brooks, #A4037, CDR, 11/14/1887; MST, MPT, 11/15/1887, SBI; Ida Washington, #B707, CDR, 9/12/1900; Eliza Boyd, an African-American housekeeper from Lycoming County was also sent to ESP for arson. See #A206, CDR, 1/17/1880; "Oyer and Terminer" and "An Arson Case," Pennsylvania, *The Sun and Lycoming Democrat*, 1/7/1880.

94. Primus, who also appears in records as Princes, was arrested along with Amanda Powell, a notorious repeat offender. Primus had no prior arrests, and this is the only one for the period. She does not appear to have been a career criminal. See #4206, CDR, 2/24/1888; MST, MPT, 2/25/1888, SBI.

95. WJ, vol. 6, 1/1889.

96. Annie Dixon or Drixon, #A3583, CDR, 1887; PL, 1/5/1887, SBI.

97. Du Bois, *The Philadelphia Negro*, 185–88.

98. Lizzie Smith, alias Walker, and Elizabeth Short were convicted of pension fraud and making false affidavits to illegally collect widows' pension money. See "United States

District Court," MPT, 2/28/1893, SBI; Lizzie Smith, #A6709, Elizabeth Short, #A6710, CDR, 2/27/1893.

99. PI, 12/13/1892, SBI; Virginia Henry, #A6584, Isaiah Miller, #A6591, CDR, 1892.

100. Harriet Lee, #A9609, CDR, 2/28/1898; "United States District Court," MPT, c. 1898, SBI.

101. See "Johanna Twiggs, colored, an old offender, was sentenced to three years in the Eastern Penitentiary, she having pleaded guilty to the larceny of clothing," MPT, c. 1895, SBI; Johanna Twiggs, #A4277, CDR, 1888, #A6126, CDR, 1891, #A8018, CDR, 1895.

102. Inmate #A740, 3/4/1881, CDR, and #A4207, 2/24/1888, CDR, CRR.

103. Inmate #A4206, CDR, 2/24/1888; MST, MPT, 2/25/1888, SBI.

104. Amanda Powell, #A4779, CDR, 3/4/1889.

105. There is evidence of this throughout the *Warden's Journals*; I delve more deeply into the matter in chapter 5, but for preliminary accounts see WJ, vol. 4, 10/2/1885; WJ, vol. 5, 3/18/1888; WJ, vol. 9, 10/7/1905.

106. Many scholars have explored this tension between black elites and the black working-class as it existed in the urban South, and while Philadelphia possessed different dynamics many of the themes overlap and can be applied. See Hunter, *To " 'Joy My Freedom,"* 145–55; Kelly, *Race Rebels*, 43–45. For an excellent exploration into the jook joints, see Katrina Hazzard-Gordon, *Jookin': The Rise of Social Dance Formations in African-American Culture* (Philadelphia: Temple University Press, 1990), 76–119. Peiss finds similar themes among working-class whites in New York; see *Cheap Amusements*, 35, 37, 45, 66–67.

107. For a discussion of prostitution in the theaters, see Claudia D. Johnson, "That Guilty Third Tier: Prostitution in Nineteenth-Century American Theaters," in *AQ* 27, no. 5, Special Issue: Victorian Culture in America (December 1975): 575–84; Steinberg also mentions this in his work; see *The Transformation of Criminal Justice*, 18–21; Du Bois, *The Philadelphia Negro*, 324.

108. Peiss, *Cheap Amusements*, 37.

109. Patricia K. Hunt, "Clothing as an Expression of History: The Dress of African-American Women in Georgia, 1880–1915," in *"We Specialize in the Wholly Impossible": A Reader in Black Women's History*, ed. Darlene Clark Hine, Wilma King, and Linda Reed (New York: Carlson Publishing, 1995), 396–97. Shane White and Graham White explain that following Emancipation blacks used clothes not only to proclaim social parity, but also to reveal their deeper desires to share in the material attractions of the larger society; see *Stylin': African American Expressive Culture from Its Beginnings to the Zoot Suit* (Ithaca: Cornell University Press, 1998), 128; Kelley, *Race Rebels*, 43–45; Peiss, *Cheap Amusements*, 62–64; Jones, *Labor of Love*, 68–72.

110. In comparing mug shots from the *Philadelphia Rogues Gallery Books* (RGB), vols. 1, 2 (PCA), I observed differences in hat styles that appeared to follow a migration pattern.

Though my current assessment is largely anecdotal, this is an area I intend to investigate more thoroughly in future work. Corresponding criminal records for the mug shots appear in the *Department of Public Safety, Bureau of Police—Detective Service* (PCA). For more about how leisure enhanced autonomy, see Kelley, *Race Rebels*, 47. Black women reformers took pains to caution young women and girls about their choice in hats because the wrong hat might give the wrong impression about their character. See Noliwe M. Rooks, *Ladies' Pages: African American Women's Magazines and the Culture That Made Them* (New Brunswick: Rutgers University Press, 2004), 50; Peiss, *Cheap Amusements*, 62–67.

111. Du Bois, *The Philadelphia Negro*, 277–82. Roger Lane finds that black women frequented bars more than white women, but on the basis of Du Bois's study in the 1890s, the numbers seem fairly equal. See Lane, *Roots of Violence*, 115–16.

112. Du Bois, *The Philadelphia Negro*, 280–82.

113. Eaton, *Special Report on Negro Domestic Service*, 469–70; Lane, *Roots of Violence*, 23–25; Gregg, *Sparks from the Anvil of Oppression*, 25–50.

114. For some examples of the disturbances and illicit nature of the spots, see PL, 6/4/1887, SB1; Du Bois, *The Philadelphia Negro*, 320–21; Hazzard-Gordon, *Jookin'*, 76, 88–91.

115. I am drawing parallels between nineteenth-century working-class black women and blacks in the early twentieth century who used similar urban spaces "to take back their bodies" after hours of backbreaking, low-wage pay. See Robin D. G. Kelley, "The Riddle of the Zoot: Malcolm Little and Black Cultural Politics during World War II," in *Malcolm X: In Our Own Image*, ed. J. Wood (New York: St. Martin's Press, 1992), 163. Sharon Harley explains that African Americans defined their identities not through their work but rather through their relationships and community roles. My argument builds upon this but posits the speakeasies as another kind of institution that allowed women whose wages and work hours isolated them to break out and create communal networks. See Sharon Harley, "When Your Work Is Not Who You Are: The Development of a Working-Class Consciousness Among Afro-American Women," in "*We Specialize in the Wholly Impossible*, ed Hine, King, and Reed, 25–27; Peiss, *Cheap Amusements*, 98.

116. Kelley, "The Riddle of the Zoot."

117. Carby, "Policing the Black Woman's Body," 739; Peiss, *Cheap Amusements*, 98; Hunter, "*To 'Joy My Freedom,*" 154.

118. These developments are similar to the process that Kevin Mumford describes as taking place in Harlem and Chicago's South Side. See *Interzones*, 34–35, and chapter 3.

119. *Annual Report of the National League*, 4.

120. Du Bois, *The Philadelphia Negro*, 45. Though few blacks in the city denied the harsh conditions in the South, their response to southern migration was lukewarm at best. African-American leaders advised blacks against moving north altogether, arguing

that the South was the true home for the newly freed population. This sentiment was fairly widespread, but among its most notable advocates was Booker T. Washington; see *Up from Slavery: An Autobiography* (1901; reprint, Oxford: Oxford University Press, 1995), "Atlanta Address."

121. Appendix, table 7.

122. Exploring Richmond, Virginia, Elsa Barkley-Brown and Gregg Kimball explain that middle-class blacks especially worried about how the "public visibility" of working-class blacks and their activities would impact race progress. This response parallels that of elite and middle-class black Philadelphians, especially with respect to their concerns about poor native-born blacks and southern migrants; see "Mapping the Terrain of Black Richmond," in *The New African American Urban History*, ed. Goings and Mohl, 97, 101.

123. Carby, "Policing the Black Woman's Body"; Barkley-Brown and Kimball, "Mapping the Terrain of Black Richmond," 101–02; Rooks, *Ladies' Pages*, 51–55; Wolcott, *Remaking Respectability*, 19–20.

124. Lane provides an excellent discussion of this population; see *William Dorsey's Philadelphia*, chaps. 6, 7.

125. Lane, *Roots of Violence*, 67.

126. "Invading the Learned Professions," TP, 8/2/1885. For a more detailed accounting of the work of elite African Americans, see chapter 1, "Work of the Afro-American Woman," in Mossell, *The Work of the Afro-American Woman*, 9–47 and chapter 9, "The Occupations of the Negro," in Du Bois, *The Philadelphia Negro*, 97–141; Richard Wright, ed., *Philadelphia Colored Directory, 1908* (Philadelphia: Philadelphia Colored Directory Co., 1907).

127. "A Great Colored Ball," TP, 3/12/1886; "Colored Journalists," TP, 8/18/1890. "The Negro by the Sea," TP, 7/15/1890.

128. I am drawing a parallel between this piece in the *Times-Philadelphia* in 1890 and the article I discussed in chapter 1, published in the *Pennsylvania Gazette* in 1829; the PG article is quoted in Lapsansky, " 'Since They Got Those Separate Churches,' " 103.

129. "The Negro by the Sea," TP, 7/15/1890.

130. PI, 10/21/1893.

131. Du Bois *The Philadelphia Negro*, 39–40; Lane, *Roots of Violence*, 45–47; Harry Silcox, "Nineteenth-Century Philadelphia Black Militant: Octavius V. Catto (1839–1871)," in *African Americans in Pennsylvania*, ed. Trotter and Smith, 198–219.

132. "The Republican Recital A Success," *Harrisburg Call*, 12 August 1896, Marlin E. Olmstead Papers, 1874–1913, Manuscript Group 153 (PHMC).

133. Pennsylvania mandated that blacks receive equal treatment from insurance and public transportation companies as well as from the hotel and hospitality industries, but, rarely enforced, the policies did little to change daily practices or biased notions. See *Penns. Laws*, 1887, 130–31. Also see Du Bois, *The Philadelphia Negro*, Appendix B, 418.

134. Wolcott, *Remaking Respectability*, 50; Michelle Mitchell discusses how racism politicized gender and sexuality in *Righteous Propagation: African Americans and the Politics of Racial Destiny after Reconstruction* (Chapel Hill: University of North Carolina Press, 2004), 7–13.

135. Gaines, *Uplifting the Race*, 2–5; Wolcott, *Remaking Respectability*, 12–20.

136. Gregg, *Sparks from the Anvil of Oppression*, 49.

137. Ibid., 46; PT, 9/29/1888, WDC #3:23.

138. Gaines, *Uplifting the Race*, xiv; Brooks-Higginbotham, *Righteous Discontent*, 187–93; Wolcott, *Remaking Respectability*, 15.

139. Barkley-Brown and Kimball, "Mapping the Terrain of Black Richmond," 102–05; Kelley, *Race Rebels*, 45–46; Hunter, *"To 'Joy My Freedom,"* 154, 198–204; Wolcott, *Remaking Respectability*, 38.

140. Frances Kellor founded the organization in 1906 in New York and Philadelphia. It was an interracial organization, and in Philadelphia a number of prominent blacks worked in the agency.

141. Gregg, *Sparks from the Anvil of Oppression*, 111.

142. *Annual Report of the National League*, 3.

143. "Local Associations: Reports to October First: Philadelphia" in *Annual Report of the National League*, 5.

144. Deborah Gray White provides a description and critique of black female reformers, especially those who were active in the National Association of Colored Women; see *Too Heavy a Load: Black Women in Defense of Themselves, 1894–1994* (New York: W. W. Norton, 1999), 70–73.

145. Gaines, *Uplifting the Race*, 166–71.

146. "Driven to Crime by Politicians," TP, 3/25/1899.

147. Du Bois, *The Philadelphia Negro*, 241.

148. A number of scholars have noted these attitudes, but texts I found most helpful regarding immorality and crime are Cheryl D. Hicks, " 'In Danger of Becoming Morally Depraved': Single Black Women, Working-class Black Families, and New York State's Wayward Minor Laws, 1917–1928," *University of Pennsylvania Law Review* 151, no. 6 (June 2003): 2077–2121 at 2086–88; Paula Giddings, "The Last Taboo," in *Words of Fire*, ed. Guy-Sheftall, 415–16.

149. Henry M. Boies, *Prisoners and Paupers: A Study of the Abnormal Increase of Criminals, and the Public Burden of Pauperism in the United States; the Causes and the Remedies* (New York: Putnam Press, 1893), 69 (LCP).

150. Ibid., 70.

151. Lane, *Roots of Violence*, 88; Rafter, *Partial Justice*, 144–49.

152. "Two Colored Graduates," PDN, 2/22/1888, and PEI, 1885, WDC #8:71.

153. RC, 4/28/1893, in *The Philadelphia Negro*, fn. 241.

154. PSBC, *Annual Reports*, 1880, 1894, 1909; also see PSBC, *Annual Reports*, 1885, 1890,

1895, 1900, 1905, 1910 (PSL); Carolyn Adams, David Bartelt, David Elesh, Ira Goldstein, Nancy Kleniewski, and William Yancy, *Philadelphia: Neighborhoods, Divisions, and Conflicts in a Postindustrial City* (Philadelphia: Temple University Press, 1991), 8–11, table 1.1.

155. Appendix, table 8; in 1880, blacks accounted for 4.3 percent of the city's population; by 1890 this number had risen to 4.4; in 1900 African Americans represented 5.4 percent and in 1910, 5.7 percent. See Adams, Bartelt, Elesh, Goldstein, Kleniewski, and Yancy, *Philadelphia*, 8–11, table 1.1.

156. Appendix, table 10; Rafter also finds this trend throughout her examinations of black women imprisoned in the South; see *Partial Justice*, 141, 154–55; Dodge, *"Whores and Thieves of the Worst Kind,"* 123–24; Anne Butler, *Gendered Justice in the American West*, 91–93.

157. Appendix, table 9.

158. Rothman, *The Discovery of the Asylum*, chapter 3, "The Challenge of Crime." Rothman's work has been criticized for oversimplifying the case, but I still find his argument quite compelling. For changing work opportunities for women in Philadelphia, see Mary Frances Cordato, "Toward a New Century: Women and the Philadelphia Centennial Exhibition, 1876," *PMHB* 107, no. 1 (January 1983): 113–35 at 126–27, 132–33.

159. Steinberg characterizes these casualties as the underemployed, landless wage laborers, chronically ill, and those who were denied opportunities on the basis of race, gender, and ethnicity; see Steinberg, *The Transformation of Criminal Justice*, 230.

160. In his discussion of laws governing morality, Lane notes that these laws in Philadelphia in particular reflected the values of white Protestants. See Lane, *Roots of Violence*, 86.

161. Black reformers warned against the dangers of drink as well, but most emphasized self-restraint. In her work on Frances Ellen Watkins Harper, Margaret Hope Bacon notes Harper's role in the Women's Christian Temperance Organization in Pennsylvania and Harper's work to desegregate the organization as well as her gentle pleas to blacks to avoid liquor because it played a central role in destabilizing the black family; see Bacon, "One Great Bundle of Humanity: Frances Ellen Watkins Harper," *PMHB* 113, no. 1 (January 1989): 21–43 at 40; Du Bois also discusses the drink habit extensively and complains bitterly about the practice among blacks; see Du Bois, *The Philadelphia Negro*, 277.

162. Ibid., 172.

163. Teeters, *The Cradle of the Penitentiary*.

164. Steinberg, *The Transformation of Criminal Justice*, 131.

165. *Penns. Laws*, 1881: two laws against sale of alcohol to minors and another law restricting people from playing pool for drinks; see no. 13 and no. 176 and no. 46; 1887, no. 135, a law to regulate the sale of wholesale liquor distributors; 1891, no. 215, an-

other law restricting alcohol; 1897, no. 76, another liquor law; 1901, a supplemental law regulating the sale of alcohol, see no. 128; *Penns. Laws*, 1903, no. 189, prevent the sale of liquor to known alcoholics; 1907, no. 200, act regulating the sale or gift of liquor to those known to be habitually addicted.

166. Lane, *Roots of Violence*, 112–14.

167. *Penns. Laws*, 1881, no. 46.

168. Lane, *Roots of Violence*, 112–16.

169. Hazzard-Gordon also discusses the "protection" money underground after-hours spots paid to local bosses and crooked politicians; see *Jookin'*, 91; Lane, *Roots of Violence*, 115.

170. Lane, *Roots of Violence*, 113–16.

171. Appendix, table 5.

172. Austin argues that racism and economic disenfranchisement led to the creation of an informal economy within the black community. Much of this informal economy revolved around unlicensed vendors and unlicensed establishments. I am using her concept and applying it to the unlicensed parlors in Philadelphia. See Regina Austin, " 'An Honest Living': Street Vendors, Municipal Regulation, and the Black Public Sphere," *Yale Law Review* 103, no. 8 (June 1994): 2119–20. Philadelphia's corruption is legendary—for a turn-of-the-century treatise on the subject, see Lincoln Steffens, "Philadelphia: Corrupt and Contented," in his book *The Shame of the Cities* (1904; reprint, New York: Hill and Wang, 1957), 134–61.

173. Lane, *Roots of Violence*, 86; Steinberg, *The Transformation of Criminal Justice*, 230–32.

174. This discussion is heavily influenced by Steinberg's important work on transformations in Philadelphia's criminal justice system. See Steinberg, *The Transformation of Criminal Justice*, 26, 37–38.

175. Sprogle, *The Philadelphia Police*, chapter 8, "The Police Free from Politics," and chapter 9, "The Force as Perfected"; Steinberg, *The Transformation of Criminal Justice*, 172.

176. See Code no. 207, Beggars, Vagrants, and Tramps, in the *Patrolman's Manual: Bureau of Police, City of Philadelphia* (Philadelphia: Issued by the Department of Public Safety, 1913), 62, in *Metropolitan Police Manuals, 1817, 1913*, ed. Richard C. Wade (New York: Arno Press, 1974).

177. See *Penns. Laws*, 1899, no. 73; Dodge also explains that prosecuting attorneys selectively tried cases which resulted in disproportionate rates for black women; see, *"Whores and Thieves of the Worst Kind,"* 70–71.

178. *Minutes of the Pennsylvania Prison Society*, vol. 7, 9/20/1883–1/24/1889, 8–9, 21–22, 26–27, 51, 83, 89, 100–102, 115–19, 129–30, 138–40, 162 (HSP).

179. Ibid., 169–80, 186–204, 209–15, 223–31, 234–45, 252–53, 266–80, 307–08. During her incarceration in a Philadelphia prison one prostitute had to exchange sexual favors with a guard in order to receive better accommodations. Her account is just one example of the kinds of abuses women needed protection from. See Maimie Pinzer,

The Maimie Papers, ed. Ruth Rosen and Sue Davidson (New York: Feminist Press, 1977), 193.

180. In his journal, Michael Cassidy noted that "Mr. Love seemed disappointed as he is one of the Benevolent cranks who think they are deserving of every consideration from every one whom they condescend to notice, Mr. Love is one of the acting committee of the Prison Society and also president of the Universal Peace Association of the United States." See WJ, vol. 5, 5/30/1886; Teeters, *They Were in Prison*.

181. Many authors have discussed this subject, but the two works that have been most helpful for my purposes are Noel Ignatiev, *How the Irish Became White* (New York: Routledge, 1995), and Roediger, *The Wages of Whiteness*.

3. Tricking the Tricks

1. Badger thieves likely did practice prostitution at some point, but there is a difference between those prostitutes who occasionally robbed patrons and those women who serially committed the crime of badger theft. I concentrate here on the latter and discuss prostitutes in another section of this chapter.

2. On April 4, 1860, Georgiana Coleman appeared before the court accused on the oath of James Madison of picking his pocket of $2.25. These charges were ignored. See PTD (4/25/1859–8/19/1860). However, in June 1860, Bill Fine brought charges against Coleman for relieving him of $10. These charges were also dismissed. She made this startling declaration at her arraignment in the Fine case. See the PL 8/23/1860, quoted in Lane, *Roots of Violence*, 107–8.

3. "Ignored" is the word that appears in the PTD.

4. Lane, *Roots of Violence*, 108–09.

5. Hine discusses some of the silences surrounding black women's interiors in "Rape and the Inner Lives of Black Women," 380–82.

6. For histories that explore the rape of black women, see Hine, ibid., and "Black Migration to the Urban Midwest"; White, *Ar'n't I a Woman?*; Carby, *Reconstructing Womanhood*; hooks, *Ain't I A Woman?*, 56–58.

7. Rosen, " 'Not That Sort of Woman,' " 268–69; Catherine Clinton, "Reconstructing Freedwomen," in *Divided Houses: Gender and the Civil War*, ed. Catherin Clinton and Nina Silber (New York: Oxford University Press, 1992), 306–19; Laura F. Edwards, *Gendered Strife and Confusion: The Political Culture of Reconstruction* (Urbana: University of Illinois Press, 1997). Patricia Hill Collins explains that by objectifying black women and recasting their experience to serve the interests of elite white men, Eurocentric paradigms depict black women as subordinate; see Collins, *Black Feminist Thought: Knowledge, Consciousness, and the Politics of Empowerment* (Boston: Unwin Hyman, 1990), 221–38.

8. The attacks, designed to degrade black women and to reinforce white patriarchy,

were frightfully common in the post-Reconstruction era. Some harrowing accounts appear in Dorothy Sterling's collection of black women's voices; see Sterling, ed., *We Are Your Sisters: Black Women in the Nineteenth Century* (New York: W. W. Norton, 1997), 344–55.

9. Hartman discusses some of the obstacles and tactics used to resubject newly freed blacks; see *Scenes of Subjection*, 116; Tate, *Domestic Allegories of Political Desire*, 10.

10. Henderson argues that black women presumably had no voice, no text, and consequently no history—that they existed historically as blank tablets to be written upon "precisely because they exist as the ultimate Other, whose absence or (non) being only serves to define the being or presence of the white or male subject." See Henderson, "Toni Morrison's *Beloved*," 322. Also see Messerschmidt, *Crime as Structured Action*, 10.

11. Black women's bodies and images were commodities for trade among mainstream society and perhaps within the African-American community as well. The practices were reminiscent of what Aime Cesaire described when he argued that in relationships of oppression, there cannot be real human contact but rather coercive binaries that eradicate humanity and make the oppressed degraded masses or products; see Cesaire, *Discourse on Colonialism*, 20–25. Also see Fanon, *Black Skins, White Masks* and *Wretched of the Earth*; hooks, *Ain't I a Woman?*, 80–86.

12. I elected not to include the photos. To view them see Deborah Willis and Carla Williams, *The Black Female Body: A Photographic History* (Philadelphia: Temple University Press, 2002), 43–44.

13. Ibid.

14. Ibid., 44. Sander Gilman provides a discussion of the sexual mythologies in his essay "Black Bodies, White Bodies: Towards an Iconography of Female Sexuality in Late-Nineteenth Century Art, Medicine and Literature," in *"Race," Writing and Difference*, ed. Henry Louis Gates Jr. (Chicago: University of Chicago Press, 1985), 231–40.

15. I also refer to the landmark Supreme Court case in 1908, *Muller v. Oregon*, which affirmed the power of the states to selectively apply protective labor laws to women and children. For an interesting history of sex-based inequality and the law, see Wendy Kaminer, *Fearful Freedom: Women's Flight from Equality*, 2nd ed. (Reading, Mass.: Addison-Wesley, 1991). For more examples of gender specific protective legislation, see the Act Against Enticing, written into the laws of Pennsylvania on May 1, 1909, in Suzanne S. Beatty, ed., *Compilation of Laws of Pennsylvania Relating to Children* (s.i.: s.n., c. 1915); *Penns. Laws*, 1909, no. 698.

16. The patrolman's manuals stipulated that when policemen discovered an alleged bawdy house that was owned or operated by a Chinese immigrant employing white women they should report the "location and name of keeper and names and addresses of women." See Code no. 215, Disorderly Houses, Bawdy Houses, Prostitution, in *Patrolman's Manual*, 62, in *Metropolitan Police Manuals*, ed. Wade, 66; Kevin J. Mum-

ford also documents the heightened policing of interracial sex parlors in Chicago and New York during the 1920s; see *Interzones*, 54–71; Nayan Shah's work examines a similar type of discrimination against Chinese immigrants in San Francisco; see *Contagious Divides: Epidemics and Race in San Francisco's Chinatown* (Berkeley: University of California Press, 2001), 77–79, 94.

17. For articles about men arrested for charges related to white slavery, see "Held White Slave by a Colored Man," EB, 3/30/1909, SB2; "A Human Spider" and "An Outrage on American Womanhood," NPG, 12/5/1885; " 'White Slave' Men Must Serve Term," MPT, MD, c. 1909, SB2; inmate #B4843 and #B1855, CRR, 1909 and 1903.

18. For evidence of this, see Cheryl Hicks's discussion about racism in the application of New York City's Wayward Minor Law in "In Danger of Becoming Morally Depraved," 2081, 2092–97.

19. "Five Years for Enticing Children," MPT, 1900, SB2, and inmate #B516, #B517, #B518, CRR, 3/10/1900; "Too Handy With a Knife," MPT, 6/18/1893, WDC #5:49 and SB1 and inmate #A7806, CDR, 1894.

20. Addie Hunton, "Negro Womanhood Defended," *The Voice of the Negro* 1, no. 7 (July 1904): 280 (SCH).

21. Within this framework Harper countered stereotypes of African-American female promiscuity—stereotypes that placed culpability on the very victims who were otherwise exonerated in the "white slavery" narratives. See P. Gabrielle Foreman, " 'Reading Aright': White Slavery, Black Referents, and the Strategy of Histotextuality in *Iola Leroy*," *Yale Journal of Criticism* 10, no. 2 (1997): 338–39.

22. Williams is quoted in Sandra Gunning, *Race, Rape, and Lynching: The Red Record of American Literature, 1890–1912* (New York: Oxford University Press, 1996), 78–81. Also see Anna Julia Cooper, 1893, "Address to the Congress of Representative Women," reprinted in *Black Women in Nineteenth-Century American Life: Their Words, Their Thoughts, Their Feelings*, ed. Bert James Loewenberg and Ruth Bogin (University Park: Pennsylvania State University Press, 1976), 329, 274–75; Giddings, *When and Where I Enter*, 86.

23. I am referring to Ida B. Wells's *A Red Record* (1895), which documents the lynching of black men in the South. Although Wells notes the hypocrisy of the white men's lynching of purported rapists, when their own crimes against black women went unabated, she does not canvass and document the rapes in the same manner.

24. Hine, "Rape and the Inner Lives of Black Women"; Carby, *Reconstructing Womanhood*, 7, 17, 37; hooks states that black men and women wrote letters to the press calling for an end to the crimes but that the cries fell on deaf ears; see *Ain't I a Woman?*, 57.

25. Painter, "Soul Murder and Slavery," 125–27. Also Ann W. Burgess and Lynda L. Holstrom, *Rape, Crisis and Recovery* (Bowie, Md: Robert J. Brady, 1979), 35–65; Thomas W. McCahill, Linda C. Meyer, and Arthur M. Fischman, *The Aftermath of Rape* (Lexington, Mass.: Lexington Books, 1979), 23–79.

26. Hine, "Rape and the Inner Lives of Black Women," 380–82.

27. Brooks-Higginbotham, *Righteous Discontent*, 186–87, 193. Though information about the impact of sexual terrorism is scare, an early case of an enslaved eighteen-year-old in Missouri provides a glimpse into the rage that the assaults engendered. See McLaurin, *Celia, A Slave*, 22–37.

28. The role of the black church and the black women's club movement have been well documented; see Brooks-Higginbotham, *Righteous Discontent*; Deborah Gray White, "The Cost of Club Work, the Price of Black Feminism," in *Visible Women: New Essays on American Activities*, ed. Nancy A. Hewitt and Suzanne Lebsock (Urbana: University of Illinois Press, 1993), and *Too Heavy A Load*, 70–73. My reference to the smaller intimate spaces is based on Farah Griffin's discussion of black women and kitchenette spaces; see Griffin, *"Who Set You Flowin'?": The African-American Migration Narrative* (New York: Oxford University Press, 1995), 76, 108, 122.

29. Apparently white men's patronage of black prostitutes had a fairly established history in Philadelphia. An early travel diary describes several black brothels and locations of black streetwalkers; see *A Guide to the Stranger* (LCP).

30. MST, MPT, c. 7/1/1902, SB2; Bessie Smith, #B1466, CRR, 7/1/1902.

31. Appendix, table 5.

32. Vice crimes sometimes underwent intense scrutiny, but at other times officers turned a blind eye on much of the city's more illicit pastimes. See Lane, *Roots of Violence*, 56–59, 109–10. Also see McCafferty, *When Bosses Ruled Philadelphia*; John Thomas Salter, *Boss Rule: Portraits in City Politics* (New York: McGraw-Hill, 1935). The city's vice commission noted that some of the worst places of vice were "political clubs" that served as hangouts for "politicians, barkeepers, pimps, etc."; see Philadelphia, Pennsylvania Vice Commission, *A Report on Existing Conditions, with Recommendations to the Honorable Rudolph Blakenburg, Mayor of Philadelphia (Philadelphia Vice Report)* (Philadelphia: The Commission, 1913), 12–13 (FL). Also see Josie Washburn, *The Underworld Sewer: A Prostitute Reflects on Life in the Trade, 1871–1909*, ed. Sharon E. Wood (Lincoln: University of Nebraska Press, 1997), chapter 3, "The Hold-Up."

33. Lane, *Roots of Violence*, 108–09.

34. Though information on the crime is limited, ESP housed the most notorious. See WJ, vol. 8, 12/9/1900; Edith Pond, #B797, CDR, 12/16/1900; Susan Denby, convicted larceny of $17, "the property of Peter Vandenberg," see PL, 7/13/1886, SBI, #A3324, CDR, July 12, 1886; "Mamie Hicks, colored, convicted of the larceny of $35 from the person of John Pisters," MPT, MST, c. 6/24/1893, SBI, A#6884, CDR, 7/23/1893; "Annie Harvey, colored, was convicted of larceny of $20 from the person of George Sloan," MPT, MST c. 11/12/1893, SBI, Annie Harvey or Hanvey, #A7111, CDR, 12/14/1893.

35. Slang for victims/patrons who solicited prostitutes.

36. Bessie Conway, #B1069, CDR, 9/16/1901.

37. MST, MPT, c. 9/17/1901, SBI.

38. See chapter II, "The Born Criminal," in Cesare Lombroso and William Ferrero, *The Female Offender* (New York: D. Appleton, 1895), 147–71.

39. Josephine Payton and Annie Reed, both repeat offenders, were convicted together, in 1896, for the theft of $25 from Adam Smith; #A8639 and #A8640, CDR, 1896, and "Quarter Sessions," MPT, C. 4/9/1896, SBI.

40. WJ, vol. 9, 3/4/1902.

41. The incident is documented, but the log does not include any motive or cause for Payton's violent outburst; see WJ, vol. 8, 7/5/1898; #A8639, CDR.

42. #A2522, CDR, 1885—listed her occupation as "Thief."

43. In this instance, Palmer forced a young white man to give her "all of the money he had, $1.50." See MST, PL, 2/12/1885, SBI.

44. ESP Reception Register noted that Palmer was a moderate drinker in 1888 and also that she had six prior criminal convictions, #A4445, CRR, 1888; PDF 5/19/1894.

45. WJ, vol. 5, 8/8/1888. A#4445, CDR, 1888—noted "House Servant" as her trade.

46. Available records indicate that she complained of not feeling well and seemed generally disturbed; see "Suicide in 'MOYA,'" PEI, 5/20/1894, and "Death in Her Cell," PI, 5/20/1894, WDC #10:23; PDF, 5/18/1894.

47. Gillis and her codefendants received two-year sentences at ESP; #A5339, #A5340, and #A5341, CDR, 1890; MPT, MST, 4/19/1890, SBI.

48. WJ, vol. 4, 1/12/1883; #A1514, #A1515, and #A1516, CDR, 1883.

49. #A8478, CDR, 1895; MST, MPT, C. 1895, SBI; #A6060 and #A6059, CDR, 1891; MPT, MST, 10/27/1891, SBI.

50. #A6060 and #A6059, CDR, 1891; MPT, MST, 10/27/1891, SBI—"running the growler" or "rushing the growler" typically referred to patrons going to neighborhood bars and carrying away pails of beer; see Lane, *Roots of Violence*, 113.

51. Marilyn Wood Hill addresses the pitfalls in discussing prostitution critically. Her observations about the gender power dynamics helped frame my thinking; see *Their Sisters' Keepers: Prostitution in New York City, 1830–1870* (Berkeley: University of California Press, 1993), 1–5. Timothy J. Gilfoyle's discussion of the slippery aspects of assessing women's prostitution was also helpful. Though both Gilfoyle's and Hill's research concentrates on New York, their critiques of urban sexuality, gender, and economic disparities apply to most large urban centers in the late nineteenth century. See Gilfoyle, *City of Eros: New York, Prostitution, and the Commercialization of Sex, 1790–1920* (New York: W. W. Norton, 1992), 1–20.

52. Using information from the vice report, I estimate that roughly a quarter of the prostitutes in the city were black women. See *Philadelphia Vice Commission, Report*, 10.

53. Ibid., 7–8.

54. Based on my findings at ESP nearly all of the women serving time on bawdy and disorderly house charges were operating the houses themselves. Moreover, the case of Helen Thomas and Mamie Brown revealed a network of female prostitutes and mad-

ams operating on Schell Street. See *Commonwealth vs. Mame Brown* and *Commonwealth vs. Helen Thomas*, Trial Transcript in the Court of Quarter Sessions and Oyer and Terminer of Philadelphia County, October Sessions, 1908, no. 375, January 5, 1909 (PCA).

55. The *Philadelphia Vice Commission* report also discussed rarer instances in which women earned as much as $20 for sex, but these prices were affiliated with call services and seemed to be more upscale than fees in most sex houses in the city; see *Philadelphia Vice Commission, Report*, 6–7, 15–16.

56. In addition to women who worked in red-light districts, a number of women drifted in and out of prostitution, depending upon economic demand or sudden loss of employment. See Ruth Rosen, *The Lost Sisterhood: Prostitution in America, 1900–1918* (Baltimore: Johns Hopkins University Press, 1982). During her trial, Mamie Brown indicated that prostitution was not her sole occupation, but rather an additional source of income in between her otherwise legitimate jobs. See *Commonwealth vs. Mame Brown*, 104. Also see the *Philadelphia Vice Commission, Report*, 16.

57. Appendix, table 5.

58. Cathy Caruth explains that unclaimed experiences of trauma result from the victim being unable to psychologically understand how and why they were victimized. In this state, victims often engage in an unconscious repetition of similar experiences as a means to remedy past traumas too painful to directly or consciously confront, psychologically or otherwise. See Caruth, *Unclaimed Experience: Trauma, Narrative, and History* (Baltimore: Johns Hopkins University Press, 1996), 7.

59. "A Police Descent: Lisbon Street Residents Arrested," MPT, 8/4/1896, WDC #11:92.

60. David Johnson, in his work on crime and policing in late nineteenth-century Philadelphia, explains that there were no rigid lines between criminals and law-abiding citizens, but rather different interactions among different types of people; see his *Policing the Urban Underworld*, 183. In her work on freed black women in Atlanta, Hunter argues that most black women were neither complete saints nor complete sinners; see "*To 'Joy My Freedom,*" 166–67; Elijah Anderson also discusses this ideological distinction in his *Code of the Street: Decency, Violence and the Moral Life of the Inner City* (New York: W. W. Norton, 2000).

61. Mumford, *Interzones*, xii–xiv, 80–92; *Philadelphia Vice Report*, section entitled, "The Responsibility of the Police," 11.

62. In his testimony, a Mr. Rogers, who lived down the street (237 Schell Street) from Helen Thomas, a brothel owner on trial, testified on her behalf. Though his answers were evasive, he appeared to be another bawdy house owner. See Testimony of Mr. Rogers, *Commonwealth vs. Helen Thomas*, *Commonwealth vs. Helen Thomas and Mame Brown*, and *Commonwealth vs. Mame Brown*, Trial Transcript in the Court of Quarter Sessions and Oyer and Terminer of Philadelphia County, October Sessions, 1908, no. 375, January 5, 1909, 91.

63. The developments parallel what Regina Austin describes in her work as the informal economy in the black community; see " 'An Honest Living,' " 2119–20.

64. MPT, MST, 11/10/1891, SBI.

65. Inmate #A6087, CDR, 1891; Martha Gibson, wid. George, h 1308 Wood Street in *Gopsill's Philadelphia City Directory, for 1890* (PCA). Wood Street was apparently a haven for bawdy houses, as arrests were also made at a white disorderly house located at 1313 Wood Street, in 1885. See Hattie Barley, Lauren Smith, Alice Urn, and Lenore Bennett in the PTD, Index, 1885.

66. WJ, vol. 5, 11/14/1888; Hester Brown, #A3800, CDR, 6/14/1887.

67. For accounts of cross-dressing, see "He Masqueraded as a Woman," *Lancaster Daily Intelligencer*, 10/5/1893 (PSL); Rosa Bonheur claimed "she would have missed all chances of success had she had to bear the weight of the skirts in fashion thirty years ago." See, "Personal Column," *Lancaster Intelligencer*, 11/3/1893; for the Philadelphia story, see, "Seeing the Elephant," NPG, 11/21/1885. This trend of whites "slumming" also occurred in New York; see Chauncey, *Gay New York*, 36–37.

68. *Philadelphia Vice Commission*, 35—section entitled, "Perversion."

69. Both Mary Bailey and Charles France were arrested and convicted of sodomy and buggery and sentenced to two-year sentences at ESP. Though the legal definition of sodomy identifies anal sex specifically, the charge of sodomy was assigned to both gay men and gay women. The term *Lesbian* was scarcely used during the period. See MST, MPT, 1/7/1891, SBI; #A5710 and #A5712, CDR, 1890; Caroll Smith-Rosenberg, *Disorderly Conduct: Visions of Gender in Victorian America* (New York: Oxford University Press, 1985), chapter 2, "The Female World of Love and Ritual Between Women in Nineteenth-Century America," 53–77. Adrienne Rich also discusses the ways in which lesbianism has been historically neglected by being discussed somewhat tangentially in respect to gay men; see "Compulsory Heterosexuality and Lesbian Existence," *Signs* (Summer 1980): 649–50; Chauncey, *Gay New York*, 39–45. Although Foucault argues that the efforts to repress prostitution and other transgressive sexual behaviors resulted in their historical documentation, he nonetheless demonstrates the repressive sexual climate of the late nineteenth century. See Michel Foucault, *History of Sexuality*, 1:4–5. Also see Isaac R. Hull, alias the "Lady Washington," #A861, CDR, 1881; " 'Lady Washington' Seriously Accused," MPT, 8/4/1896, WDC #11:92. Middle Alley frequently came up in news accounts and arrest dockets; for examples, see Kate Johnson and Maggie Cannon, arrested at a disorderly house on 627 Middle Alley, PTD, 1895. Certain streets, particularly Schell, Guliema, Alaska, Minster, Lisbon, and Hurst, were among the most notorious for crime and illicit entertainments. Also see *Commonwealth vs. Helen Thomas and Mame Brown*; Du Bois, *The Philadelphia Negro*, 60–63; and Lane, *Roots of Violence*, 107, 121.

70. I agree with Chauncey's conclusion that policing of these groups sprang up because their sexuality challenged traditional Victorian notions of sex and gender; see his

"From Sexual Inversion to Homosexuality: The Changing Medical Conceptualization of Female 'Deviance,'" in *Passion and Power: Sexuality in History*, ed. Kathy Peiss and Christina Simmons (Philadelphia: Temple University Press, 1989), 108.

71. Barbara Omolade, "Hearts of Darkness," in *Words of Fire*, ed. Guy-Sheftall, 371, and Barbara Smith, "Toward a Black Feminist Criticism," *Conditions: Two* 1, no. 2 (October 1977): 25–52.

72. Lee's name appears throughout the coverage as either Emily or Emma. Her prison intake records list her name as Emily, #B3005, CRR, 10/25/1905.

73. "Mrs. Stella Weldon Brutally Murdered by Miss Emily Lee," SD, 3/15/1905 (PHMC).

74. Lisa Duggan talks a great deal about this phenomenon in her work on media constructions of sex and sexuality at the turn of the twentieth century; see *Sapphic Slashers: Sex, Violence, and American Modernity* (Durham and London: Duke University Press, 2000), chapter 1.

75. SD, 3/15/1905.

76. Ibid.

77. This case typifies George Chauncey's assertion of the "myth of invisibility." Though his discussion concentrates on gay men's openness in the early twentieth century, his critique and observations also appear to hold true for African-American lesbians. See Chauncey, *Gay New York*, 3–4.

78. "The Emma Lee Case: Sensation of the Hour," SD 10/14/1905. This kind of tacit acceptance is not entirely uncommon in black history; it seemed to be a facet of Rebecca Primus's and Addie Brown's relationship in the late nineteenth century, and Eric Garber notes that blacks in the 1920s in Harlem displayed fairly tolerant attitudes toward "black gays and lesbians," though he notes that they still endured difficulties from both blacks and whites. See Garber, "A Spectacle in Color," 319–21, 322–25; *Beloved Sisters and Loving Friends*.

79. Chauncey, *Gay New York*, 3–4.

80. Though Cheryl Clarke examines interracial sexual relations between women, her basic premise that lesbianism for black women existed as an inherent site of resistance can be applied to the Lee case; see "Lesbianism: An Act of Resistance," 242–44.

81. Also the pen names are those of characters from classic eighteenth-century novels: Gil Blas is the central figure in a work by the French author LeSage, and Sancho Panza (the actual press has "Panzo" but I have changed it to Panza because I believe this is an error) was the name of Don Quixote's faithful squire. See Alain-René LeSage, *The Adventures of Gil Blas of Santillane*, and Miguel de Cervantes Saavedra, *The History of the Renowned Don Quixote de la Mancha*.

82. "Gil Blas's Final Resume of the Emma Lee Affair," SD, 4/29/1905.

83. "The Sancho Panzo-Gil Blas Controversy: Gil Blas Answered," SD, 5/13/1905.

84. Duggan, *Sapphic Slashers*, "Introduction."

85. Gaines, *Uplifting the Race*, 166–71.

86. Richie, *Compelled to Crime*, "Introduction"; Wolcott, *Remaking Respectability*, 19–20, 50; Barkley-Brown and Kimball, "Mapping the Terrain of Black Richmond," 97, 101; see also Broder, *Tramps, Unfit Mothers, and Neglected Children*, 131–32; Mitchell, *Righteous Propagation*, 12–13.

87. See *"Ida Howard Sentenced."*

88. Messerschmidt, *Crime as Structured Action*, chapter 2, "Hustler"; Jeffrey Adler discusses a similar concept in his work on black violence in Chicago when he links certain crimes to an "honor based culture" which influenced social mobility in the North and Midwest during the great migration; see Adler, "The Negro Would Be More Than an Angel to Withstand Such Treatment": African American Homicide in Chicago, 1875–1910," in *Lethal Imagination: Violence and Brutality in American History*, ed. Michael A. Bellesiles (New York: New York University Press, 1999), 296.

89. I gleaned some of these observations from prior work with at-risk teens in juvenile facilities in New York in 1992. Dialogues with women imprisoned at SCI-Muncy, Pennsylvania, in 1995 also powerfully informed my understanding of the scope and function of violence in women's lives. I also find Paulo Freire's work especially helpful; see his *Pedagogy of the Oppressed*, trans. Myra Bergman Ramos (New York: Continuum International, 1986).

90. "Too Handy With a Knife," MPT, 6/18/1893, WDC #5:49 and SB1; #A7806, CDR, 1894; "George Prattis, colored, was convicted of attempting to commit a felonious assault on Annie Clark, also colored. Sentenced to two years and three months in Eastern State Penitentiary," MPT, MD, c. 1895, SB1; #A8412, CDR, 1895.

91. Roger Lane explained that reformers and grand juries repeatedly called for the elimination of formal trials and procedures for what they thought were trivial incidents, especially wife beating, "which accounted for about a fifth of all recorded crimes against the person"; see Lane, *Roots of Violence*, 86.

92. "Oyer and Terminer," MPT, MD, c. 1902, SB2; Ella Johnson, #B1342, CDR, 3/31/1902.

93. "Killed Man With a Lighted Lamp," MPT, MD, c. 1902, SB2; Lucinda Johnson, #B1682, CDR, 7/15/1902; "Common Pleas Court: Prisoners Sentenced," West Chester, Penn., *Daily Local News*, 26 October 1910 (PSL); Clara Chaffin, #B5573, CRR, 10/24/1910.

94. MST, MPT, c. 1903, SB2, Mamie (or Mame) Johnson, #B1775, CRR, 11/9/1902.

95. Messerschmidt, *Crime as Structured Action*, chapter 2, "Hustler."

96. Over eight months, newspapers chronicled the shocking murder and preceding events. Cutler's image underwent multiple transformations, as her character shifted from that of the typical black femme fatale to that of an intelligent young woman who was horribly betrayed by Knight. Moreover, the accounts also published otherwise scarce excerpts from her trial transcripts. See "Fatal Jealousy," PI 4/23/1885; "A Woman to Hang," PI, 10/17/1885; "In Behalf of Annie Cutler," RC 11/7/1885, WDC #3:32.

97. News accounts listed Cutler's home and her employment as a domestic working for the Mettlers on 835 Race Street. This address was confirmed as that of Joseph Mettler of Mettler Bros. in *Gopsill's Philadelphia City Directory for 1884*.

98. Also verified in *Gopsill's Philadelphia City Directory for 1884*.

99. PI, 10/17/1885; RC 11/7/1885, WDC #3:32.

100. This is the letter as it appeared in the *Philadelphia Evening Item*. See MST, PEI, 1885, WDC #3:32; #A3013, CDR, CRR, 10/16/1885.

101. PI 4/23/1885.

102. Ibid, PEI, 5/18/1885, WDC #3:3; PL 10/17/1885, Sb1. Evelyn Brooks-Higginbotham's research on black Baptist women demonstrates the binary nature of a politics of respectability. I use Brooks-Higginbotham's analysis to show that everyday working-class black women also upheld these problematic notions/definitions of womanhood—in many respects to their detriment. See Brooks-Higginbotham, *Righteous Discontent*, 173–80.

103. Omolade, "Hearts of Darkness," 372.

104. Rafter, *Partial Justice*, 155.

105. Cutler was initially denied sympathy, but subsequent pleas and the intervention of the Pennsylvania Prison Society helped sway popular opinion and eventually the court. See PI 10/17/1885; RC 11/7/1885, WDC #3:32; EB 10/17/1885 (TUA).

106. WJ, vol. 5, 5/30/1886.

107. Smith-Rosenberg, *Disorderly Conduct*, 153–59; Elizabeth Pleck, "A Mother's Wages: Income Earning Among Married Italian and Black Women, 1896–1911," in *The American Family in Social-Historical Perspective*, ed. Michael Gordon, 2nd ed. (New York: St. Martin's Press, 1978), 490–510.

108. TP 8/13/1885; "The Child Stealer," PI 8/13/1885; #A2830, CRR, 9/15/1885.

109. Theodore Hershberg and Henry Williams, "Mulattoes and Blacks: Intragroup Color Differences and Social Stratification in Nineteenth-Century Philadelphia," in *Philadelphia*, ed. Hershberg, 392–428.

110. Testimony of Mary Wood at Winson's trial. See "On Trial for Her Life," *Harrisburg Patriot*, 10/27/1898 (PSL).

111. Testimony of Laura Smith at Albert Smith's trial. See "Al Smith Found Guilty of Murder," *Harrisburg Patriot*, 1/16/1899—this comment reprinted in Smith's trial.

112. According to Monica J. Evans, outlaws operated outside the law because justice did not serve them; in many ways, black female criminals acted as outlaws in this sense; see "Stealing Away: Black Women, Outlaw Culture and the Rhetoric of Rights," in *Critical Race Theory: The Cutting Edge*, ed. Richard Delgado (Philadelphia: Temple University Press, 1995), 503.

113. Tabbs's name appears as both Mary Hannah Tabbs and Hannah Mary Tabbs. In most prison dockets the former is recorded, so I use this in lieu of press accounts that relied on Hannah Mary. For the information about her maiden name and nativity, see PI 2/21/1887; Mary Hannah Tabbs, #A3928, CDR, 9/28/1887.

114. "The Butchered Corpse," EB 2/23/1887.

115. "A Woman for a Clue," TP, 2/20/1887; "The Woman Found," TP 2/22/1887.

116. TP 2/22/1887.

117. Ibid.; the article also states, "When they lived in Cornwells she got jealous if he joked with her young niece."

118. "Annie Richardson Found," EB 3/3/1887.

119. TP 2/22/1887.

120. EB 2/23/1887.

121. TP 2/22/1887.

122. TP 3/3/1887.

123. "Wilson's Trial," EB 6/31/1887.

124. "John H. Tabbs, cook, h, 1642 Richard Street," in *Gopsill's Philadelphia City Directory for 1885*; "Wilson's Trial," *Philadelphia Evening Bulletin*, 31 June 1887.

125. The *Ledger* and *Inquirer* report that Wilson also worked at the Brock Estate, but the *Bulletin* reported Wilson worked as a butcher in the city, and just before the commission of the crime he was employed in an upholstery shop. EB 2/23/1887.

126. TP 2/22/1887.

127. "The Eddington Puzzle," EB 2/22/1887, EB 3/3/1887.

128. EB 6/31/1887.

129. "The Mystery Solved," PI 2/23/1887; "Murder Confessed," TP 2/23/1887; PL 2/23/1887.

130. "The Gains Murder," EB 6/1/1887.

131. "Local Affairs," TP 6/4/1887.

132. Ibid.

133. EB 2/24/1887.

134. EB 2/23/1887; EB 3/1/1887.

135. TP 3/3/1887.

136. #A3928, CDR, 9/28/1887.

4. Roughneck Women, Pale Representations, and Dark Crimes

1. bell hooks, *Ain't I a Woman?*, 81–82.

2. These caricatures work together to proffer traditional social mores. Lisa Duggan's work examines constructions of lesbians in modern America and explores the cultural significance on a national scale. See Duggan, *Sapphic Slashers*, 4–6. For a discussion of "Mammy and Jezebel," see White, *Ar'n't I a Woman?*, chapter 1. Also see Nell Painter, *Sojourner Truth: A Life, A Symbol* (New York: W. W. Norton, 1996).

3. "Negro Women Rob and Kill Farmer in Den," *Philadelphia North American*, 9/13/1908; SB2. Peter Jackson argues that predominant notions of black masculinity encompass a contrived image of black men as dangerous, threatening, and predatory characters. This contrived representation is imbued with white projections of

hyper heterosexuality. I agree with Jackson's assessment and find that a similar argument applies to images of black women. See Jackson, "Black Males: Advertising and the Cultural Politics of Masculinity," *Gender, Place and Culture* 1, no. 1 (1994): 49–59.

4. Though no red-light district existed in Philadelphia, certain streets and alleyways were notorious havens of prostitution and vice. Helen Thomas is referred to as both Helen and Ella in news accounts and in the case trial transcripts, and Mamie Brown is referred to as both Mamie and Mame. See *Commonwealth vs. Helen Thomas and Mame Brown* and *Commonwealth vs. Mame Brown*, Trial Transcript in the Court of Quarter Sessions and Oyer & Terminer of Philadelphia County, October Sessions, 1908, no. 375, January 5, 1909 (PCA).

5. *North American*, 9/13/1908. Moreover, witness accounts, included in additional coverage, charged that "the man started to hit Miss Helen . . . and she told Miss Mame to get the hatchet" and portrayed Madden as the aggressor. See "Boy Describes Murder," EB 1/4/1909, SB3.

6. *Commonwealth vs. Brown*, 73–74.

7. My aim here is not to dispute Madden's age, but to call attention to the ways in which the press framed his age and profession to make the women seem that much more depraved—failing to acknowledge that the sixty-five-year-old man trolling the Tenderloin was drunk and looking for black prostitutes. See *Commonwealth vs. Thomas*, 2.

8. "Ella Thompson," RC 9/16/1908, SB2.

9. RC 9/16/1908, SB2.

10. Helen Thomas, #B4778, and Mamie Brown, #B4779, CRR, 3/3/1909. A Mr. Weil, manager of the Theatrical Hotel on 204–6 North Franklin Street, testified that Brown was employed as a chambermaid in his hotel eight months prior to her arrest. See *Commonwealth vs. Brown*, 104.

11. Testimony of Officer George Merriman, *Commonwealth vs. Brown*, 61.

12. Testimony of the defendant, Mame Brown, *Commonwealth vs. Brown*, 73–74.

13. Ibid, *Commonwealth vs. Brown*, 75–76.

14. Ibid, *Commonwealth vs. Brown*, 77–79. Thomas did not take the stand, though her police statement was read into evidence during her trial. See Testimony of Frank Paul, *Commonwealth vs. Helen Thomas and Mame Brown*, 68–69.

15. In each case witnesses did not notice bruises until Madden reached the hospital, indicating that the fatal injuries could have been sustained from his fall on pavement. See Testimony of Dr. Handiwork and Dr. Awdsworth in *Commonwealth vs. Thomas*, 45.

16. #B4778, #B4779, CRR, 3/3/1909.

17. Ibid., *North American*, 9/13/1908; "Convict Negress of Manslaughter," *North American*, 1/7/1909, SB3.

18. Turn-of-the-century America witnessed the invention of a national rhetoric of white supremacy and domesticity; see Duggan, *Sapphic Slashers*, 13–16, and Laura Wexler,

Tender Violence: Domestic Visions in an Age of U.S. Imperialism (Chapel Hill: University of North Carolina Press, 2000), 30–31.

19. Duggan, *Sapphic Slashers*, 13–16; Wexler, *Tender Violence*, 30–31.

20. Quoted in Wexler, *Tender Violence*, 31.

21. Barnes, *The Repression of Crime*, 253–54; Steinberg, *The Transformation of Criminal Justice*, 230–34.

22. Stephen Kantrowitz, *Bell Tillman and the Reconstruction of White Supremacy* (Chapel Hill: University of North Carolina Press, 2000), 2. Though Kantrowitz is exploring Tillman's use of the farmer trope as both an idea and a constituency, I am using the phrase to discuss the role of the white family in the construction of both white supremacy and domesticity.

23. Because whites felt jeopardized by the increasing social mobility of those groups that were beyond the pale of whiteness, safeguarding mainstream hegemony became a key facet of the new notion of domesticity. Bederman, *Manliness and Civilization*, 11–15; Duggan, *Sapphic Slashers*, 13–16; Sander Gilman, *Difference and Pathology: Stereotypes of Sexuality, Race and Madness* (Ithaca: Cornell University Press, 1985).

24. Cesare Lombroso, *The Female Offender* (1895); Boies, *Prisoners and Paupers*, and Rafter, *Creating Born Criminals*; also see Rothman, *The Discovery of the Asylum*, 84–85; Daryl Michael Scott, *Contempt and Pity: Social Policy and the Image of the Damaged Black Psyche, 1880–1996* (Chapel Hill: University of North Carolina Press, 1997), 1–2.

25. Senator John T. Morgan, "The Race Question in the United States," *Arena*, no. 10 (September 1890): 395–98.

26. Henderson, "Toni Morrison's *Beloved*," 322.

27. Samuel Dennison describes this racial retrogression; see *Scandalize My Name: Black Imagery in American Popular Music* (New York: Garland, 1982), 254, 354.

28. According to M. M. Manring, who explains that the mammy cartoon first appeared on a sack of pancake flour in 1889, the caricature represented the desire as well as the reality of white male control over black and white women; see *A Slave in a Box: The Strange Career of Aunt Jemima* (Charlottesville: University Press of Virginia, 1998), 23; Hartman, *Scenes of Subjection*; Tate, *Domestic Allegories of Political Desire*, 10–11.

29. Manring, *A Slave in a Box*, 23.

30. Kevin Gaines charges that whites used popular culture as a public forum to exorcise their anxieties about blacks and to promote racist initiatives; see *Uplifting the Race*, 67–75.

31. Ibid. Though Eric Lott's work does not explore the full implications of white men's infatuation with black women through the ritual of cross-dressing, his work offers insightful analysis of the homosocial aspects of minstrelsy; see *Love and Theft: Blackface Minstrelsy and the American Working Class* (New York: Oxford University Press, 1993), 27, 53–55, 86, 117, 120–22, 161–68.

32. Dennison, *Scandalize My Name*, 287–89.

33. Giddings, "The Last Taboo," 414–27.

34. "The 'Black Patti,'" PI 11/1892 WDC #5:49. After confronting racism in the entertainment industry, Sissieretta Joyner Jones, "the Black Patti," formed her own company. The Patti Troubadours performed an eclectic mixture of musical styles ranging from opera to ragtime. For more on Jones, see "Jones, Sissieretta Joyner" in *Black Women in America: An Historical Encyclopedia*, vol. A–L, 2nd ed, ed. Darlene Clark Hine, Elsa Barkley Brown, and Rosalyn Terborg-Penn (Bloomington: Indiana University Press, 1994), 654–55; also the Dime Museum flyer highlighting "Colored Minstrels" and "8 Pickaniny Dancers" among the forty entertainers advertised. See "Dockstader's Original Colored Minstrels," MPT, c. 1892, WDC #2:19.

35. MST, TP 12/25/1892, WDC #5:49.

36. "Jaspar's Wooing," TP 2/16/1891; MST, *N.J. Trenton Times*, 11/5/1885, WDC# 9:78; Manring, *A Slave in a Box*, 23–23.

37. Gaines, *Uplifting the Race*, 67–69; Lane, *William Dorsey's Philadelphia*, 6, 14, 33–36.

38. See "A Raving Maniac," PEI, 6/3/1890, WDC #10:86. Other examples of this are "George Smith, a South Carolina negro, was sentenced to six years imprisonment in the Eastern Penitentiary to-day by Judge Johnson for horse-stealing," RC, 9/29/1903, SB2—though according to his intake Smith was a Maryland native, #B2022, CDR, 1903; "Long Term For Negroes," MPT, c. 1904, SB2.

39. Apparently an investigative report, the account published a litany of significant findings about blacks, among them the conclusion that a "darky is yet to be born who would not be willing to subsist for the rest of his lifetime upon an exclusive diet of pork, corn bread, cabbage, buttermilk and watermelon." "The Negro as a Fatalist," EB 5/2/1888, WDC #7:65.

40. Kimmel, *Manhood in America*, 9, 83–89.

41. Duggan, *Saphic Slashers*, 33–35; Walkowitz also exposes how the investigative tactics of W. T. Stead surrounding various sex crimes and scandals translated into higher sales; see *City of Dreadful Delight*, 125–31.

42. This is evident from scanning the papers, but it is also mentioned in Gerald Baldasty, "The Nineteenth-Century Origins of Modern American Journalism," in *Three Hundred Years of the American Newspaper*, ed. John B. Hench (Worcester: American Antiquarian Society, 1991), 407, 415.

43. Allen Steinberg discusses the connection between politics and criminal justice— marking ways that key players in both the criminal justice system and politicians and Democratic and Republican papers supported court officers in their respective parties; see *The Transformation of Criminal Justice*, 92–115. Moreover, a number of members of the Pennsylvania Prison Society were justices, and other members of Philadelphia's older elite maintained strong ties to presses. See Teeters, *They Were In Prison*; Duggan, *Sapphic Slashers*, 37–38.

44. Walkowitz discusses this notion throughout her work, but sums it up concisely when

she explains that a key press mogul sought to "create a single moral majority out of an expanded, heterogeneous public"; see *City of Dreadful Delight*, 130; Karen Halttunen, *Murder Most Foul: The Killer and the American Gothic Imagination* (Cambridge, Mass: Harvard University Press, 1998), 3; and Hall, *Things of Darkness*.

45. Lisa Duggan explains this in her work when she writes, "Located at the intersection of law, which defined the interests and powers of state institutions, and the press, which circulated meanings through nationwide networks, trial stories were especially potent nationalizing narratives"; see *Sapphic Slashers*, 62, 2–4.

46. Ayers, *Vengeance and Justice*, 238–41. Black women's attempts to secure better wages and higher levels of autonomy rattled white citizens. As in many northern cities, in Philadelphia whites rued the increasing presence of black women. For evidence of black women's demographics, see Du Bois, *The Philadelphia Negro*, 66–69.

47. Table 7, chapter 2.

48. I am borrowing Chandra Mohanty's phrase "social indicator"; I am applying it in the sense that late-nineteenth-century presses perpetuated racist dialogues about African Americans by using coded language and symbols. See Chandra Mohanty, ed., "Under Western Eyes," in *Third World Women and the Politics of Feminism*, ed. Ann Russo and Lourdes Torres (Bloomington: Indiana University Press, 1991).

49. The names appeared in print as either Wakefield Gaines or Gains, Mary Hannah Tabbs or Hannah Mary Tabbs; #A3928, CDR, 9/28/1887.

50. "The Mystery Solved," PI, 2/23/1887 (FL). According to the *Times-Philadelphia*, Tabbs was "quite black and of medium height. She has one front tooth missing. She is not a good looking colored woman": "The Woman Found," TP, 2/22/1887 (VP). There is no mention of Tabbs's lacking a front tooth in descriptive intake registers at ESP.

51. TP 2/22/1887. Cornel West charges that researchers must examine how whiteness is a "politically constructed parasitic" on blackness; see "The New Cultural Politics of Difference," 30–32.

52. PI 2/23/1887. The *Ledger*, though rarely characterizing Tabbs as a mulatto, frequently acknowledged the victim's mixed race. Moreover, George Wilson, Tabbs's accomplice, originally described as a mulatto, was upon his arrest also referred to as "colored." See "The Mystery Surrounding the Finding of the Dismembered Body at Eddington Apparently Solved," PL 2/23/1887, SBI; and "The Killing of Wakefield Gaines," PL, 6/1/1887, SBI.

53. "A Crazy Cook," NPG, 11/28/1885 (VP).

54. The caricature was similar to those that Shawn Michelle Smith discusses in her work; see *Photography on the Color Line: W. E. B. Du Bois, Race, and Visual Culture* (Durham: Duke University Press, 2004), 80–86.

55. Southern propaganda primarily identified two types of black women. One who rightly understood her role as a servant and one whose ambitious participation in the labor force and profane attempts at "playing the lady" betrayed her lawlessness. Also,

in Atlanta whites mounted negative campaigns against black washerwomen organizing against racist white employers. See Hunter, "*To 'Joy My Freedom,*" 191, 194–95,
213–18.

56. "Stabbed by a Woman," TP, 2/20/1890.

57. TP, 2/20/1890.

58. The disparity in the level of violence when Smith's race was thought to be black
demonstrates the ways in which white patriarchy in Philadelphia stigmatized black
women. This point resonates with Nancy Hartsock's critique of Foucault; she points
out that dominant white male discourses divide up the world, positioning white males
as central, omnipotent subjects. This logic also constructs "marginal others" with
negative qualities. See Hartsock, "Foucault on Power," 158–62.

59. Similarly, in 1893, the *Ledger*, reporting on a badger crime, never addressed the so-
cial relationship between the two convicted parties, an African-American woman,
Emma Archey, and a white man, Henry Good. See "Trials Before Judge Livingston,"
PL, 11/21/1893, SB1. The records indicate that Archey and Good were well acquainted.
The pair had both served prior sentences at the Lancaster County Prison in addition to their sentences at ESP. See Emma Archey, #A7152, and Henry Good, #A7154,
CDR, 11/21/1893. The *Inquirer* account attaches race and invokes violence, an implied
characteristic of blackness, as the cause of the row, explaining simply that "Pearl's
temper got the best of her." Finally, in a later article, the *Inquirer* amended its details,
reporting that Smith stabbed "Samuel Crippen, colored." See "Probable Murder in
the Slums," PI, 12/7/1890. According to ESP intake and descriptive discharge records,
Smith was a white woman. The *Philadelphia County Prisoners for Trial Docket*, however, listed Smith's race as black, and Crippen's race remains a mystery. See Pearl
Smith, #A5659, CDR, 12/5/1890; DDD, 5/5/1892. Also see November 1, 1890, "B, Pearl
Smith," PTD. The ambiguities about Smith's race suggest that she was a mulatto who
was able to pass for white.

60. "The Sentence Must Stand," MST, c. 1890, SB1; John Riley, #A5953, CDR, 7/16/1891.
My point is that the judge's definition, in accord with the notions of true womanhood, was predicated upon whiteness and white femininity. African-American
women, as a consequence of their very being, could not be easily assimilated, included, or considered as a part of the mainstream definition of womanhood. For a
critical discussion of this, see Brooks-Higginbotham, *Righteous Discontent*, 185–229.

61. PI 2/23/1887; TP 2/22/1887.

62. "Killed by Jealous Woman," TP, 10/25/1884. Also see Jacquelyn Dowd Hall, *Revolt
Against Chivalry: Jessie Daniel Ames and the Women's Campaign Against Lynching* (New
York: Columbia University Press, 1979), xx–xxviii. Sander Gilman explains that the
black female body—or the Hottentot—became the icon and image of the prostitute,
or the sexualized female. Gilman enhances his discussion by examining how the categories were constructed to represent specific qualities. My aim is to point out how

black women's images in Philadelphia's presses were constructed as wild and sexually lascivious. See Gilman, "Black Bodies, White Bodies," in *"Race," Writing, and Difference*, ed. Gates, 233. Other examples of black female violence are "Ella Reed, colored was convicted of assault and battery with intent to kill Henrietta Murray, also colored, whom she stabbed six times with a penknife," MST, C. 7/1895, SBI; Ella Reed, #A8218, CDR, 7/10/1895; MST, MPT, C. 3/1902, SB2; Ella Johnson, #B1342, CDR, 3/31/1902.

63. "Magistrate Smith Blushed," PI, 8/10/1890. In his examination of gay and lesbian subculture in jazz age Harlem, Eric Garber explains how the more illicit aspects of the music and performative arts, though creating a space for black gays and lesbians, also facilitated white spectatorship. In other words, the same sex relationships, song lyrics, and live sexual acts also made black gay life a spectacle—a commodity for white patrons and onlookers. Although Garber focuses on the 1920s, the 1890 piece chronicling an exchange between a black woman and a white judge operates on a similar level. See Garber, "A Spectacle in Color," 318–31.

64. PI 4/23/1885; PI 8/12/1885; PI 8/13/1885; #A2830, CRR, 9/15/1885.

65. "Accused of Murder: Colored woman alleged to have poisoned a colored child," *Lancaster Intelligencer*, Monday, 5/18/1903 (PSL); Bella Beary, #B2010, CRR, 9/26/1903.

66. Although sources are sparse, evidence suggests that independent African-American newspapers also adhered to these negative representations. The black independent press's adherence to biased depictions of black female criminals demonstrates how pervasive the notions of racial reasoning were/are—and that often, as Lubiano points out, "even those individuals who are its objects are not exempt from thinking about the world through its [politically elite] prism." See Lubiano, "Introduction," *The House that Race Built*, vii.

67. "Mrs. Stella Weldon Brutally Murdered by Miss Emily Lee," SD 3/25/1905; Emily Lee, #B3005, CRR, 10/25/1905.

68. "Charge of Murder Against Mother," PL, 12/29/1885, SBI. Gaskin was not sent to ESP, but instead to the state asylum in Norristown; see Annie Gaskin, PTD, 12/29/1885. An article on Jane Potter, a white woman accused of infanticide in 1891, sketched her as a pitiable figure who was "unmarried . . . her mother had been dead for some time, and . . . she, being the oldest child, took care of her father's house and three younger children." The social stigma attached to unwed motherhood disappears behind the young woman's tragic circumstances. See "Young Girl Sentenced for Infanticide Two Years," MPT, 9/24/1891, SBI.

69. PI 8/13/1885. Depictions of Derry's clothes are also significant because in the late nineteenth century women's clothes were regarded as an indication of social status and morality. Clothes were designed to complement but also to cover and restrict the movement of women's breasts, hips, etc. See Lee Hall, *Common Threads: A Parade of American Clothing* (Boston: Bulfich Press Book, 1992).

70. PI 8/12/1885.

71. Following Taggart's sentencing, the judge bemoaned the proceedings, as "it represented in no sense his conception of her guilt or any intention to take the life of her son, but that it should be impressed on the public what a serious matter it was to endanger or take the life of another." "The Penalty for Her Angry Act," PI, 4/25/1893; Mary Taggart, #A6769, CDR and CRR, 1/20/1893. Such sentiments starkly contrasted with the judge's remarks to Martha Davis, an African-American woman convicted of attempting to poison her employers, who, according to the judge, "deserve[d] no mercy." "A Family Poisoned," PI, 11/21/1890, SBI; Martha Davis in PTD, Index, 11/1/1890.

72. "Jennie Rothermel Gets Five Years," MPT, c. 1899, SBI; Jennie Rothimel, #A9838, CDR, 8/4/1898.

73. Similarly, when Mrs. Heffner, a white female and convicted professional abortionist, was arrested again after serving five years at ESP for setting up an illegal abortion clinic, press coverage was minimally disparaging. Heffner, or Hoeffner, was referred to as a "widow" with a wealthy clientele. See *North American*, c. 1890, SBI; Maria Heffner or Hoeffner, #A2737, CDR, 7/3/1885; PI 10/29/1905 (SB2).

74. "Follow Her in Death," MPT, c. 1902, SB2; Katherine Ness, #B1250, CDR, CRR, 1/11/1902; "Josephine Smith, Alias Mallison, Sentenced to 12 years," PI, 12/12/1892; Josephine Smith, #6583, CDR, 12/19/1892.

75. Papers documented cases of cross-dressing women who performed men's work and even attempted to marry other women. The instances of female love in press accounts were filtered through a narrative lens that pitted "mannish-women" as forever outmatched when they competed with normal white men for female affection. In this narrative, female sexual-inverts typically resorted to violence when their affections were cast aside—their female lovers choosing instead to be with white men. See Duggan, *Sapphic Slashers*, "Introduction."

76. "Shot Down Woman Who Spurned Her," PL, c. 1901, SB2; Alice Hitchings or Hutchings, #B1016, CDR, CRR, 6/14/1901; Duggan, *Sapphic Slashers*, 51–60.

77. "Five Years for Mrs. Hitchings," MPT, c. 1901, SB2.

78. Even though in Hutchings's case the doctors are being used to garner sympathy for her—by insisting that her attraction to women is a mental disorder—they were eroding white female sexual autonomy. Jacquelyn Zita explains, linking sexual deviance to pathologies, whether mental or physical, required a new authority—the modern medical expert—that saw the body as a thing controlling and defining the stricken homosexual; see Zita, *Body Talk: Philosophical Reflections on Sex and Gender* (New York: Columbia University Press, 1998), 88.

79. The documenting of black male violence relied upon gratuitous tales of "drunken" fighting over "craps" games. A 1902 article, exaggerating the destructive nature of African-American masculinity, implied a deficit of morality by revealing that the

altercation "over a game of craps" occurred on Christmas Day; see "Too Free with Their Knives," MPT, c. 1902, SB2; #B1223, CDR, 1902. Don Belton, ed., "Introduction," in *Speak My Name: Black Men on Masculinity and the American Dream* (Boston: Beacon Press, 1995), 2; also see Robert Staples, *Black Masculinity: The Black Man's Role in American Society* (San Francisco: Black Scholar Press, 1982). Newspapers blended depictions of black men as foolish and inferior, but also as "deliberate and cold-blooded" in their offending. For example, see "Harris Shoots Three Men," PI, 6/10/1890; MST, MPT c. 1901, SBI.

80. "Lynched at Midnight," TP, 3/6/1886; "LYNCH HIM! THE CRY," RC, 9/29/1903, SB2; Frank Jackson, #B2039, CRR, 10/16/1903; William Dorsey would document that no efforts were undertaken to discover Mingo Jack's murderers. See Lane, *William Dorsey's Philadelphia*, 46.

81. Though her work examined the alleged rape of white women by black men, Jacquelyn Dowd Hall points out that rape and rumors of rape operated as a type of acceptable popular pornography in the South; see *Revolt Against Chivalry*, xxvii.

82. "Soon Identified: William Lingear Declared by Witnesses to Have Assaulted Mrs. Shaw," MPT, c. 1901, SB2; William Linyear, #B123, CDR, 4/6/1899; "Five Years for a Footpad: Witnessed Clashed, But Jury Found Linyear Guilty," MPT, c. 1901, SBI.

83. Ibid, *Record*, 29 September 1903.

84. "Ready to Kill Their Victim," TP 2/27/1900; George Holmond sentenced to eighteen years, James Cummings sentenced to eleven years; #B526 and #B527, CDR, 2/29/1900.

85. "Extreme Penalty for Negro," MPT, c. 1906, SB2; #B3248, CRR, 1906.

86. Ibid.

87. The *Record*, at the turn of the century, published a story titled "Black Fiends in Prison." It alleged that the two black men with "intentions of assaulting Miss Cooper," a white woman, "were foiled in their terrible design." The paper reported that Cooper "heroically" escaped through her bedroom window. See "Woman Fought Negro Robber in Cemetery," MPT, c. 1904, SB2; Henry Jenkins, #B2162, CRR, 1904; "Women's Battle for Life," RC, 4/1/1902, SB2; Thomas Gibbs, #B1395, CRR, 4/29/1902.

88. "Tried to Kill for a Quarter: A Murderous Negro Fatally Stabbed Prominent Montgomery Country Farmer," MPT, 1899, SBI. Though news accounts printed his first name as Charles, in prison registers it is listed as Henry. See Henry Fortune, #B326, CDR, 10/5/1899.

89. "Hard Fight for His Life," RC, 7/20/1900, SBI; Charles Truxton or Truxson, #B703, CRR, 9/18/1900. Lynne Segal describes how blackness is scripted as the color of dirty secrets about sex—notions relentlessly represented in images of black men as well as black women; see Segal, *Slow Motion: Changing Masculinities, Changing Men* (New Brunswick: Rutgers University Press, 1990). Also see Michael Eric Dyson, *Reflecting Black: African American Cultural Criticism* (Minneapolis: University of Minnesota

Press, 1993), and John Remu, "Racism, Black Masculinity and the Politics of Space," and Michael Kimmel, "Beyond Sex and Gender: Masculinity, Homosexuality and Social Theory," in *Men, Masculinities and Social Theory*, ed. Jeff Hearn and David Morgan (London: Unwin Hyman, 1990).

90. Roediger, *The Wages of Whiteness*, 30.

91. Prison records at ESP overwhelmingly characterized all inmates, white and black, as possessing dark or ruddy complexions. Bertillon roll books measured the sizes of inmates' craniums, and intake registers listed information about inmates' marital statuses, educational levels, economic statuses, and alcohol intake. See BHB, 1895–1937.

92. William H. Tucker, *The Science and Politics of Racial Research* (Urbana: University of Illinois Press, 1994), 34.

93. "Widow Colefish Sent to Prison," PI, 10/21/1893; Discharged 12/1/1893; PTD, 10/10/1893.

94. "Judge Denounces Assailant of Girl," MPT, 1902, SB2; Balton Bokvick, #B1566, CRR, 9/26/1902; "Scored a Killing Immigrant" RC, 9/14/1903, SB2; Jose Dimario, #B1971, CRR, 9/14/1903; "Second Degree, the Verdict," MPT, c. 1901, SB2; John Kirsinjko, #B929, CDR, 4/15/1901.

95. "Time for Shooting Americans Is Past," MPT, 1/4/1900, SB2; Von Govonda, #B470, CDR, 1/4/1900.

96. "Victim of the Slasher Appears," TP, 12/7/1899. I discuss Lombroso in detail in chapter 5.

97. Ibid.

98. "Spiedle Held Without Bail," MPT, c. 1908, SB2; #B4075, CRR, 1908; "Girl Tells of Pathetic Tragedy in Her Lowly Life," MPT, 1900, SB1; William Jimie, #B602, CDR, 5/15/1900. Notions of biological determinism described men as possessing more savage passions. Though these theories stressed control, shifts in society lessened these expectations. I am arguing that these changes released men/masculinity from certain morals and behavioral constraints—constraints often placed upon and upheld by women.

99. "Solar Plexus Blow Ends a Man's Life," MPT, c. 1901, SB2; Thomas B. McGrath, #B1156, CDR, 10/25/1901.

100. However, despite exclusion from whiteness for crimes of extreme violence, white male criminals retained the possibility of redemption and a modicum of dignity, as reports included the defendants' histories of decency and their calm acceptance of verdicts. In a few rape cases, though articles railed against the white perpetrators, the accounts nonetheless included information from family or friends testifying that an alleged assailant's "general reputation and character for chastity were good." See "The Sentence Must Stand," MPT, c. 1890, SB1. The story also noted that "the right of the children and girls of this great city should be protected." Also see "M'Manus Sentenced," PL, c. 1890, SB1. In the case of Winan Hull, a white man convicted of murder

in the second degree, press characterizations avoided portrayals of him as ruthlessly lacking remorse but simply reported that he "received the verdict calmly." See "Hull Found Guilty Murder 2d Degree," PI, 10/15/c. 1901, SBI; Winan Hull, #B1154, CDR, 10/21/1901.

101. Chapter 1 explores this history.

102. "The Sentence Must Stand," MPT, c. 1890, SBI.

103. African-American women on average received longer sentences: white women received, on average, prison sentences of 8.5 months, and black women received sentences averaging 14.1 months. Black men also received slightly longer sentences, 14.8 months on average, than white men, who averaged 12.4. Although Du Bois attributed sentencing discrepancies to social positions and whites' connections "in procuring . . . pardons or lighter sentences," he could not ignore the possibility that "there is apt to be a certain presumption of guilt when a Negro is accused, on the part of the police, public and judges." See Du Bois, *The Philadelphia Negro*, 249; and Lane, *Roots of Violence*, 88.

104. In a number of news reports, the words and roles of judges conveyed specific mainstream values and political agendas. For example, in a small piece covering the sentencing of a black male rapist, in response to the light sentence handed down, accounts quoted the judge as explaining, "Only the color and ignorance of the convicted man saved him from extreme penalty of the law." Throughout the limited news coverage of crimes against black women, the white judges, investigators, and other officials operated as the voices and symbols for righteous whiteness. The article concluded, "The judge's leniency does not support the theory that justice is more harsh to the negro than to the white man," MPT, SB2.

105. "A Murder in St. Mary Street," PL, 4/24/1886, SBI.

106. PL 4/24/1886, SBI.

107. Ibid.

108. PL 4/10/1887, SBI.

109. PL 4/19/1887, SBI.

110. "Admits Killing Woman: Negro Youth Leaves it to Court to Fix Degree of Crime," RC, 12/15/1908, SB2; Robert Halestock, #4620, CRR, 1908.

111. Cesaire, *Discourse on Colonialism*, 20–25.

112. "Negro Kills Woman, Then Shoots Self," PI, 1/20/1909; "Kills Woman; Tries to Die, But Will Live," *North American*, 1/20/1909, SB2; "Declares Slayer Feigned Insanity," *North American*, 4/3/1909, SB2; "Negro on Trial for Murder," RC, 4/2/1909, SB2; "20 Years for Murder," *Ledger*, 4/3/1909, SB3.

113. bell hooks discusses these caricatures; see *Ain't I a Woman?*, 81–85.

114. Walkowitz, *City of Dreadful Delight*, 4–5.

5. Deviant by Design

1. Because this case uses confidential patient files the prisoner's name has been changed and all information that might reveal her true identity has been omitted; WJ, vol. 6.

2. For an example of her work, see Dorothea Dix, *An Address by a Recent Female Visiter* [sic] *to the Prisoners in the Eastern State Penitentiary* (Philadelphia: Joseph and William Kite, 1844), 6–8 (LCP). Also Lyn Gamwell and Nancy Tomes, *Madness in America: Cultural and Medical Perceptions of Mental Illness Before 1914* (Ithaca: Cornell University Press, 1995), 55–56; Nancy Tomes, *The Art of Asylum-Keeping: Thomas Story Kirkbride and the Origins of American Psychiatry* (Philadelphia: University of Pennsylvania Press, 1994).

3. WJ, vol. 6.

4. PIA, Admissions Register, Female Patients, Indexed, #2777.

5. WJ, vol. 7; WJ, vol. 8.

6. Dodge, *"Whores and Thieves of the Worst Kind,"* 42, 68–70.

7. Boies, *The Science of Penology*, 14; Cole, *Suspect Identities*, 3; Dodge, *"Whores and Thieves of the Worst Kind,"* 47.

8. Teeters and Shearer, *The Prison at Philadelphia, Cherry Hill*, 83–85.

9. Owen Lewis, *The Development of American Prisons and Prison Customs, 1776–1845* (New York: Prison Society of New York, 1922), 29; *Second Annual Report of the Board of Commissioners of Public Charities of the State of Pennsylvania; to which is appended the Report of the General Agent and Secretary, Transmitted to the Legislature, January 4, 1872* (Harrisburg: B. Singerly, State Printer, 1873), xxvii (PHMC); Roberts Vaux, *Notices of the Original, and Successive Efforts to Improve the Discipline of the Prison at Philadelphia, and to Reform the Criminal Code of Pennsylvania: With A Few Observations on the Penitentiary System* (Philadelphia: Kimber and Sharpless, 1826), 58–60 (LCP).

10. Rothman, *The Discovery of the Asylum*, 78, 79–83.

11. Teeters and Shearer, *The Prison at Philadelphia, Cherry Hill*, 13; Teeters, *They Were in Prison*, xi. Michael Hindus demonstrates that northern states had an organized penal system largely because of a rigid Puritan background; the cultural hegemony which was sufficient for its northern natives was inadequate to control the increasing numbers of immigrants and transient workers. While I agree with Hindus's analysis that the development of the more secure forms of penal justice was designed to reinforce a white, Protestant cultural hegemony, I believe that the increase in the number of prisons was also about confining the growing numbers of freed blacks after Emancipation. See Hindus, *Prison and Plantation*, xxvii; Foucault, *Discipline and Punishment*, 215.

12. Teeters and Shearer, *The Prison at Philadelphia, Cherry Hill*, 17–20.

13. *The Pennsylvania System of Separate Confinement Explained and Defended* (Philadelphia: J. B. Chandler Printer, 1867), 3–4, 68.

14. Rothman, *The Discovery of the Asylum*, 82–83.

15. The Prison Society and a number of penal reformers believed that silence, strict separation of inmates, hard labor, and prayer would rehabilitate criminals and ultimately save their souls. See Teeters, xi; and, *The Pennsylvania System of Separate Confinement Explained and Defended*, 3–4.

16. Foucault, *Discipline and Punish*, 200–215.

17. A quote from Richard Vaux, a warden at ESP, at the National Prison Conference in July, 1888. See, *The 30th Anniversary Commemorative History: The Bureau of Correction and its Institutions*, by Judith R. Smith, Pennsylvania Bureau of Correction, printed at SCI-Huntingdon, Second Printing: August, 1983.

18. *The Eastern State Penitentiary of Pennsylvania: An Investigation by Authority of the Legislature, Book No I: Testimony of First Day, Thursday, May 13th, 1897* (hereafter ESP *Investigation*), 58.

19. Teeters, *The Prison at Cherry Hill*, 137.

20. Lewis, *Development of American Prisons*, 124.

21. ESP *Investigation*, bk. 1, 61; Eugenia C. Lekkerkerker, *Reformatories for Women in the United States* (Groningen: J. B. Wolters, 1931), 312. Also, the records do not list women's prison attire in detail; this description is based on pictures of ESP female inmates.

22. ESP *Investigation*, bk. 1, 12.

23. Ibid., bk. 1., 91; WJ, vol. 9, 3/1904.

24. Teeters and Shearer, *The Prison at Philadelphia, Cherry Hill*, 98–99.

25. *Second Annual Report of the Board of Commissioners of Public Charities*, xxvii.

26. Warden's Testimony, ESP *Investigation*, bk. 1; *Twenty-First Annual Report of the Board of Commissioners of Public Charities*, 239.

27. Judith R. Smith, 21.

28. WJ, vol. 4, 3/12/1883.

29. Ibid.

30. Teeters and Shearer, *The Prison at Philadelphia, Cherry Hill*, 68.

31. Ibid., 93–112, 113–32; Charles Dickens denounced the institution in his travel diary, *American Notes for General Circulation* (Philadelphia: Lea and Blanchard, 1842), (LCP).

32. Rothman, *The Discovery of the Asylum*, 237–52; Rafter, *Creating Born Criminals*, 123–24; Boies, *Prisoners and Paupers*, 42–64, 65–87, 170–203, and *The Science of Penology*; this shift mirrors those taking place in psychiatric hospitals as well—rather than accept the failure of treatments or confront issues plaguing the institutions, they "inculcated a taste for the fashionable theory of eugenics." See Ian Robert Dowbiggin, *Keeping America Sane: Psychiatry and Eugenics in the United States and Canada 1880–1940* (Ithaca: Cornell University Press, 1997), 21–22.

33. Rafter, *Creating Born Criminals*, 57, 86–89.

34. Charles Darwin, *The Descent of Man and Selection in Relation to Sex* (London: J. Murray, 1871) (VP); Frances Alice Kellor, "Criminal Anthropology in Its Relation to Criminal Jurisprudence," in *American Journal of Sociology* 4, no. 4 (January 1899): 515–27 at 516–18. Lombroso lists four basic categories: born criminals, occasional criminals, hysterical (insane) criminals, and criminals who commit crimes of passion; see Lombroso and Ferrero, *The Female Offender*, chaps. 12–15.

35. Cole, *Suspect Identities*, 23–24; Rafter, *Creating Born Criminals*, 86–89.

36. I discuss this in chapter 4.

37. Rafter, *Creating Born Criminals*, 36–38.

38. Lane, *William Dorsey's Philadelphia*, 34.

39. Lombroso and Ferrero, *The Female Offender*, 111–13.

40. See Carby, "Policing the Black Woman's Body," 738–55.

41. Kellor, "Southern Colored Girls in the North," 585 (SCH); *Annual Report of the National League for the Protection of Colored Women* (New York, 1910), 3–5 (SCH); Dodge, *"Whores and Thieves of the Worst Kind,"* 47.

42. Rafter, *Creating Born Criminals*, 86–89, 119.

43. Boies, *Prisoners and Paupers*, 73; Rafter, *Creating Born Criminals*, 118–19.

44. R. L. Dugdale, *"The Jukes": A Study in Crime, Pauperism, Disease and Heredity, also Further Studies of Criminals* (New York: G. P. Putnam's Sons, 1877), v (LCP).

45. Rafter, *Creating Born Criminals*, 57, 69–84.

46. I am borrowing and building upon JoAnne Brown's critique of the theories; see *The Definition of a Profession* (Princeton: Princeton University Press, 1992), 12–13; Rafter, *Creating Born Criminals*, 88.

47. Marouf Arif Hasain, Jr., *The Rhetoric of Eugenics in Anglo-American Thought* (Athens: University of Georgia Press, 1996), 4.

48. Frances Alice Kellor, "Criminal Anthropology in Its Relation to Criminal Jurisprudence. II," in *American Journal of Sociology* 4, no. 5 (March 1899): 630–48 at 643–44.

49. For examples of Wells-Barnett's lynching studies, see Wells-Barnett, *Southern Horrors and Other Writings*.

50. William Freeman was called to be a juror in a case against a black woman accused of the murder of a white man. See *Commonwealth vs. Helen Thomas and Mame Brown, in the Court of Quarter Sessions and Oyer and Terminer of Philadelphia County, October Sessions, 1908, no. 375, January 4, 1908*, v–7. Freeman was not selected to serve, but the personal opinion he disclosed was shared by everyday citizens, police, prison administrators, and criminologists alike.

51. Cole, *Suspect Identities*, 35–49.

52. Eastern's CDR and CRR are replete with examples of this, especially between 1880 and 1910; Matthew Frye Jacobson, *Whiteness of a Different Color: European Immigrants and the Alchemy of Race* (Cambridge, Mass: Harvard University Press, 1998), 142–46.

53. I am modifying Foucault's argument that in repressing and admonishing certain be-

haviors reformers ultimately canonized the acts and brought them into high relief. See Michel Foucault, *Madness and Civilization: A History of Insanity in the Age of Reason*, trans. Richard Howard (New York: Vintage Books, 1988), 82–83; also see Foucault, *The Order of Things: An Archaeology of the Human Sciences* (New York: Vintage Books, 1994).

54. *Penns. Laws* (1889), no. 109 (PHMC).

55. The *Bertillon Hand Books* at Eastern State Penitentiary span 1895 to 1937; *Department of Public Safety, Bureau of Police—Detective Service, Register of Description of Criminals, 1892–1897, 1902–1907* (PCA).

56. Cole, *Suspect Identities*, 19–22.

57. Shawn Michelle Smith, *American Archives: Gender, Race, and Class in Visual Culture* (Princeton: Princeton University Press, 1999), 68–93.

58. Ibid., 68–93.

59. *Rogues Gallery Books*, 4 vols., c. 1880–1920 (PCA); Sander Gilman's critique of the ways in which photography framed insanity helped shape my thinking in this area; see *Seeing the Insane* (Lincoln: University of Nebraska Press, 1982), 164, 184–90; the work of Deborah Willis and Carla Williams—particularly their descriptions of the ways photographers posed black female bodies—also sharpened my thinking about the false objectivity of images: see Willis and Williams, *The Black Female Body*, 21–24, 117–23; Shawn Michelle Smith makes a similar point in exploring Du Bois's own "mug shots" of blacks at the turn of the century: see *Photography on the Color Line*, 41–47.

60. Shawn Michelle Smith also notes how the *Rogues Gallery Books* came to highlight the boundaries of middle-class identities; see *American Archives*, 68–71.

61. Teeters and Shearer, *The Prison at Philadelphia, Cherry Hill*, 89–90.

62. Charles Raymond, a forty-two-year-old white man, went to ESP for embezzlement in 1895; see CDR, 1895.

63. Appendix, table 11.

64. Appendix, table 12.

65. Appendix, table 9.

66. Appendix, table 13.

67. *ESP Investigation*, bk. 1, 63, 58–60.

68. Ibid., 63, 86.

69. Overseers used inmates as "runners" to help with tasks; see WJ, vol. 4, 3/9/1883; JW, vol. 5, 1/29/1887; WJ, vol. 9, 1/9/1906.

70. Lewis, *Development of American Prisons*, 125.

71. WJ, vol. 4, 5/20/1882, 6/15/1882, 6/20/1882, 7/3/1885, 8/10/1885.

72. WJ, vol. 4., 10/2/1885; Cornelia Crapper, #A2125, CDR, 5/2/1884.

73. WJ, vol. 4., 10/2/1885.

74. WJ, vol. 5, 3/18/1888; Laura Williams, #A3768, CDR, 5/16/1887; WJ, vol. 7, 3/21/1898.

75. Lewis, *Development of American Prisons*, 240. The high mortality rate appears to have

been a historic trend: in the 1830s blacks died at almost four times the rate of whites; see *8th Annual Report of the Board of Inspectors of the State Penitentiary for the Eastern District of Pennsylvania, 1837* (Philadelphia, 1838), 12; *9th Annual Report of the Inspectors of the State Penitentiary for the Eastern District of Pennsylvania, 1838* (Philadelphia, 1839), 13.

76. WJ, vol. 9, 10/7/1905; Irene Archey, #B2983, CRR, 10/3/1905.

77. This theme permeated the 1897 investigation; see *ESP Investigation, 1897*; Harry Elmer Barnes provides a detailed discussion of the interwoven development of punishing criminals and treating prisoners who went mad or used insanity as a part of their defense; see *The Evolution of Penology*, 341–44.

78. *Twenty-First Annual Report of the Board of Commissioners of Public Charities of the Commonwealth of Pennsylvania for 1890; also the Report of the General Agent and Secretary Statistics, and the Report of the Committee on Lunacy* (Harrisburg: Edwin K. Meyers, State Printer, 1891), 231.

79. *ESP Investigation*, bk. 1, 143. Teeters and Shearer, *The Prison at Philadelphia, Cherry Hill*, 149.

80. Anne Butler asserts that the penitentiary served as one more societal location where black women "found that race propelled a wide spectrum of policies reinforcing social, economic, and political control over minority groups"; see *Gendered Justice in the American West*, 93; in other cities black women's exclusion from female reformatories as opposed to custodial institutions further highlights the racist double standard in the prison system; see Rafter, *Partial Justice*, 131–46.

81. WJ, vol. 6, 10/29/1891; WJ, vol. 5, 8/8/1888, 10/8/1888.

82. WJ, vol. 4, 6/2/1883.

83. WJ, vol. 4, 1/20/1883.

84. WJ, vol. 4, 4/5/1884; Mary Ann Sells, #A2070, CDR, 1884; WJ, vol. 5, 10/28/1886; Anne Cleary, #A3490, CDR, 1886; WJ, vol. 5, 9/26/1887.

85. WJ, vol. 7, 4/24/1893; Mary Taggart, #A6769, CDR, 1893.

86. WJ, vol. 6, 6/3/1889.

87. WJ, vol. 4, 9/14/1885; WJ, vol. 5, 3/21/1886.

88. WJ, vol. 7, 5/27/1893; Josephine Smith, alias Mallison, #A6583, CDR, 1893; WJ, vol. 4, 4/24/1884.

89. I believe Cassidy was aiming for "superfluities." See WJ, vol. 4, 3/3/1885; Sarah Scott, #A2565, CDR, 3/3/1885.

90. *ESP Investigation*, bk. 1, 41; PIA, Admissions Register, 1852–1929, Female Patients, Indexed, # 4052. Because this example uses confidential patient information, the prisoner's name has been changed and the prisoner's identification numbers have been omitted.

91. PIA, Medical Case Book, Female Departments, 1902–15, vol. xv, indexed, 140.

92. *ESP Investigation*, bk. 1, 41.

93. WJ.

94. *The Mamie Papers*, ed. Ruth Rosen and Sue Davidson (New York: Feminist Press, 1977), 193; Rafter, *Partial Justice*, 9, 19.

95. Rafter, *Partial Justice*, 9, 19.

96. Teeters and Shearer, *The Prison at Philadelphia, Cherry Hill*, 101.

97. WJ, vol. 4, 11/8/1885.

98. *ESP Investigation*, bk. 1, 5/13/1897.

99. WJ, vol. 4, 7/11/1885.

100. WJ, vol. 8, 7/5/1898; WJ, vol. 9, 4/15/1902; 8/11/1909.

101. Jacquelyn Zita explains that homophobia is really a "border crisis" on the part of heterosexuals; see *Body Talk*, 39. In their investigation of sexuality, D'Emilio and Freedman noted that the period's expanding sexuality frightened and undermined traditional white middle-class morality: see *Intimate Matters*, 172–73. Also Domna C. Stanton describes sexual identities as being fluid and, though capable of being singular, always possessing an ability to expand or contract: see "Introduction," *Discourses of Sexuality*, 7–8. I am building on her ideas as well as on those of the other authors cited to suggest that the prison administrators were threatened, repulsed, and also excited by the more transgressive forms of sexuality demonstrated by the inmates at ESP.

102. Foucault explains how power is not absolute and that it can be wielded by and through those who are subjected. I am building on this notion and arguing that prisoners exerted their own power by provoking criminal behavior from their jailers—in their efforts to repress the prisoners the overseers often resorted to unofficial or illegal tactics. See Foucault, *Discipline and Punish*, "The Body of the Condemned."

103. WJ, vol. 5, 3/8/1888; John O'Donnell, #A4221, CDR, 1890.

104. Cassidy's actions also reflect a shift from characterizing homosexuality as a sin to regarding it as a criminal, but also a mental/behavorial, problem. Though George Chauncey, Jr. calls the role of science into question when accounting for such a shift, he does discuss the transformation; see "From Sexual Inversion to Homosexuality," 87–89; he also explores the utility of the scientific rhetoric: see 103–08.

105. WJ, vol. 9, 8/22/1903; Solomon Reed, #B951, CRR, 1901.

106. WJ, vol. 6, 2/11/1890, 9/20/1890; Henry Compton, #A5226, CDR, 1890.

107. WJ, vol. 5, 2/27/1888.

108. WJ, vol. 9, 3/4/1902.

109. WJ, vol. 9, 2/3/1902. Cassidy's behavior may also reflect the double standard in discussions of same-sex "aberration"; women who did not conform to proper sex and gender roles were regarded as "hypersexual" and pathological; however, sodomy among men was regarded as vastly more taboo. Estelle B. Freedman notes that though a 1915 sexologist discussed female abnormality, for male sexual deviance he suggested readers "should leave the unpleasant subject alone." See Estelle B. Freedman, " 'Uncontrolled Desires': The Response to the Sexual Psychopath, 1920–1960," in *Passion and Power*, ed. Peiss and Simmons, 202.

110. Teeters and Shearer, *The Prison at Philadelphia, Cherry Hill*, 86.

111. Butler, *Gendered Justice in the American West*, 34; Dodge, *"Whores and Thieves of the Worst Kind,"* 51.

Conclusion

1. Chapter 1; Holt, *The Problem of Race*, 8, 21–22, 27–28.

2. I discuss this in chapter 1.

3. Darlene Clark Hine and Kathleen Thompson, *A Shining Thread of Hope: The History of Black Women in America* (New York: Broadway Books, 1998); White, "The Cost of Club Work," and *Too Heavy a Load*.

4. Boies, *Prisoners and Paupers*, 42–64, 65–87, 170–203; Kellor, "Criminal Anthropology in Its Relation to Criminal Jurisprudence. II," 643–44.

5. *The Trial of Alice Clifton* (LCP).

6. Smith, *Photography on the Color Line; A Small Nation of People: W. E. B. Du Bois and African American Portraits of Progress*, Library of Congress, with Essays by David Levering Lewis and Deborah Willis (New York: Amistad, 2003), 30–34; Mitchell, *Righteous Propagation*.

7. See University Archives and Records Center, University of Pennsylvania, UPT 50 A 374S, Saddie Tanner Mossell Alexander, Record Group, 1817, 1858–1985.

8. Marc Stein, *City of Sisterly and Brotherly Loves: Lesbian and Gay Philadelphia, 1945–1972* (Philadelphia: Temple University Press, 2004), 17.

9. For works that discuss these shifting social dynamics, see Genna Rae McNeil, *Charles Hamilton House and the Struggle for Civil Rights* (Philadelphia: University of Pennsylvania Press, 1983); Joanne Meyerowitz, ed., *Not June Cleaver: Women and Gender in Postwar America, 1945–1960* (Philadelphia: Temple University Press, 1994); Martin B. Duberman, *Stonewall* (New York: Plume, 1994).

10. This section relies on Ron Avery's work on infamous crimes in Philadelphia; see Avery, *City of Brotherly Mayhem: Philadelphia Crimes and Criminals* (Philadelphia: Otis Books, 1997), 75–79, 81–86; for Sykes, see EB 12/8/1944, 12/14/1944, 1/29/1945, 2/1/1945, 3/12/1945, 3/13/1945, 3/15/1945, 10/14/1946; for Levin, see EB 1/11/1948, 1/12/1949, 1/13/1949, 1/29/1949, 3/17/1949 — also see Stein, *City of Sisterly and Brotherly Loves*, 116–19.

11. Avery, *City of Brotherly Mayhem*, 75–79, 80–82; Raymond Pace Alexander Record Group, 1880–1975, Alexander Family Papers, 1817–1985, UPT 50 A374R, University Archives and Records Center, University of Pennsylvania — Scrapbook, 1948 — Corrine Sykes Case (VP).

12. Avery, *City of Brotherly Mayhem*, 75–79, 81–86.

13. Chauncey, *Gay New York*, 359–60; Freedman, " 'Uncontrolled Desires,' " 199–225.

14. EB 3/17/1949.

15. Ibid.

16. Ibid.

17. EB 12/14/1944.

18. Savage, *Broadcasting Freedom*, 2–3, 21; Thomas J. Sugrue, *The Origins of the Urban Crisis: Race and Inequality in Postwar Detroit*, (Princeton: Princeton University Press, 1996), 8–10.

19. "Corrine Sykes Remembered," on *All Things Considered*, April 3, 1988. NPR's Vertamae Grosvenor discussed the case and its impact on the North Philadelphia neighborhood where she grew up—specifically, she talks about black domestics' responses to the case and also the treatment they received as a result of the case.

20. Davis, *Women, Race and Class*; Jones, *Labor of Love, Labor of Sorrow*.

21. Adams, Bartelt, Elesh, Goldstein, Kleniewski, and Yancy, *Philadelphia*, 8–11, table 1.1.

22. Of the thirty women to receive the death penalty in the United States between 1900 and 1950, twelve were African American; two were listed as "other." See M. Watt Espy and John Ortiz Smylka, "Executions in the U.S. 1608–1987: The Espy File" (Inter-University Consortium for Political and Social Research, 1994).

23. Dodge, *"Whores and Thieves of the Worst Kind,"* 123–24; Rafter, *Partial Justice*, 154–55; Butler, *Gendered Justice*, 91–93.

24. U.S. Department of Justice, Office of Justice Programs, Bureau of Justice Statistics, *Women Offenders*, revised 10/03, NCJ 175688, 7.

25. Patrick-Stamp, "Numbers That Are Not New," 95–128; Rowe, "Women's Crime and Criminal Administration in Pennsylvania," 109; *Pennsylvania Department of Corrections: Female Offenders* (Report published by the Pennsylvania Department of Corrections, February 2003), 1. With respect to the parenthetical section, I am referring to the war on drugs and the mandatory sentencing laws that have resulted.

26. In 1999, the United States Bureau of Justice Statistics published data showing that nearly six of every ten women in state prisons experienced physical or sexual abuse in their past; see *Pennsylvania Department of Corrections*. In her contemporary research on battered black women and crime, Beth Richie found that early childhood victimization and exposure to violence also played a significant factor in black women's crimes and their subsequent incarceration. See chapter 3, "Gender-Identity Development," in Richie, *Compelled to Crime*, esp. 46–47.

27. This essay not only discusses the way in which black women's images were used in the media—particularly how caricatures of black "Welfare Queens" were deployed during debates over welfare spending—but also contains a superb analysis of how images of black women are used as foils for whiteness and masculinity. See Lubiano, "Black Ladies, Welfare Queens, and State Minstrels."

28. I discuss this at some length in the introduction—but here I am referring to the legacy of black scholarship that was as much about black empowerment as it was about documenting the lives and culture of people.

29. My work moves away from the politics of respectability that often operate in

African-American history and Black Studies. For a discussion of respectability, see Brooks-Higginbotham, *Righteous Discontent*, 186–87, 193; Gaines, *Uplifting the Race*, 5; Kali N. Gross, "Examining the Politics of Respectability in African American Studies," *University of Pennsylvania Almanac* 43, no. 28 (April 1, 1997): 15–16.

30. Black women are the fastest growing prison population; in addition, disproportionate numbers of black women and children live below the poverty line. Black women are also suffering from some the highest rates of infection for HIV/AIDS; see Center for Disease Control and Prevention, "HIV/AIDS among African Americans" (February 2005); Phill Wilson, "In the Fight of Our Lives: Notes on the AIDS Crisis in the Black Community"; and Julianne Malveaux, "Still at the Periphery: The Economic Status of African Americans," in *Race and Resistance: African Americans in the 21st Century*, ed. Herb Boyd (Cambridge, Mass: South End Press, 2002). I list these things not to paint black women as victims but rather to call attention to the very real social issues plaguing black women—and to argue that these conditions are related to black women's criminal offending.

31. Discrimination in policing, arrests, convictions, and sentencing remains systemic and largely unabated, and alternatives to prison are woefully inadequate and underfunded. Some works that explore these issues are Rudolph Alexander, Jr., and Jacquelyn Gyamerah, "Differential Punishing of African Americans and Whites Who Possess Drugs: A Just Policy or a Continuation of the Past?," *Journal of Black Studies* 28 (September 1997): 97–111; A. V. Alfieri, "Prosecuting Race," *Duke Law Journal* 48 (April 1999): 1157–1264; R. L. Austin and M. D. Allen, "Racial Disparity in Arrest Rates as an Explanation of Racial Disparity in Commitment to Pennsylvania's Prisons," *Journal of Research in Crime and Delinquency* 37 (May 2000): 200–220; R. Bachman, "Victim's Perceptions of Initial Police Responses to Robbery and Aggravated Assault: Does Race Matter?" *Journal of Quantitative Criminology* 12 (December 1996): 363–90; David Barsamian, "Angela Davis: African American Activist on Prison-Industrial Complex," *The Progressive* 65 (February 2001): 33–38; Jennifer E. Smith, "ONAMOVE: African American Confronting the Prison Crisis," in *Still Lifting, Still Climbing: African American Women's Contemporary*, ed. Kimberly Springer (New York: New York University Press, 1999), 219–34.

BIBLIOGRAPHY

Primary Sources

Alexander, Raymond Pace, Record Group, 1880–1975, Alexander Family Papers, 1817–1985, UPT 50 A374R, University Archives and Records Center, University of Pennsylvania—Scrapbook, 1948—Corrine Sykes Case.

Alexander, Saddie Tanner Mossell, Record Group, 1817, 1858–1985, University Archives and Records Center, University of Pennsylvania, UPT 50 A 374S.

Second Annual Report of the Board of Commissioners of Public Charities of the State of Pennsylvania; to which is appended the Report of the General Agent and Secretary, Transmitted to the Legislature, January 4, 1872. Harrisburg: B. Singerly, State Printer, 1873.

Annual Report of the National League for the Protection of Colored Women. New York, 1910.

Beatty, Suzanne S., ed., *Compilation of Laws of Pennsylvania Relating to Children.* S.l.: s.n., c. 1915.

Beccaria, Cesare. *On Crimes and Punishments, and Other Writings.* Edited by Richard Bellamy. Translated by Richard Davies, Virginia Cox, Richard Bellamy. Cambridge: Cambridge University Press, 1995.

Boies, Henry. *Prisoners and Paupers: A Study of the Abnormal Increase of Criminals, and the Public Burden of Pauperism in the United States.* New York: Putnam, 1893.

———. *The Science of Penology: The Defense of Society Against Crime.* New York: G. P. Putnam's Sons, 1901.

Commonwealth vs. Helen Thomas, Commonwealth vs. Helen Thomas and Mame Brown, and *Commonwealth vs. Mame Brown,* Trial Transcript in the Court of Quarter Sessions and Oyer and Terminer of Philadelphia County, October Sessions, 1908, no. 375, January 5, 1909, 91.

Commonwealth vs. Mame Brown and the *Commonwealth vs. Helen Thomas,* Trial Transcript in the Court of Quarter Sessions and Oyer and Terminer of Philadelphia County, October Sessions, 1908, no. 375, January 5, 1909.

Darwin, Charles. *The Descent of Man and Selection in Relation to Sex.* London: J. Murray, 1871.

de Cervantes Saavedra, Miguel. *The History of the Renowned Don Quixote de la Mancha.* 1719.

Department of Public Safety, Bureau of Police—Detective Service, c. 1880–1900.

Dickens, Charles. *American Notes for General Circulation.* Philadelphia: Lea and Blanchard, 1842.

Dix, Dorothea. *An Address by A Recent Female Visiter* [sic] *to the Prisoners in the Eastern State Penitentiary.* Philadelphia: Joseph and William Kite, 1844.

Dubois, Silvia. *Silvia Dubois, A Biografy of the Slav Who Whipt Her Mistress and Gand Her Freedom,* by C. W. Larison. Edited by Jared C. Lodbell. New York: Oxford University Press, 1988.

Du Bois, W. E. B. *The Philadelphia Negro: A Social Study.* 1899. Reprint, Philadelphia: University of Pennsylvania Press, 1996.

———. *The Souls of Black Folk: Essays and Sketches.* 2nd ed. Chicago: A. C. McClurg, 1903.

Dugdale, R. L. "*The Jukes": A Study in Crime, Pauperism, Disease and Heredity, also Further Studies of Criminals.* New York: G. P. Putnam's Sons, 1877.

The Eastern State Penitentiary of Pennsylvania: An Investigation by Authority of the Legislature, Book no. I: Testimony of First Day, Thursday, May 13th, 1897.

Eaton, Isabel "*Special Report on Negro Domestic Service in the Seventh Ward, Philadelphia.*" In *The Philadelphia Negro: A Social Study.* 1899. Reprint, Philadelphia: University of Pennsylvania Press, 1996.

Flanders, Henry, and James T. Mitchell. *Statutes at Large of Pennsylvania: From 1682 to 1801.* 18 vols. Harrisburg, Penn.: 1896–1915.

Forten, James. *Series of Letters by a Man of Colour, 1813.* In *Pamphlets of Protest: An Anthology of Early African American Protest Literature, 1790–1860,* edited by Richard Newman, Patrick Rael, and Phillip Lapsansky. New York: Routledge, 2001.

Gopsill's Philadelphia City Directory for 1884, 1885, 1890, 1900.

A Guide to the Stranger, or Pocket Companion for the Fancy, Containing a List of the Gay Houses and Ladies of Pleasure in the City of Brotherly Love and Sisterly Affection. Philadelphia, c. 1849.

Hunton, Addie. "Negro Womanhood Defended." *The Voice of the Negro* 1, no. 7 (July 1904).

A Just and True Account of the Prison of the City and County of Philadelphia; Accompanied With the Rules, Regulations, Manners, Customs, and Treatment of the untried Prisoners, who have the misfortune Of being Committed to this place For Trial. 1820.

Kellor, Frances. "Criminal Anthropology in Its Relation to Criminal Jurisprudence." *American Journal of Sociology* 4, no. 4 (January 1899): 515–27.

———. "Criminal Anthropology in Its Relation to Criminal Jurisprudence, II." *American Journal of Sociology* 4, no. 5 (March 1899): 630–48.

————. "Southern Colored Girls in the North: The Problem of Their Protection." *Charities* 15 (March 18, 1905).

Laws of the General Assembly of the State of Pennsylvania, Harrisburg, Penn., 1881–1909.

LeSage, Alain-René. *The Adventures of Gil Blas of Santillane.* 1759.

Lombroso, Cesare, and William Ferrero. *The Female Offender.* New York: D. Appleton, 1895.

McMichael, Charles B., ed. *The Municipal Law of Philadelphia: A Digest of the Charters, Acts of Assembly, Ordinances, and Judicial Decisions Relating Thereto, from 1701 to 1887.* Philadelphia: J. M. Power Wallace, 1887.

Minutes of the Pennsylvania Prison Society, vol. 7.

Mossell, Gertrude N. F. *The Work of the Afro-American Woman.* 2nd ed. 1908. Reprint, New York: Oxford University Press, 1988.

A Narrative of the Proceedings of Black People, During the Late, Awful Calamity in Philadelphia. 1794.

Olmstead, Marlin E., Papers, 1874–1913. Manuscript Group 153 (PHMC).

Patrolman's Manual: Bureau of Police, City of Philadelphia (Philadelphia: Issued by the Department of Public Safety, 1913), in *Metropolitan Police Manuals, 1817, 1913.* Edited by Richard C. Wade. New York: Arno Press, 1974.

The Pennsylvania System of Separate Confinement Explained and Defended. Philadelphia: J. B. Chandler Printer, 1867.

Purvis, Robert. *Appeal of Forty Thousand Citizens Threatened with Disfranchisement, to the People of Pennsylvania*, 1837.

Rayne, Martha Louise. *What a Woman Can Do.* Detroit: F. B. Dickerson, 1883.

A Report on Existing Conditions, with Recommendations to the Honorable Rudolph Blakenburg, Mayor of Philadelphia. Philadelphia Vice Report. Philadelphia: The Commission, 1913.

Rush, Benjamin. *Enquiry into the Effects of Public Punishments upon Criminals, and upon Society; Read in the Society for Promoting Political Enquiries, Convened at the House of His Excellency Benjamin Franklin, Esquire, in Philadelphia, March 9th, 1787.* Philadelphia, 1787.

Salmon, Lucy M. *Domestic Service.* London: Macmillan, 1897.

Sprogle, Howard O. *The Philadelphia Police, Past and Present.* Philadelphia, 1887.

Steffens, Lincoln. *The Shame of the Cities.* 1904. Reprint, New York: Hill and Wang, 1957.

To the Honourable The Senate and House of Representatives of the Commonwealth of Pennsylvania, in General Assembly Met: The Memorial of the Subscribers, free people of colour, residing in the County of Philadelphia. 1832.

The Trial of Alice Clifton for the Murder of her Bastard-Child, At the Court of Oyer and Terminer and General Gaol Delivery, held at Philadelphia, on Wednesday the 18th of April 1787.

Turnbull, Robert. *A Visit To The Philadelphia Prison: Being An Accurate and Particular Ac-*

count of the Wise and Humane Administration Adopted in Every Part of that Building. 1796.

Twenty-First Annual Report of the Board of Commissioners of Public Charities of the Commonwealth of Pennsylvania for 1890; also the Report of the General Agent and Secretary Statistics, and the Report of the Committee on Lunacy. Harrisburg, Penn.: Edwin K. Meyers, State Printer, 1891.

Vaux, Roberts. *Notices of the Original, and Successive Efforts to Improve the Discipline of the Prison at Philadelphia, and to Reform the Criminal Code of Pennsylvania: With A Few Observations on the Penitentiary System.* Philadelphia: Kimber and Sharpless, 1826.

Walker, David. *David Walker's Appeal: To the Coloured Citizens of the World, but in particular, and very expressly, to those of the United States of America.* 1830. Reprint, with an introduction by James Turner. Baltimore: Black Classic, 1993.

Washington, Booker T. *Up from Slavery: An Autobiography.* 1901. Reprint, Oxford: Oxford University Press, 1995.

Watson, John F. *Annals of Philadelphia: Being a Collection of Memoirs, Anecdotes, and Incidents of the City and Its Inhabitants from the Days of the Pilgrim Founders.* Philadelphia, 1830.

Wright, Richard, Jr. *The Negro in Pennsylvania: A Study in Economic History.* 1912. New York: Arno Press, 1969.

U.S. Bureau of the Census, Thirteenth Census, 1910, Population.

Secondary Sources

Adams, Carolyn, David Bartelt, David Elesh, Ira Goldstein, Nancy Kleniewski, and William Yancy. *Philadelphia: Neighborhoods, Divisions, and Conflicts in a Postindustrial City.* Philadelphia: Temple University Press, 1991.

Adler, Jeffrey S. "'The Negro Would Be More Than an Angel to Withstand Such Treatment': African American Homicide in Chicago, 1875–1910." In *Lethal Imagination: Violence and Brutality in American History*, edited by Michael A. Bellesiles. New York: New York University Press, 1999.

Alexander, Rudolph, Jr., and Jacquelyn Gyamerah. "Differential Punishing of African Americans and Whites Who Possess Drugs: A Just Policy or a Continuation of the Past?" *Journal of Black Studies* 28 (September 1997): 97–111.

Alfieri, A. V. "Prosecuting Race." *Duke Law Journal* 48 (April 1999): 1157–1264.

Anderson, Elijah. *Code of the Street: Decency, Violence and the Moral Life of the Inner City.* New York: W. W. Norton, 2000.

Armstrong, Erica. "Negro Wenches, Washer Women, and Literate Ladies: The Transforming Identities of African American Women in Philadelphia, 1780–1854." Ph.D. diss., Columbia University, 2000.

Austin, Regina. "'An Honest Living': Street Vendors, Municipal Regulation, and the Black Public Sphere." *Yale Law Review* 103, no. 8 (June 1994): 2119–20.

————, and M. D. Allen. "Racial Disparity in Arrest Rates as an Explanation of Racial Disparity in Commitment to Pennsylvania's Prisons." *Journal of Research in Crime and Delinquency* 37 (May 2000): 200–220.

Avery, Ron. *City of Brotherly Mayhem: Philadelphia Crimes and Criminals*. Philadelphia: Otis Books, 1997.

Ayers, Edward. *Vengeance and Justice, Crime and Justice in the 19th Century South*. New York: Oxford University Press, 1984.

Bachman, R. "Victim's Perceptions of Initial Police Responses to Robbery and Aggravated Assault: Does Race Matter?" *Journal of Quantitative Criminology* 12 (December 1996): 363–90.

Bacon, Margaret Hope. "One Great Bundle of Humanity: Frances Ellen Watkins Harper." *PMHB* 113, no. 1 (January 1989): 21–43.

Baldasty, Gerald. "The Nineteenth-Century Origins of Modern American Journalism." In *Three Hundred Years of the American Newspaper*, edited by John B. Hench. Worcester: American Antiquarian Society, 1991.

Barkley-Brown, Elsa, and Gregg Kimball. "Mapping the Terrain of Black Richmond." In *The New African American Urban History*, edited by Kenneth W. Goings and Raymond A. Mohl. Thousand Oaks: Sage Press, 1996.

Barnes, Harry Elmer. *The Repression of Crime: Studies in Historical Penology*. New York: George H. Duran, 1926.

————. *The Evolution of Penology in Pennsylvania: A Study in American Social History*. Indianapolis: Bobbs-Merrill, 1927.

Barnes, Harry Elmer, and Negley K. Teeters. *New Horizons in Criminology: The American Crime Problem*. New York: Prentice-Hall, 1946.

Barsamian, David. "Angela Davis: African American Activist on Prison-Industrial Complex." *The Progressive* 65 (February 2001): 33–38.

————. *The Reason Why the Colored American is not in the World's Columbian Exposition: The Afro-American's Contribution to Columbian literature*, edited by Robert W. Rydell. Urbana: University of Illinois Press, 1999.

Bederman, Gail. *Manliness and Civilization: A Cultural History of Gender and Race in the United States, 1880–1917*. Chicago: University of Chicago Press, 1995.

Bell, Patricia Scott. "Debunking Sapphire: Towards a Non-Racist and Non-Sexist Social Science." In *All the Women are White, All the Blacks are Men, But Some of Us Are Brave: Black Women's Studies*, edited by Gloria T. Hull and Barbara Smith. Old Westbury, N.Y.: Feminist Press, 1982.

Belton, Don, ed. "Introduction." *Speak My Name: Black Men on Masculinity and the American Dream*. Boston: Beacon Press, 1995.

Berger, Maurice, ed. "Introduction." In *Constructing Masculinity*, edited by Brian Walls and Simon Watson. New York: Routledge, 1995.

Berry, Mary Frances. *Black Resistance, White Law: A History of Constitutional Racism*. 2nd ed. New York: Penguin Books, 1994.

Blockson, Charles L. *Philadelphia: 1639–2000*. Charleston: Arcadia Press, 2000.

Broder, Sherri. *Tramps, Unfit Mothers, and Neglected Children: Negotiating the Family in Late Nineteenth-Century Philadelphia*. Philadelphia: University of Pennsylvania Press, 2002.

Brody, Jennifer DeVere. *Impossible Purities: Blackness, Femininity, and Victorian Culture*. Durham and London: Duke University Press, 1998.

Brooks-Higginbotham, Evelyn. "Beyond the Sound of Silence: Afro-American Women in History." *Gender and History* 1 (1989): 50–67.

———. "African American Women's History and the Metalanguage of Race." *Signs* 17, no. 21 (1992): 251–77.

———. *Righteous Discontent: The Women's Movement in the Black Baptist Church, 1880–1920*. Cambridge, Mass.: Harvard University Press, 1993.

Brown, JoAnne. *The Definition of a Profession*. Princeton: Princeton University Press, 1992.

Brown, Kathleen M. *Good Wives, Nasty Wenches, and Anxious Patriarchs: Gender, Race, and Power in Colonial Virginia*. Chapel Hill: University of North Carolina Press, 1996.

Burgess, Ann W., and Lynda L. Holstrom. *Rape, Crisis and Recovery*. Bowie, Md.: Robert J. Brady, 1979.

Burt, Nathaniel, and Wallace E. Davies. "The Iron Age, 1876–1095." In *Philadelphia: A 300 Year History*, edited by Russell F. Weigley. New York: W. W. Norton, 1982.

Butler, Anne. *Gendered Justice in the American West: Women Prisoners in Men's Penitentiaries*. Urbana: University of Illinois Press, 1997.

Butler, Judith. *Gender Trouble: Feminism and the Subversion of Identity*. New York: Routledge, 1990.

Camp, Stephanie. *Closer to Freedom: Enslaved Women and Everyday Resistance in the Plantation South*. Chapel Hill: University of North Carolina Press, 2004.

Carby, Hazel V. *Reconstructing Womanhood: The Emergence of the Afro-American Woman Novelist*. New York: Oxford University Press, 1987.

———. "Policing the Black Woman's Body in an Urban Context." *Critical Inquiry* 18, no. 4 (Summer 1992): 738–55.

Carlisle, Marcia. "Disorderly City, Disorderly Women: Prostitution in Ante-Bellum Philadelphia." *PMHB* (October 1986): 549–69.

Caruth, Cathy. *Unclaimed Experience: Trauma, Narrative, and History*. Baltimore: Johns Hopkins University Press, 1996.

Cesaire, Aime. *Discourse on Colonialism*. Translated by Joan Pinkham. New York: Monthly Review Press, 1955.

Center for Disease Control and Prevention. "HIV/AIDS among African Americans" (February 2005).

Chauncey, George, Jr. "From Sexual Inversion to Homosexuality: The Changing Medical Conceptualiziation of Female 'Deviance.'" In *Passion and Power: Sexuality in History*, edited by Kathy Peiss and Christina Simmons. Philadelphia: Temple University Press, 1989.

————. *Gay New York: Gender, Urban Culture, and the Making of the Gay Male World, 1890–1940*. New York: Basic Books, 1994.

Clark, Dennis. "The Philadelphia Irish: Persistent Presence." In *The Peoples of Philadelphia: A History of Ethnic Groups and Lower-Class Life, 1790–1940*, edited by Allen F. Davis and Mark H. Haller. Philadelphia: University of Pennsylvania Press, 1998.

Clarke, Cheryl. "Lesbianism: An Act of Resistance." In *Words of Fire: An Anthology of African-American Feminist Thought*, edited by Beverly Guy-Sheftall. New York: New York Press, 1995.

Clinton, Catherine. "Reconstructing Freedwomen." In *Divided Houses: Gender and the Civil War*, edited by Catherine Clinton and Nina Silber. New York: Oxford University Press, 1992.

Cohen, David. "Social Injustice, Sexual Violence, Spiritual Transcendence: Constructions of Interracial Rape in Early American Crime Literature, 1767–1817." *WMQ*, 3rd ser., 56, no. 3 (July 1999): 481–526.

Cole, Simon. *Suspect Identities: A History of Fingerprinting and Criminal Identification*. Cambridge, Mass.: Harvard University Press, 2001.

Collins, Patricia Hill. *Black Feminist Thought: Knowledge, Consciousness, and the Politics of Empowerment*. Boston: Unwin Hyman, 1990.

Cooper, Anna Julia. *A Voice from the South*. 1892. Reprint, New York: Oxford University Press, 1988.

Cordato, Mary Frances. "Toward a New Century: Women and the Philadelphia Centennial Exhibition, 1876." *PMHB* 107, no. 1 (January 1983): 113–35.

Cott, Nancy F. *The Grounding of Modern Feminism*. New Haven: Yale University Press, 1987.

Davis, Angela Y. *Women, Race and Class*. New York: Random House, 1981.

DeLauretis, Teresa. *Technologies of Gender: Essays, Theory, Film, and Fiction*. Bloomington: Indiana University Press, 1987.

D'Emilio, John, and Estelle B. Freedman. *Intimate Matters: A History of Sexuality in America*. New York: Harper and Row, 1988.

Dennison, Samuel. *Scandalize My Name: Black Imagery in American Popular Music*. New York: Garland, 1982.

Dodge, L. Mara. *"Whores and Thieves of the Worst Kind": A Study of Women, Crime, and Prisons, 1835–2000*. Dekalb: Northern Illinois University Press, 2002.

Dowbiggin, Ian Robert. *Keeping America Sane: Psychiatry and Eugenics in the United States and Canada, 1880–1940*. Ithaca: Cornell University Press, 1997.

Duberman, Martin B. *Stonewall*. New York: Plume, 1994.

Duggan, Lisa. *Sapphic Slashers: Sex, Violence, and American Modernity*. Durham and London: Duke University Press, 2000.

Dyson, Michael Eric. *Reflecting Black: African American Cultural Criticism*. Minneapolis: University of Minnesota Press, 1993.

Edwards, Laura F. *Gendered Strife and Confusion: The Political Culture of Reconstruction*. Urbana: University of Illinois Press, 1997.

Espy, M. Watt, and John Ortiz Smylka. "Executions in the U.S. 1608–1987: The Espy File." Inter-University Consortium for Political and Social Research, 1994.

Evans, Monica J. "Stealing Away: Black Women, Outlaw Culture and the Rhetoric of Rights." In *Critical Race Theory: The Cutting Edge*, edited by Richard Delgado. Philadelphia: Temple University Press, 1995.

Fanon, Frantz. *Black Skin, White Masks*. Translated by Charles Lam Markmann. New York: Grove Press, 1967.

———. *The Wretched of the Earth*. Preface by Jean-Paul Sartre. Translated by Constance Farrington. New York: Grove Press, 1968.

Fields, Barbara J. "Ideology and Race in American History." In *Region, Race, and Reconstructing: Essays on C. Vann Woodward*, edited by J. Morgan Kousser and James McPherson. New York: Oxford University Press, 1982.

Foner, Eric. *Tom Paine and Revolutionary America*. New York: Oxford University Press, 1976.

Foreman, P. Gabrielle. " 'Reading Aright': White Slavery, Black Referents, and the Strategy of Histotextuality in *Iola Leroy*." *Yale Journal of Criticism* 10, no. 2 (1997): 327–54.

Foucault, Michel. *Madness and Civilization: A History of Insanity in the Age of Reason*. Translated by Richard Howard. New York: Vintage Books, 1988.

———. *The History of Sexuality: An Introduction*. Volume 1. Translated by Robert Hurley. New York: Vintage Books, 1990.

———. *The Order of Things: An Archaeology of the Human Sciences*. New York: Vintage Books, 1994.

———. *Discipline and Punish: The Birth of the Prison*. 2nd ed. Translated by Alan Sheridan. New York: Vintage Books, 1995.

Freedman, Estelle B. " 'Uncontrolled Desires': The Response to the Sexual Psychopath, 1920–1960." In *Passion and Power: Sexuality in History*, edited by Kathy Peiss and Christina Simmons. Philadelphia: Temple University Press, 1989.

Freire, Paulo. *Pedagogy of the Oppressed*. Translated by Myra Bergman Ramos. New York: Continuum International, 1986.

Friedman, Lawrence M. *A History of American Law*. New York: Touchstone Book, 1985.

———. *Crime and Punishment in American History*. New York: Basic Books, 1993.

Gaines, Kevin. *Uplifting the Race: Black Leadership, Politics, and Culture in the Twentieth Century*. Chapel Hill: University of North Carolina Press, 1996.

Gamwell, Lyn, and Nancy Tomes. *Madness in America: Cultural and Medical Perceptions of Mental Illness Before 1914*. Ithaca: Cornell University Press, 1995.

Garber, Eric. "A Spectacle in Color: The Lesbian and Gay Subculture of Jazz Age Harlem." In *Hidden From History*, edited by Martin Duberman, Martha Vicinus, and George Chancey. New York: Meridian Book, 1989.

Giddings, Paula. *When and Where I Enter: The Impact of Black Women on Race and Sex in America*. New York: Bantam Books, 1988.

———. "The Last Taboo." In *Words of Fire: An Anthology of African-American Feminist Thought*, edited by Beverly Guy-Sheftall. New York: New York Press, 1995.

Gilfoyle, Timothy J. *City of Eros: New York, Prostitution, and the Commercialization of Sex, 1790–1920*. New York: W. W. Norton, 1992.

Gilman, Sander. *Difference and Pathology: Stereotypes of Sexuality, Race and Madness*. Ithaca: Cornell University Press, 1985.

———. "Black Bodies, White Bodies: Towards an Iconography of Female Sexuality in Late-Nineteenth Century Art, Medicine and Literature." In *"Race," Writing and Difference*, edited by Henry Louis Gates, Jr. Chicago: University of Chicago Press, 1985.

Goings, Kenneth W., and Gerald Smith. " 'Unhidden Transcripts': Memphis and African American Agency, 1862–1920." In *The New African American Urban History*, edited by Kenneth W. Goings and Raymond A. Mohl. Thousand Oaks: Sage Press, 1996.

Golab, Caroline. "The Immigrant and the City: Poles, Italians, and Jews in Philadelphia, 1870–1920." In *The Peoples of Philadelphia: A History of Ethnic Groups and Lower-Class Life, 1790–1940*, edited by Allen F. Davis and Mark H. Haller. Philadelphia: University of Pennsylvania Press, 1998.

Gough, Robert J. "The Philadelphia Economic Elite at the End of the Eighteenth Century." In *Shaping a National Culture: The Philadelphia Experience, 1750–1800*, edited by Catherine E. Hutchins. Winterthur, Del.: Henry Francis du Pont Winterthur Museum, 1994.

Green, Venus. *Race on the Line: Gender, Labor and Technology in the Bell System, 1880–1980*. Durham: Duke University Press, 2001.

Gregg, Robert. *Sparks from the Anvil of Oppression: Philadelphia's African Methodists and Southern Migrants, 1890–1940*. Philadelphia: Temple University Press, 1993.

Griffin, Farah Jasmine. *"Who set you flowin'?": The African-American Migration Narrative*. New York: Oxford University Press, 1995.

Griffin, Farah Jasmine, ed. *Beloved Sisters and Loving Friends: Letters from Rebecca Primus of Royal Oak, Maryland, and Addie Brown of Hartford, Connecticut, 1854–1868*. New York: Alfred A. Knopf, 1999.

Gross, Kali N. "Examining the Politics of Respectability in African American Studies." In *University of Pennsylvania Almanac* 43, no. 28 (April 1, 1997): 15–16.

Grosvenor, Vertamae. "Corrine Sykes Remembered." *All Things Considered*, NPR, April 3, 1988.

Gunning, Sandra. *Race, Rape, and Lynching: The Red Record of American Literature, 1890–1912*. New York: Oxford University Press, 1996.

Hall, Jacquelyn Dowd. *Revolt Against Chivalry: Jessie Daniel Ames and the Women's Campaign Against Lynching*. New York: Columbia University Press, 1979.

Hall, Kim F. *Things of Darkness: Economies of Race and Gender in Early Modern England*. Ithaca: Cornell University Press, 1995.

Hall, Lee. *Common Threads: A Parade of American Clothing*. Boston: Bulfich Press, 1992.

Halttunen, Karen. *Murder Most Foul: The Killer and the American Gothic Imagination*. Cambridge, Mass.: Harvard University Press, 1998.

Harley, Sharon. "When Your Work Is Not Who You Are: The Development of a Working-Class Consciousness Among Afro-American Women." In *"We Specialize in the Wholly Impossible": A Reader in Black Women's History*, edited by Darlene Clark Hine, Wilma King, and Linda Reed. New York: Carlson, 1995.

Harris, Leslie. *In the Shadow of Slavery: African Americans in New York City, 1626–1863*. Chicago: University of Chicago Press, 2003.

Hartman, Saidiya. *Scenes of Subjection: Terror, Slavery, and Self-Making in Nineteenth-Century America*. New York: Oxford University Press, 1997.

Hartsock, Nancy. "Foucault on Power: A Theory for Women?" In *Feminism/Postmodernism*, edited by Linda Nicolson. New York: Routledge, 1990.

Hasain, Marouf Arif, Jr. *The Rhetoric of Eugenics in Anglo-American Thought*. Athens: University of Georgia Press, 1996.

Hazzard-Gordon, Katrina. *Jookin': The Rise of Social Dance Formations in African-American Culture*. Philadelphia: Temple University Press, 1990.

Hemphill, C. Dallett. *Bowing to Necessities: A History of Manners in America, 1620–1860*. New York: Oxford University Press, 1999.

Henderson, Mae G. "Toni Morrison's *Beloved*: Re-membering the Body as Historical Text." In *Discourses of Sexuality: From Aristotle to AIDS*, edited by Domna C. Stanton. Ann Arbor: University of Michigan Press, 1992.

Hershberg, Theodore, ed. "Free Blacks in Antebellum Philadelphia: A Study of Ex-Slaves, Freeborn, and Socioeconomic Decline." In *Philadelphia: Work, Space, Family, and Group Experience in the Nineteenth Century, Essays Toward an Interdisciplinary History of the City*. Oxford: Oxford University Press, 1981.

Hicks, Cheryl D. "'In Danger of Becoming Morally Depraved': Single Black Women, Working-class Black Families, and New York State's Wayward Minor Laws, 1917–1928." *University of Pennsylvania Law Review* 151, no. 6 (June 2003): 2077–2121.

Higginbotham, A. Leon. *In the Matter of Color: The Colonial Period*. New York: Oxford University Press, 1978.

———. *Shades of Freedom: Racial Politics and Presumptions of the American Legal Process*. New York: Oxford University Press, 1996.

Hill, Marilyn Wood. *Their Sisters' Keepers: Prostitution in New York City, 1830–1870*. Berkeley: University of California Press, 1993.

Hindus, Michael S. *Prison and Plantation: Crime, Justice and Authority in Massachusetts and South Carolina, 1767–1878*. Chapel Hill: University of North Carolina Press, 1980.

Hine, Darlene Clark. "Black Migration to the Urban Midwest: The Gender Dimension, 1915–1945." In *The Great Migration in Historical Perspective: New Dimensions of Race, Class, and Gender*, edited by Joe William Trotter, Jr. Bloomington: Indiana University Press, 1991.

BIBLIOGRAPHY

———. "Rape and the Inner Lives of Black Women in the Middle West: Preliminary Thoughts on the Culture of Dissemblance." In *Words of Fire: An Anthology of African-American Feminist Thought*, edited by Beverly Guy-Sheftall. New York: New York Press, 1995.

Hine, Darlene Clark, Elsa Barkley Brown, and Rosalyn Terborg-Penn, eds. *Black Women in America: An Historical Encyclopedia*. Volume A–L. 2nd ed. Bloomington: Indiana University Press, 1994.

Hine, Darlene Clark, and Kathleen Thompson. *A Shining Thread of Hope: The History of Black Women in America*. New York: Broadway Books, 1998.

Hofstadter, Richard. *The Age of Reform*. New York: Vintage Books, 1995.

Holt, Thomas C. *The Problem of Race in the 21st Century*. Cambridge, Mass.: Harvard University Press, 2000.

hooks, bell. *Ain't I a Woman?: Black Women and Feminism*. Boston: South End Press, 1981.

———. *Talking Back: thinking feminist, thinking black*. Boston: South End Press, 1989.

Hull, Gloria T. " 'Lines She Did Not Dare': Angelina Weld Grimké, Harlem Renaissance Poet." In *The Lesbian and Gay Studies Reader*, edited by Henry Abelove, Michèle Aina Barale, and David M. Halperin. New York: Routledge, 1993.

Hunt, Patricia K. "Clothing as an Expression of History: The Dress of African-American Women in Georgia, 1880–1915." In *"We Specialize in the Wholly Impossible": A Reader in Black Women's History*, edited by Darlene Clark Hine, Wilma King, and Linda Reed. New York: Carlson, 1995.

Hunter, Tera. *"To 'Joy My Freedom": Southern Black Women's Lives and Labors After the Civil War*. Cambridge, Mass.: Havard University Press, 1997.

———. "The 'Brotherly Love' for Which This City Is Proverbial Should Extend to All: The Everyday Lives of Working-Class Women in Philadelphia and Atlanta in the 1890s." In *W. E. B. Du Bois, Race and the City*: The Philadelphia Negro *and Its Legacy*, edited by Michael B. Katz and Thomas J. Sugrue. Philadelphia: University of Pennsylvania Press, 1998.

Ignatieff, Michael. *A Just Measure of Pain: The Penitentiary in the Industrial Revolution, 1750–1850*. New York: Columbia University Press, 1980.

Ignatiev, Noel. *How the Irish Became White*. New York: Routledge, 1995.

Jackson, Peter. "Black Males: Advertising and the Cultural Politics of Masculinity." *Gender, Place and Culture* 1, no. 1 (1994): 49–59.

Jacobson, Matthew Frye. *Whiteness of a Different Color: European Immigrants and the Alchemy of Race*. Cambridge, Mass.: Harvard University Press, 1998.

Johnson, Claudia D. "That Guilty Third Tier: Prostitution in Nineteenth-Century American Theaters." *AQ* 27, no. 5, Special Issue: Victorian Culture in America (December 1975): 575–84.

Johnson, David R. *Policing the Urban Underworld: The Impact of Crime on the Development of the American Police, 1800–1887*. Philadelphia: Temple University Press, 1979.

Johnson, David R. "Crime Patterns in Philadelphia, 1840–70." In *The Peoples of Philadelphia: A History of Ethnic Groups and Lower-Class Life, 1790–1940*, edited by Allen F. Davis and Mark Haller. Philadelphia: University of Pennsylvania Press, 1998.

Jones, Jacqueline. *Labor of Love, Labor of Sorrow: Black Women, Work, and the Family from Slavery to the Present*. New York: Basic Books, 1985.

———. *The Dispossessed: America's Underclasses from the Civil War to the Present*. New York: Basic Books, 1992.

———. "'Lifework' and Its Limits: The Problem of Labor in *The Philadelphia Negro*." In *W. E. B. Du Bois, Race and the City*: The Philadelphia Negro *and Its Legacy*, edited by Michael B. Katz and Thomas J. Sugrue. Philadelphia: University of Pennsylvania Press, 1998.

Jordan, Winthrop. *White Over Black: American Attitudes Towards the Negro, 1550–1812*. Baltimore: Penguin Books, 1969.

———. *The White Man's Burden: Historical Origins of Racism in the United States*. Oxford: Oxford University Press, 1974.

Kaminer, Wendy. *Fearful Freedom: Women's Flight from Equality*. 2nd ed. Reading, Mass.: Addison-Wesley, 1991.

Kantrowitz, Stephen. *Ben Tillman and the Reconstruction of White Supremacy*. Chapel Hill: University of North Carolina Press, 2000.

Kehl, James A. *Boss Rule in the Gilded Age: Matt Quay of Pennsylvania*. Pittsburgh: University of Pittsburgh Press, 1981.

Kelley, Robin D. G. *Hammer and Hoe: Alabama Communists During the Great Depression*. Chapel Hill: University of North Carolina Press, 1990.

———. "The Riddle of the Zoot: Malcolm Little and Black Cultural Politics during World War II." In *Malcolm X: In Our Own Image*, edited by J. Wood. New York: St. Martin's Press, 1992.

———. *Race Rebels: Culture, Politics, and the Black Working Class*. New York: Free Press, 1994.

Kimmel, Michael S. "Beyond Sex and Gender: Masculinity, Homosexuality and Social Theory." In *Men, Masculinities and Social Theory*, edited by Jeff Hearn and David Morgan. Boston: Unwin Hyman, 1990.

———. *Manhood in America: A Cultural History*. New York: Free Press, 1996.

Klepp, Susan E. "Seasoning and Society: Racial Differences in Mortality in Eighteenth-Century Philadelphia." *WMQ*, 3rd. ser., 51, no. 3, Mid-Atlantic Perspectives (July 1994): 473–506.

Kolchin, Peter. *Unfree Labor: American Slavery and Russian Serfdom*. Cambridge, Mass.: Harvard University Press, 1987.

Lapsansky, Emma. "'Since They Got Those Separate Churches': Afro-Americans and Racism in Jacksonian Philadelphia." In *Americans in Pennsylvania: Shifting Historical Perspectives*, edited by Joe William Trotter, Jr. and Eric Ledell Smith. Harrisburg: Penn-

sylvania Historical and Museum Commission; University Park: Pennsylvania State
University Press, 1997.

Lane, Roger. *The Roots of Violence in Black Philadelphia, 1860–1900*. Cambridge, Mass.:
Harvard University Press, 1986.

———. *William Dorsey's Philadelphia and Ours: On the Past and Future of the Black City
in America*. New York: Oxford University Press, 1991.

———. *Violent Death in the City: Suicide, Accident, and Murder in Nineteenth-Century
Philadelphia*. Columbus: Ohio State University Press, 1999.

Lasch-Quinn, Elisabeth. *Black Neighbors: Race and the Limits of Reform in the American
Settlement House Movement, 1890–1945*. Chapel Hill and London: University of North
Carolina Press, 1993.

Lekkerkerker, Eugenia C. *Reformatories for Women in the United States*. Groningen: J. B.
Wolters, 1931.

Lerner, Gerder, ed. *Black Women in White America: A Documentary History*. New York:
Vintage Books, 1992.

Lewis, David Levering, and Deborah Willis. *A Small Nation of People: W. E. B. Du Bois and
African American Portraits of Progress*. Library of Congress. New York: HarperCollins,
2003.

Lewis, Earl. *In Their Own Interest: Race, Class, and Power in Twentieth-Century Norfolk,
Virginia*. Berkeley: University of California Press, 1991.

Lewis, Owen. *The Development of American Prisons and Prison Customs, 1776–1845*. New
York: Prison Society of New York, 1922.

List, Karen. "The Post-Revolutionary Woman Idealized: Philadelphia Media's Republican
Motherhood." *Journalism Quarterly* 66, no. 1 (Spring 1989): 65–75.

Loewenberg, Bert James, and Ruth Bogin. *Black Women in Nineteenth-Century American
Life: Their Words, Their Thoughts, Their Feelings*. University Park: Pennsylvania State
University Press, 1976.

Lott, Eric. *Love and Theft: Blackface Minstrelsy and the American Working Class*. New York:
Oxford University Press, 1993.

Lubiano, Wahneema. "Black Ladies, Welfare Queens, and State Minstrels." In *Race-ing
Justice, En-gendering Power: Essays on Anita Hill, Clarence Thomas, and the Construction
of Social Reality*, edited by Toni Morrison. New York, Pantheon Books, 1992.

Lubiano, Wahneema, ed. "Introduction." *The House that Race Built: Black Americans, U.S.
Terrain*. New York: Pantheon Books, 1997.

Malcolm X. *The Autobiography of Malcolm X*. New York: Grove Press, 1965.

Malveaux, Julianne. "Still at the Periphery: The Economic Status of African Americans."
In *Race and Resistance: African Americans in the 21st Century*, edited by Herb Boyd.
Cambridge, Mass.: South End Press, 2002.

Manring, M. M. *A Slave in a Box: The Strange Career of Aunt Jemima*. Charlottesville:
University Press of Virginia, 1998.

McCaffery, Peter. *When Bosses Ruled Philadelphia: The Emergence of the Republican Machine, 1867–1933*. University Park: Pennsylvania State University Press, 1993.

McCahill, Thomas W., Linda C. Meyer, and Arthur M. Fischman. *The Aftermath of Rape*. Lexington, Mass.: Lexington Books, 1979.

McDowell, Deborah. "'The Changing Same': Generation Connections and Black Women Novelists." In *Reading Black, Reading Feminist*, edited by Henry Louis Gates, Jr. New York: Meridian Press, 1990.

McLaurin, Melton. *Celia, A Slave: A True Story*. New York: Avon Books, 1991.

McNeil, Genna Rae. *Charles Hamilton Houston and the Struggle for Civil Rights*. Philadelphia: University of Pennsylvania Press, 1983.

Melosh, Barbara, ed. "Introduction." *Gender and American History Since 1890*. New York: Routledge, 1993.

Meranze, Michael. *Laboratories of Virtue: Punishment, Revolution, and Authority in Philadelphia, 1760–1835*. Chapel Hill: University of North Carolina Press, 1996.

Messerschmidt, James W. *Crime as Structured Action: Gender, Race, Class, and Crime in the Making*. London: Sage Publications, 1997.

Meyerowitz, Joanne, ed. *Not June Cleaver: Women and Gender in Postwar America, 1945–1960*. Philadelphia: Temple University Press, 1994.

Miller, Fredric, et al. *Still Philadelphia: A Photographic History, 1890–1940*. Philadelphia: Temple University Press, 1983.

Mitchell, Michele. "Silences Broken, Silences Kept: Gender and Sexuality in African-American History." *Gender and History* 11, no. 3 (November 1999): 433–44.

———. *Righteous Propagation: African Americans and the Politics of Racial Destiny after Reconstruction*. Chapel Hill: University of North Carolina Press, 2004.

Mohanty, Chandra, ed. "Under Western Eyes." In *Third World Women and the Politics of Feminism*, edited by Ann Russo and Lourdes Torres. Bloomington: Indiana University Press, 1991.

Morgan, Edmund. "Slavery and Freedom: The American Paradox." *Journal of American History* 59, no. 1 (June 1972): 5–29.

Morgan, Jennifer. "'Some Could Suckle Over Their Shoulder': Male Travelers, Female Bodies, and the Gendering of Racial Ideology, 1500–1770." *WMQ*, 3rd ser., 54, no. 1 (January 1997): 167–92.

Morrison, Toni. "Unspeakable Things Unspoken: The African American Presence in American Literature." *Michigan Quarterly Review* 28, no. 1 (Winter 1989): 1–34.

———. *Playing in the Dark: Whiteness and the Literary Imagination*. Cambridge, Mass.: Harvard University Press, 1992.

Mott, Frank Luther. *American Journalism: A History of Newspapers in the United States Through 1690–1950*. Rev. ed. New York: Macmillan, 1950.

Mumford, Kevin J. *Interzones: Black/White Sex Districts in Chicago and New York in the Early-Twentieth Century*. New York: Columbia University Press, 1997.

Nash, Gary B. *Forging Freedom: The Formation of Philadelphia's Black Community, 1720–1840*. Cambridge, Mass.: Harvard University Press, 1988.

———, and Jean Soderlund. *Freedom by Degrees: Emancipation in Pennsylvania and Its Aftermath*. New York: Oxford University Press, 1991.

———. "Slaves and Slave Owners in Colonial Philadelphia." In *African Americans in Pennsylvania: Shifting Historical Perspectives*, edited by Joe William Trotter, Jr. and Eric Ledell Smith. Harrisburg: Pennsylvania Historical and Museum Commission; University Park: Pennsylvania State University Press, 1997.

———. *First City: Philadelphia and the Forging of Historical Memory*. Philadelphia: University of Pennsylvania Press, 2002.

Omolade, Barbara. "Hearts of Darkness." In *Words of Fire: An Anthology of African-American Feminist Thought*, edited by Beverly Guy-Sheftall. New York: New York Press, 1995.

Oshinsky, David M. *"Worse Than Slavery": Parchman Farm and the Ordeal of Jim Crow Justice*. New York: Free Press, 1996.

Padgug, Robert. "Sexual Matters: On Conceptualizing Sexuality in History." In *Passion and Power: Sexuality in History*, edited by Kathy Peiss and Christina Simmons. Philadelphia: Temple University Press, 1989.

Painter, Nell. *Exodusters: Black Migration to Kansas After Reconstruction*. New York: Alfred A. Knopf, 1976.

———. *The Narrative of Hosea Hudson, His Life as a Negro Communist in the South*. Cambridge, Mass.: Harvard University Press, 1979.

———. *Standing at Armageddon: The United States, 1877–1919*. New York: W. W. Norton, 1987.

———. "Soul Murder and Slavery: Toward a Fully Loaded Cost Accounting." In *U.S. History as Women's History: New Feminist Essays*, edited by Linda K. Kerber, Alice Kessler-Harris, and Kathryn Kish Sklar. Chapel Hill: University of North Carolina Press, 1995.

———. *Sojourner Truth: A Life, A Symbol*. New York: W. W. Norton, 1996.

Patrick-Stamp, Leslie. "Numbers That Are Not New: African Americans in the Country's First Prison, 1790–1835." *PMHB* 119 (1995): 95–128.

Peiss, Kathy. *Cheap Amusements: Working Women and Leisure in Turn-of-the-Century New York*. Philadelphia: Temple University Press, 1986.

Pennsylvania Department of Corrections: Female Offenders. Report published by the Pennsylvania Department of Corrections, February 2003.

Pleck, Elizabeth. "A Mother's Wages: Income Earning Among Married Italian and Black Women, 1896–1911." In *The American Family in Social-Historical Perspective*, edited by Michael Gordon. 2nd ed. New York: St. Martin's Press, 1978.

Rafter, Nicole Hahn. *Partial Justice: Women, Prisons, and Social Control*. New Brunswick: Transaction Publishers, 1990.

Rafter, Nicole Hahn. *Creating Born Criminals.* Urbana: University of Illinois Press, 1997.

Remu, John. "Racism, Black Masculinity and the Politics of Space." In *Men, Masculinities and Social Theory,* edited by Jeff Hearn and David Morgan. Boston: Unwin Hyman, 1990.

Rich, Adrienne. "Compulsory Heterosexuality and Lesbian Existence." *Signs: Journal of Women in Culture and Society* (Summer 1980): 631–60.

Richie, Beth E. *Compelled to Crime: The Gender Entrapment of Battered Black Women.* New York: Routledge, 1996.

Roediger, David. *The Wages of Whiteness: Race and the Making of the American Working Class.* Cambridge, Mass.: Harvard University Press, 1991.

Rooks, Noliwe M. *Ladies' Pages: African American Women's Magazines and the Culture That Made Them.* New Brunswick: Rutgers University Press, 2004.

Rosen, Hannah. " 'Not That Sort of Women': Race, Gender and Sexual Violence." In *Sex, Love, Race: Crossing Boundaries in North American History,* edited by Martha Hodes. New York: New York University Press, 1999.

Rosen, Ruth, and Sue Davidson. *The Mamie Papers.* New York: Feminist Press, 1977.

———. *The Lost Sisterhood: Prostitution in America, 1900–1918.* Baltimore: Johns Hopkins University Press, 1982.

Rothman, David. *The Discovery of the Asylum: Social Order and Disorder in the New Republic.* Boston: Little, Brown and Company, 1971.

Rowe, G. S. "Women's Crime and Criminal Administration in Pennsylvania, 1763–1790." *PMHB* 109 (1985): 335–68.

———. "Black Offenders, Criminal Courts, and Philadelphia Society in the Late Eighteenth-Century." *Journal of Social History* 22 (Summer 1989): 685–712.

Rubin, Gayle. "Thinking Sex: Notes for a Radical Theory of the Politics of Sexuality." In *Pleasure and Danger: Exploring Female Sexuality,* edited by Carol S. Vance. London: Pandora Press, 1989.

———. "The Traffic in Women: Notes on the 'Political Economy' of Sex." In *Feminism and History,* edited by Joan Wallach Scott. New York: Oxford University Press, 1996.

Ruth, David E. *Inventing the Public Enemy: The Gangster in American Culture, 1918–1934.* Chicago: University of Chicago Press, 1996.

Salinger, Sharon V. *To Serve Well and Faithfully: Labor and Indentured Servants in Pennsylvania, 1682–1800.* Bowie, Md.: Heritage Books, 2000.

Salter, John Thomas. *Boss Rule: Portraits in City Politics.* New York: McGraw-Hill, 1935.

Savage, Barbara. *Broadcasting Freedom: Radio, War, and the Politics of Race, 1938–1948.* Chapel Hill: University of North Carolina Press, 1999.

Scott, Daryl Michael. *Contempt and Pity: Social Policy and the Image of the Damaged Black Psyche, 1880–1996.* Chapel Hill: University of North Carolina Press, 1997.

Segal, Lynne. *Slow Motion: Changing Masculinities, Changing Men.* New Brunswick: Rutgers University Press, 1990.

Shah, Nayan. *Contagious Divides: Epidemics and Race in San Francisco's Chinatown*. Berkeley: University of California Press, 2001.

Silcox, Harry. "Nineteenth-Century Philadelphia Black Militant: Octavius V. Catto (1839–1871)." In *African Americans in Pennsylvania: Shifting Historical Perspectives*, edited by Joe William Trotter, Jr. and Eric Ledell Smith. Harrisburg: Pennsylvania Historical and Museum Commission; University Park: Pennsylvania State University Press, 1997.

Slaughter, Thomas P. *Bloody Dawn: The Christiana Riot and Racial Violence in the Antebellum North*. New York: Oxford University Press, 1991.

Smith, Barbara. "Toward a Black Feminist Criticism." *Conditions: Two* 1, no. 2 (October 1977): 25–52.

Smith, Billy G. *The "Lower Sort," Philadelphia's Laboring Peoples, 1750–1800*. Ithaca: Cornell University Press, 1990.

———. "Black Family Life in Philadelphia from Slavery to Freedom." In *Shaping a National Culture: The Philadelphia Experience, 1750–1800*, edited by Catherine E. Hutchins. Winterthur, Del.: Henry Francis du Pont Winterthur Museum, 1994.

Smith, Billy G., and Richard Wojtowicz. *Blacks Who Stole Themselves: Advertisements for Runaways in the Pennsylvania Gazette, 1728–1790*. Philadelphia: University of Pennsylvania Press, 1989.

Smith, Jennifer E. "ONAMOVE: African American Confronting the Prison Crisis." In *Still Lifting, Still Climbing: African American Women's Contemporary*, edited by Kimberly Springer. New York: New York University Press, 1999.

Smith, Judith R. *The 30th Anniversary Commemorative History: The Bureau of Correction and Its Institutions*. Pennsylvania Bureau of Correction, Printed at SCI-Huntingdon, 2nd printing. August 1983.

Smith, Shawn Michelle. *American Archives: Gender, Race, and Class in Visual Culture*. Princeton: Princeton University Press, 1999.

———. *Photography on the Color Line: W. E. B. Du Bois, Race, and Visual Culture*. Durham: Duke University Press, 2004.

Smith-Rosenberg, Caroll. *Disorderly Conduct: Visions of Gender in Victorian American*. Oxford: Oxford University Press, 1985.

Soderlund, Jean R. "Black Women in Colonial Pennsylvania." In *African Americans in Pennsylvania: Shifting Historical Perspectives*, edited by Joe William Trotter, Jr. and Eric Ledell Smith. Harrisburg: Pennsylvania Historical and Museum Commission; University Park: Pennsylvania State University Press, 1997.

Stansell, Christine. *City of Women: Sex and Class in New York, 1789–1860*. Urbana: University of Illinois Press, 1987.

Stanton, Domna C., ed. "Introduction." *Discourses of Sexuality: From Aristotle to AIDS*. Ann Arbor: University of Michigan Press, 1992.

Staples, Robert. *Black Masculinity: The Black Man's Role in American Society*. San Francisco: Black Scholar Press, 1982.

Stein, Marc. *City of Sisterly and Brotherly Loves: Lesbian and Gay Philadelphia, 1945–1972*. Philadelphia: Temple University Press, 2004.

Steinberg, Allen. *The Transformation of Criminal Justice: Philadelphia, 1800–1880*. Chapel Hill: University of North Carolina Press, 1989.

Sterling, Dorothy, ed. *Speak Out in Thunder Tones: Letters and Other Writings by Black Northerners, 1787–1865*. New York: Da Capo Press, 1998.

Stewart, Maria. *America's First Black Woman Political Writer: Essays and Speeches*. Edited and introduced by Marilyn Richardson. Bloomington: University of Indiana Press, 1987.

Sugrue, Thomas. "The Peopling and Depeopling of Early Pennsylvania: Indians and Colonists, 1680–1720." *PMHB*, 106 (1992) 3–31.

———. *The Origins of the Urban Crisis: Race and Inequality in Postwar Detroit*. Princeton: Princeton University Press, 1996.

Sutherland, John F. "Housing the Poor in the City of Houses." In *The Peoples of Philadelphia: A History of Ethnic Groups and Lower-Class Life, 1790–1940*, edited by Allen F. Davis and Mark Haller. Philadelphia: University of Pennsylvania Press, 1998.

Tate, Claudia. *Domestic Allegories of Political Desire: The Black Heroine's Text at the Turn of the Century*. New York: Oxford University Press, 1992.

Teeters, Negley K. *They Were In Prison: A History of the Pennsylvania Prison Society 1787–1937*. Philadelphia: John C. Winston, 1937.

———. *The Cradle of the Penitentiary: The Walnut Street at Philadelphia, 1773–1835*. Philadelphia, 1955.

———, and John D. Shearer. *The Prison at Philadelphia, Cherry Hill: The Separate System of Penal Discipline, 1829–1913*. New York: Columbia University Press, 1957.

Thompson, E. P. *The Making of the English Working-Class*. New York: Vintage Books, 1963.

Thompson, Peter. *Rum Punch and Revolution: Taverngoing and Public Life in Eighteenth-Century Philadelphia*. Philadelphia: University of Pennsylvania Press, 1999.

Tomes, Nancy. *The Art of Asylum-Keeping: Thomas Story Kirkbride and the Origins of American Psychiatry*. Philadelphia: University of Pennsylvania Press, 1994.

Trotter, Joe. *Black Milwaukee: The Making of an Industrial Proletariat, 1915–45*. Urbana: University of Illinois Press, 1985.

Turner, Edward R. *The Negro in Pennsylvania, Slavery—Servitude—Freedom*. Washington: American Historical Association, 1911.

U.S. Department of Justice, Office of Justice, Bureau of Justice Statistics. *Prisoners in 2002*. 07/03 NCJ 200248.

———. *Women Offenders*. Revised 10/03. NCJ 175688.

Varbero, Richard. "Philadelphia's South Italians in 1920s." In *The Peoples of Philadelphia: A History of Ethnic Groups and Lower-Class Life, 1790–1940*, edited by Allen F. Davis and Mark H. Haller. Philadelphia: University of Pennsylvania Press, 1998.

Walkowitz, Judith. *City of Dreadful Delight: Narratives of Sexual Danger in Late-Victorian London*. Chicago: University of Chicago Press, 1992.

Wallach, Joan. "Gender: A Useful Category of Historical Analyses." In *Feminism and History*, edited by Joan Scott Walllach. New York: Oxford University Press, 1996.

Washburn, Josie. *The Underworld Sewer: A Prostitute Reflects on Life in the Trade, 1871–1909*. Edited by Sharon E. Wood. Lincoln: University of Nebraska Press, 1997.

Wells-Barnett, Ida B. *Southern Horrors and Other Writings: The Anti-lynching Campaign of Ida B. Wells, 1892–1900*. Edited with an introduction by Jacqueline Jones Royster. Boston: Bedford Books, 1997.

West, Cornel. "The New Cultural Politics of Difference." In *Out There: Marginalization and Contemporary Cultures*, edited by Russell Ferguson, Martha Gever, Trinh T. Min-ha, and Cornel West. Cambridge, Mass.: MIT Press, 1990.

White, Deborah Gray. "The Cost of Club Work, the Price of Black Feminism." In *Visible Women: New Essays on American Activities*, edited by Nancy A. Hewitt and Suzanne Lebsock. Urbana: University of Illinois Press, 1993.

———. *Ar'n't I a Woman?: Female Slaves in the Plantation South*. New York: W. W. Norton, 1999.

———. *Too Heavy A Load: Black Women in Defense of Themselves, 1894–1994*. New York: W. W. Norton, 1999.

White, Shane, and Graham White. *Stylin': African American Expressive Culture from Its Beginnings to the Zoot Suit*. Ithaca: Cornell University Press, 1998.

———. "The Death of James Johnson." *AQ* 51, no. 4 (1999): 753–95.

Willis, Deborah, and Carla Williams. *The Black Female Body: A Photographic History*. Philadelphia: Temple University Press, 2002.

Wilson, Phill. "In the Fight of Our Lives: Notes on the AIDS Crisis in the Black Community." In *Race and Resistance: African Americans in the 21st Century*, edited by Herb Boyd. Cambridge, Mass.: South End Press, 2002.

Winch, Julie. *Philadelphia's Black Elite: Activism, Accommodation and the Struggle for Autonomy, 1787–1848*. Philadelphia: Temple University Press, 1988.

Winch, Julie, ed. *The Elite of Our People: Joseph Willson's Sketches of Black Upper-Class Life in Antebellum Philadelphia*. University Park: Pennsylvania State University Press, 2000.

Wolcott, Victoria. *Remaking Respectability: African American Women in Inter-war Detroit*. Chapel Hill: University of North Carolina Press, 2001.

Wood, Peter. " 'Impatient of Oppression': Black Freedom Struggles on the Eve of White Independence." *Southern Exposure* 12, no. 6 (1984): 10–16.

Woodson, Carter G. *The Mis-Education of the Negro*. Washington, D.C.: Associated Publishers, 1933.

Zita, Jacquelyn N. *Body Talk: Philosophical Reflections on Sex and Gender*. New York: Columbia University Press, 1998.

INDEX

abolitionist movement, 13–14, 24–26, 30–31, 36–38

Act for the Gradual Abolition of Slavery, 25–27, 39

Act for the Identification of Habitual Criminals, 136–37, 188n.20

Act for the Trial of Negroes, 21–22

Act to Provide Civil Rights for All People, 48

African Americans: elite class of, 10, 178n.39; as first penitentiary inmates, 129; racist hereditary studies of, 133–38

African-American scholarship and empowerment, 1–2, 155–56

agency and prostitution, 82

Alberts, Margaret, 125

Albright, Mick, 73

alcohol regulations and race, 67–71, 198n.161, 198n.165, 199n.169

Alexander, Sadie Tanner Mossell, 152

alienation and larceny, 10

Allen, Richard, 29

AME Mother Bethel Church, 52, 54

Archey, Emma, 215n.59

Archey, Irene, 141

Armstrong, Hattie, 97

Austin, Regina, 199n.172

autonomy: of black women, 44–46; leisure activities and, 59–61, 194n.110

badger crimes, 72–73, 77–81, 101, 200n.1; media coverage of, 215n.59; white justice system and, 123–25

Bailey, Mary, 84, 206n.69

Ball, Gil, 69

Barber, Percy V., 42, 188n.14

Bartholomew, John and Mary, 15–17

Beacham, Arthur, 78

Beary, Bella, 116

Beccaria, Cesare, 31

Bertillon, Alphonse, 136–37

Bertillon Hand Books, 137–38

Beveridge, Albert J., 106

black activism and black scholarship, 2

black church and community, 27–29

black community: black church and, 27–29; black female criminals and, 4

black female criminals: biases of justice system against, 123–25; birthplace data on, 160; community and, 4; conditions for, at Eastern State, 140–46; crime characteristics and origins of, 161; current *vs.* historical characterizations of, 150–56; employment data on, 158; historical understanding of, 3, 174n.15; in Jacksonian America, 33–34; popular culture images of, 11, 178n.43; psychic damage of, 6, 155, 176n.26, 228n.26; scholarship on, 155–56, 228n.28

"Black Fiends in Prison," 218n.87

black male criminals and race, 118–21

black newspapers, crime coverage in, 116, 216n.66

black scholarship: black activism and, 2; heroic aspects of, 3, 173n.12; political empowerment through, 1–2, 156–57

black women: demonization of, 112–19; depictions of, by African-American elites, 64–65; excluded from republican womanhood, 35, 186n.111; history of, 6, 176n.25; HIV/AIDS and, 229n.30; housing discrimination against, 8–9, black women (*continued*)

10; laundry work and, 50; moral stigmatization of, 35–38, 65–71, 74–77, 124–25, 197n.148; narcotics crimes of, 155, 228n.25; objectification of, 200n.7; property crimes by, 34–35, 155, 228n.25; racist hereditary studies of, 133–38; sex crimes and, 10, 73–77, 155, 178n.41, 228n.26; Southern propaganda on, 113–14, 214n.55; suicides of, 53–54, 80, 141, 145–46, 193n.86, 204n.46; victimization of, 74–77; violence and, 5–6, 72–100, 176n.24, 208n.89. *See also* exploitation of black women

Blum, Gabe, 46–47

Boies, Henry, 66, 127, 134

Bokwick, Balton, 121–22

Bowser, David, 62

Boyd, Eliza, 193n.93

Brock, William, 94

Broder, Sherri, 186n.112

Brody, Jennifer DeVere, 175n.23

Brooks, Louisa, 55, 58, 193n.93

Brooks-Higginbotham, Evelyn, 209n.102

brothels and sex parlors: alternative sexual practices in, 83–84; of Chinese immigrants, 75, 201n.16; women as managers of, 82–84, 204n.54. *See also* prostitution

Brown, Addie, 186n.114, 207n.78

Brown, Mamie, 102–5, 204n.51, 211nn.4, 5, 10

brutality against prison inmates, 145–46

Burn, Catherine, 142

Burrows, Harriet, 142

Bush, William, 124–25

business operations: brothels run by women as, 82–84; lack of licenses for, 69–71

Butler, Annie, 225n.80

Byrne, Thomas, 137

capitalism and black female criminals, 3, 174n.16

Carey, Mathew, 30

caricatures: of African Americans, 107–11, 123–25, 152–55, 212n.28, 228n.27; of crime, 125–26; of immigrants, 122–23

Caruth, Cathy, 205n.58

Cassidy, Michael, 41–42, 128, 132, 138, 140, 142–43, 146, 150, 200n.180, 226nn.104, 109

Catto, Octavius V., 63

Cesaire, Aime, 201n.11

Chauncey, George Jr., 207n.77, 226n.104

Chinese immigrants: employment opportunities for, 40; sex laws focused on, 75, 201n.16

Christianity: as class signifier, 20; conversion of blacks to, 19–20

church communities: class issues in, 64–65; as support networks, 52, 54, 77, 203n.28

citizenship: black female criminals and, 2–3; black women's adaptation to, 44–46; history of, for African Americans, 8, 38; race, gender, and sexuality and, 9; supremacist ideology and, 106–7

Civil Rights Act, repeal of (1883), 64

Civil War: black crime rates during, 34, 186n.105; end of slavery and, 39

Clarke, Cheryl, 207n.80

class issues: abolitionist movement and, 30–31; black elite urban reform and, 61–65, 195nn.120, 122; for black female criminals, 4, 11; black social networks and, 58–59, 194n.106; in criminology and penology, 133–38, 148–49; among Eastern State inmates, 140–46; entertainment preferences and, 58–61, 194n.106; in justice system, 35–38; in Philadelphia, 19, 180n.32; in post-Reconstruction era, 8–9, 10; supremacist ideology and, 106–7; terminology of, 178n.39; urbanization and influence of, 67–68

Clay, Edward, 35–36, 108

Clifton, Alice, 9, 151; revolutionary ideology and case of, 25–26; trial of, 14–18, 23–24, 38, 40

clothing of working-class African Americans, 59–61, 194n.109

Colefish, Helen, 121

Coleman, Georgiana, 72, 200n.2

Collins, Patricia Hill, 200n.7

Colored Amazon stereotype: in black newspapers, 116, 216n.66; historical and current versions of, 150–51; homosexual constructs in, 118; legacy of, 152–56; media portrayal of, 101–5, 111–19, 125–26; supremacist ideology and, 105–7; white justice system and, 123–25

Colored Barbers' Mutual Aid Association, 63

Committee on Lunacy, 127

commodification of black identity, 11

Consolidation Act of 1854, 37–38, 67, 69–70

Conway, Bessie, 78–80

Conway, Martha, 80–81

Cook, Johanna, 80

Cooper, Anna Julia, 1, 173n.11

corruption and African Americans, 169–71, 199n.172

Costill, Mary Ann, 34–35

Court of Oyer and Terminer, 110–11

courts, colonial, segregation of, 21–22

Crapper, Cornelia, 141

"Crazy Cook, A," 113

crime control rhetoric and judicial reform, 31

crime reporting, 125–26
criminal behavior: Bertillon measurement and identification system for, 136–37; black elite stereotypes of, 64–65; colonial justice system and, 24–25; crime class concept and, 133–38; demographics of, of black women, 43; employment discrimination and racism as factors in, 51–54; housing segregation and, 51–54; images of, in popular culture and media, 108–11; in Jacksonian America, 33–34; logic and consequences of, for black women, 99–100; migrant *vs.* native-born patterns of, 62–65; as "Negro problem," 65–71; penology and, 128–49; post-Reconstruction era definitions of, 8–9; as racial characteristic, 20; racist hereditary studies of, 133–38; varieties of, 54–58; as viable choice for black women, 41–43, 188n.7; violent patterns of, 88, 208n.88
criminal records as historical sources, 4–5
Crippen, Archie, 114–15, 215nn.58, 59
cross-dressing: in black-owned sex parlors, 83–84, 206n.67; among white female criminals, 117–18
cultural influences: on black women criminals, 6; on class issues, 20; on crime, 66; on penal philosophy, 129–33, 221n.111; supremacist ideology and, 106–7. *See also* popular culture
Cummings, James, 119–20, 218n.84
Cutler, Annie, 90–93, 105, 208n.96, 209n.97

Davis, Annie, 115, 216n.63
Davis, Martha, 217n.71
Defender, The, 85–87, 116
democracy and supremacist ideology, 106–7
Denny, James, 101
Derry, Ellen, 93, 116–17, 216n.69
deviance: of immigrants, 121–23; race and penology as factors in, 127–49
Dickens, Charles, 222n.31
Dix, Dorothea, 127
domestic respectability: barriers to, for African Americans, 87–94; farmer trope in construction of, 102–6, 212n.22; supremacist ideology and, 105–7, 211n.18, 212n.23; treatment of inmates and, 142
domestic service: black female criminality and, 40–44, 154–55, 188nn.6, 7; criminal behavior patterns influenced by, 54–58, 154–55; manipulation of black women's participation in, 113–19; racially based job segregation in, 46–54; specialization and grading of, 49–54, 192n.67

domestic violence and black women, 89–94, 208n.91
Dorsey, William, 218n.80
Dubois, Sylvia, 15
Du Bois, W. E. B., 1, 39, 48, 52, 87–88; mug shots by, 224n.59; on race-based sentencing patterns, 220n.103
Dugdale, Richard, 135
Duggan, Lisa, 207n.75, 214n.45
Duke of York's Laws, 19

Eakins, Thomas, 74
Eastern State Penitentiary: age statistics on prisoners in, 158; black female recidivism rates in, 56, 157; classification of black female crime at, 159; closing of, 149; crime classifications at, 164; demographics of inmates of, 55–56, 140; dilapidated conditions at, 141; disciplinary problems at, 127; Fannie Smiley at, 41–42; living conditions of inmates of, 130–33, 138, 140–46, 222n.21; marital status of inmates of, 159; mortality rates at, 141–42, 224n.75; nativity of inmates of, 165; occupations of inmates of, 163; opening of, 129; penal philosophy at, 130–33; punishment regimens at, 144–45; race and gender statistics on inmates of, 162; records of, 57, 104, 128, 136, 223n.52; relations between administrators and inmates of, 142–44; staff shortages at, 132; statistics on badger theft from, 78, 203n.34; treatment of inmates of, 7–9, 11, 145–46; violence against inmates of, 89, 208n.90; women inmate demographics in, 162
Eastern State Penitentiary Convict Descriptive Register, 175n.21
economic conditions: for black elites, 63–65; black entrepreneurship and, 29–30; black female crime and, 3, 41–43, 73; black migration as result of, 44–46; of black prostitutes, 81–84, 204n.51, 205n.55, 56; culture of violence and, 5, 176n.24; discrimination as factor in, 40–43, 48–49; patterns of entertainment and, 58–61; racialized commercial exchange and, 107–11; status of prisoners based on, 140
education of women inmates, 1–2
elites: African-American, 36, 61–65; legal system's protection of, 24, 67–71, 182n.60; political influence of, 69–71
emancipation, 39; control of freed blacks through prison system after, 129–33, 221n.111; vulnerability of black women after, 73–77

Hogan, Jennie, 142

Holmond, George, 119–20, 218n.84

homophobia: black female criminals in context of, 3, 174n.16; prison control of sodomites and, 146–48

homosexuality: African-American subculture of, 216n.63; among white female criminals, 117–18, 217nn.75, 78; prison control of sodomites and, 146–48; prostitution in black-owned sex parlors and, 83–84, 206nn.69, 70; stereotypes and myths about, 2, 172n.7. *See also* lesbianism

hooks, bell, 173n.12, 178n.43

hotel and hospitality industry, racial inequalities in, 63, 196n.133

House of Correction, 41

House of Refuge, 41

housing discrimination: against black women, 8–9, 10; concentration of African-American populations by, 51–54, 192n.73; deterioration of urban housing and, 52–54

Howard, Frank, 80

Howard, Ida, 88, 142

Hulburt, Bliss O., 89

Hunter, Tera, 176n.25, 205n.60

Hunton, Addie, 75

Hutchings, Alice, 118, 148, 217n.78

immigrants: criminalized images and identities of, 121–23; domestic services jobs taken by, 49–50; employment opportunities for, 48–49, 191n.56; housing segregation of, 52–53, 192n.73; urbanization and, 46–48, 190n.46

indentured servants: former slaves as, 27–29, 36; legal protections for, 24

infantilization of migrant black women, 65, 197n.144

inferiority myths and black scholarship, 2

Institute for Colored Youth, 52

insurance industry: defrauded by black female criminals, 55; racial inequalities in, 63, 196n.133

Iola Leroy, 76

Jackson, James, 89

Jackson, Peter, 210n.3

Jacksonian America: crime patterns in, 33–38, 67–68; justice system in, 33–34

"Jaspar's Wooing: How the Colored Preacher and 'Sis' Tilda Did Their Brief Courtship," 109

Jefferson Medical College, 63

job segregation: gender-based patterns of, 29–30, 46–47, 190n.48; racially-based patterns of, 49–54. *See also* employment discrimination

Johnson, Carrie, 115

Johnson, David, 205n.60

Johnson, Ella, 89

Johnson, Lucinda, 89

Johnson, Mamie, 89–90, 136

Jones, Absalom, 29

Jones, Grace, 89

Jones, Kate, 80

Jones, Sissieretta, 109, 213n.34

jook joints, 59–61

justice system: African-American perceptions of, 83–84, 205n.60, 209n.112; African Americans as lawyers in, 152; badger thieves overlooked by, 72–73; black female criminals in, 2–3, 156, 229n.31; black women's manipulation of, 94–99; class bias in, 35–38; in Jacksonian America, 33–34; in Philadelphia, 7–9, 70–71, 199n.174; race, gender, and sexuality in, 9, 65–71, 152–55; in South, 44–46, 174n.15; ties of, to media and political establishments, 110–11, 213n.43; white dominance of, 123–25. *See also* legal system

Kane, Edward, 122–23

Kantrowitz, Stephen, 212n.22

Kelley, Robin, 188n.21

Kellor, Frances, 135–36, 197n.140

Knight, William H., 90–92

labor issues: black male criminality and, 119–21; convict labor problems, 141–42; gender-based job segregation and, 29–30, 46–54, 67, 190n.48; manipulation of black women's participation in, 113–19; post-Reconstruction era changes in, 8, 10; racial clashes over, 36–38; strikes in Philadelphia and, 46–47; unfree labor terminology, 13, 179n.1. *See also* slavery

Lane, Roger, 195n.111, 208n.91

Lane, Stephen, 81

larceny: law against, in Jacksonian America, 34; patterns of, in black female criminals, 55–58; poverty as motivation for, 10, 41, 73; recidivism of offenders of, 56–58

Larson, Peter, 80

laundry work and black women, 50

Law and Order League, 68–69

Lee, Bert, 85

Lee, Emily, 84–87, 116

Lee, Harriet, 56

legal system: alcohol regulations and, 67–68,

legal system (*continued*)
198n.161, 198n.163, 199n.169; badger theft and, 78–81; black women and, 3; historical analysis of, 9; race and citizenship in, 30; as threat to black women, 20–21, 67, 70–71, 199n.177; white slavery laws and, 74–75. *See also* justice system

leisure activities and identity, 59–61, 195nn.110, 111

Lenni Lenape Indians, 19, 181n.33

lesbianism: African-American attitudes on, 85–87, 207nn.77, 78, 79, 80; in African-American sex parlors, 83–84, 206nn.69, 70; cultural constructions of, 101–2, 210n.2; prison anti-sodomy practices and, 148–49, 226n.109; among white female criminals, 117–18, 217nn.75, 78

Levin, Seymour, 152–55

Lewis, John D., 62

"Life in Philadelphia" series, 35, 186n.112

List, Karen, 186n.111

Lloyd, Rachel, 29

Lombroso, Cesare, 122, 133–34, 137, 223n.34

Lott, Eric, 212n.31

Lubiano, Wahneema, 174n.16, 216n.66

Lynch, W. A. (Rev.), 47

lynching: of black male criminals, 119–21; justified by habitual criminality, 136

Madden, Anthony, 102–5, 211nn.7, 15

Mann Act, 75

marriage in African-American culture: badger thievery and, 81; prisoners at Eastern State Penitentiary and, 159; as route to domestic stability, 93–94

"Marvelous and Horrible: Superstitious Lore of the Old Negroes, The," 109

masculinity: of black males, stereotypes of, 119–21, 210n.4; of whites, and justice and prison systems, 123–25, 146–48

Mathews, Annie, 75

McDowell, John Henry, 146–47

McLaurin, Melton, 178n.41

media coverage: of black male crime, 116–21; by black newspapers, 116–19, 216n.66; Colored Amazon stereotype in, 101–5, 111–19; of crime, 113–19, 215n.58, 216n.66; as historical resource, 5, 175n.22; images of race, gender, and sexuality in, 178n.42; of lynchings, 119–21; mythologization of gangsters in, 178n.42; racial stereotyping in, 66–67, 101–2; of sex and sexuality, 85–86, 207n.74, 215n.62; of

sex crimes, 122–23, 153–55, 219n.100; sources for crime reporting in, 125–26; supremacist ideology and content of, 107–11; white female criminals in, 116–17, 217nn.71, 72, 73. *See also* caricatures

mental institutions, reform of, 127–28. *See also* names of specific institutions

Merriman, George, 104

migration patterns of blacks: post-Revolutionary restrictions on, 30, 184n.84; stereotypes concerning, 64–65; urban reform and, 62–65

Miller, Isaiah, 55–56

Mingo Jack, 119–20, 218n.80

minstrelsy, supremacist ideology in, 107–11, 212n.31

Mis-Education of the Negro, The, 1–2

Mitchell, Michele, 176n.25

Mohanty, Chandra, 214n.48

monastic practices in penal philosophy, 129–33

morality: of African-Americans, in popular culture, 109–11; conceptions of, by black elites, 62–65; domesticity and African-American conceptions of, 87–94; stigmatizing constructions of, 112–19. *See also* moral stigmatization of black women

moral stigmatization of black women, 35–38; in policing and justice systems, 65–71, 124–25, 197n.148; through rape and sexual assault, 74–77

Morgan, John T., 107

Muelbronner Act, 141–42

mug shot photography, 137–39, 224n.59

Muller v. Oregon, 201n.15

Mumford, Kevin, 195n.118

"myth of invisibility," homosexuality and, 207n.77

narcotics crimes of black women, 155, 228n.25

National Association for the Advancement of Colored People, 152

national identity and supremacist ideology, 106–7

National League for the Protection of Colored Women, 64–65, 197n.140

National Police Gazette, 83, 113

nativism and criminalization of immigrants, 121–23

"Negro as a Fatalist," 109, 213n.39

Negro Courts, 21–22, 26, 150

Ness, Kate, 117

newspapers. *See* media coverage; names of individual newspapers

North American, 102, 105, 175n.22

objectification and sexual exploitation of black women, 200n.7

Palmer, Sarah, 80, 204nn.43, 44, 46
patriarchy: of African-American reformers, 64, 197n.134; black male laborers and, 120–21; domestic violence as sign of, 89; sexual assault and, 200n.8
Patti Troubadours, 213n.34
Payton, Josephine, 79–80, 204nn.39, 41
penitentiary records as historical source, 5
Penn, William, 19, 181n.33
Pennsylvania Gazette, 36
"Pennsylvania Insane Asylum," 42, 106, 117, 127, 143–44, 216n.68
Pennsylvania Prison Society for Alleviating the Miseries of Prisoners, 32, 67, 70–71, 93, 130–33, 209n.105, 213n.43, 222n.15
Pennsylvania Village for Feeble Minded Women, 106
penology, 127–49; class issues in, 133–38; paradigms of, 148–49; philosophy and praxis in, 129–33; restoration of white masculinity through, 146–48. *See also* prisons, prison populations
pension fraud by black female criminals, 55–56, 193n.98
Philadelphia: black community in, 27–32; black elites in, 62–65; black migration to, 44–46; corruption in, 34–35, 169–71, 186n.110, 199nn.172, 174; economics of slavery in, 19–20; minstrel shows in, 109–11; police and justice systems in, 67–71; post-Reconstruction labor patterns in, 10; prison history of, 6–9; racial tensions in, 36–38, 46–54, 152–55; Seventh Ward of, as black community center, 52–54; slave demographics in, 13–14; vice crimes in, 81–84
Philadelphia County Prison, 41–42, 188n.7; demographics of women prisoner in, 162; race and gender statistics on, 159; records of, 57
Philadelphia County Prisoners for Trial Docket, 175n.21
Philadelphia Evening Bulletin, 101, 154, 175n.22
Philadelphia Inquirer, 114–16, 175n.22, 215n.59
Philadelphia Press, 175n.22
Philadelphia Public Ledger, The, 34, 72, 125, 175n.22, 215n.59. See also *Philadelphia Public Ledger and Transcript*
Philadelphia Public Ledger and Transcript, 175n.22. See also *Philadelphia Public Ledger, The*
Philadelphia Record, 103–4, 125, 175n.22, 218n.87

Philadelphia Rogues Gallery Books, 194n.110
"Philadelphia Slices" series, 186n.112
Philadelphia Vice Commission, 84, 205n.55
Phillips, Henry L., 54
Pierson, Matilda, 142
Pinzer, Mamie, 144
Plessy v. Ferguson, 64
Pole, Edward, 17, 23
policing: African-American perceptions of, 83, 205n.60; habitual criminal behavior created by, 128; racism and, 65–71, 137–38
political empowerment: African-American scholarship as tool for, 1–2, 155–56, 228n.28; black prostitution and, 82–84; justice system and, 110, 213n.43; marginalization of black lawmakers and, 63–65; vice crimes as tool for, 81–84, 204n.51
popular culture: black female criminals in, 5, 10–11, 175n.23, 178n.42; black male criminal in, 118–21; supremacist ideology and, 107–11
post-Reconstruction era: criminal justice system in, 174n.15; Philadelphia in, 7
Potter, Jane, 216n.68
poverty: black female criminality as symptom of, 4, 40, 71; larceny and, 10; urbanization and, 50–54, 62–65
Powell, Amanda, 56–57, 193n.95
power relations: at Eastern State penitentiary, 138, 140–46; in post-Reconstruction Philadelphia, 9; slavery laws as expression of, 20–25; white masculinity and prisons and, 146–48. *See also* political empowerment
pregnancy in prisons, 143–44
presentment of 1693, 20–22
Primus, Hannah, 56
Primus, Rebecca, 55, 186n.114, 193n.94, 207n.78
prisons, prison populations: African Americans and, 34, 125, 155, 220n.103; black women in, 2–3, 12, 155–56, 229n.30; characterization of inmates in records of, 121–23, 219n.91; habitual criminal behavior created in, 128; history of, in Philadelphia, 6–9; insanity among inmates of, 58, 194n.105; institutionalization of, for black Americans, 26–32; matrons in, 70–71; penal philosophy and praxis in, 129–33, 221n.111; popular cultural images of, 11; social and judicial reform of, 31–32; as source of criminality, 12; system of sexual favors in, 199n.179
Professional Criminals in America, 137
property crimes by black women, 34–35, 155, 228n.25
prostitution: African Americans and, 59, 82–84, 194n.107, 205n.55, 205n. 56, 206nn.69,

sexuality: black stereotypes of, 102, 210n.3; empowerment of black women through prostitution and, 81–84, 204n.51; gender politics and, 8; inmates' expression of, as protest, 145–46, 226n.101; politicization of, 64, 197n.134; popular culture images of, 10–11, 108–11, 115–19, 178n.42, 215nn.62, 63; in slave laws, 9; stereotypes of black women and, 62–65, 77–81; stigmatizing constructions of, 112–19; supremacist ideology and notions of, 106–7

sexual morality: black women's concealment of, 76–77; racial and gender double standard in, 23–24

Shaffer, John, 16–17

shoplifting: by black female criminals, 55–56; gender stereotypes of, 143

shopping patterns of working-class African Americans, 59

Short, Elizabeth, 55–56, 193n.98

"Shot Down Woman who Spurned Her," 118

Shotwell, Sadie, 43

silent meditation in penal philosophy, 129–33, 222n.15

Simmons, Ellis, 152–53

skin color as social indicator, 112–19, 214nn.48, 51

Skinner, Edward, 80

slavery: abolition of, 39; black wage laborers' transition from, 120–21; caricatures of, 107–11, 212n.28; in colonial Pennsylvania, 18–25; domestic service as substitute for, 41–43; economics of, 20; historical demographics on, 13–14; impact of, on morality, 35, 66, 186n.111; laws concerning, 9, 20–21; living conditions in, 15–16; rape and violence against black women during, 73–77; sexism and racism in laws concerning, 22–25

Smiley, Fannie, 41–43, 55, 188n.16

Smith, Albert, 93–94

Smith, Bessie, 78

Smith, Josephine, 143

Smith, Lizzie, 55–56, 193n.98

Smith, Pearl, 114–15, 215nn.58, 59

Smith, Shawn Michelle, 214n.54, 224nn.59, 60

social context of crime, 3–4; black female criminal and, 9–10, 40–43,150–56; black prostitution and, 82–84; hierarchy of justice system and, 123–25; inmate social status and prison life, 142; moral stigma of black women and, 35–36; popular culture and press as influences on, 107–11; prison system as social engineering and, 129–33; during Reconstruction, 40; supremacist ideology and, 106–7

social Darwinism and class-based criminology, 133–38

social networks: of badger thieves, 81; of black prostitutes, 82–84, 204n.54; black women's creation of, 58–61, 77

social rituals and class issues, 20

sodomy laws: African-American prostitution and, 84, 206n.69; prison system's control of sodomites and, 146–48

solitary confinement, 129–30

Southern migration: black elites' criticism of, 61–65, 195n.120; gender-based patterns in, 44–46

spatial mobility: housing discrimination as barrier to, 51–54, 192n.73; slavery's restrictions on, 15–16, 20, 179n.13

Stanton, Domna C., 226n.101

State Correctional Institution, Muncy: establishment of, 149; violence discussed by inmates at, 88, 208n.89; women's education program in, 1, 171n.2

State Institution for the Feeble Minded of Western Pennsylvania, 106

statistical database on black female criminals, 5, 175n.21

Stead, W. T., 213n.41

Steinberg, Allen, 199n.174, 213n.43

stereotypes: of African-American degeneracy, 65–71; of African-American psyche, 109–10; of black female migrant workers, 63–65; black scholarship as tool against, 2, 155–56; of immigrants, 121–23; moral stereotypes of black women, 35–38, 186n.111–12; in racist hereditary criminal studies, 133–38; sex crimes as representations of, 74–81, 202n.21; of sexuality of black women, 62–65, 77–81; supremacist ideology and evolution of, 105–7

strikebreakers, African-American, 46–47

suicides of African-American women, 53–54, 80, 193n.86, 204n.46; at Eastern State Penitentiary, 141, 145–46

supremacist ideology: impact of, on black women, 105–7; in popular culture and press, 107–11

surveillance tactics and habitual criminal behavior, 128

Sutherland, John F., 192n.73

Sykes, Corrine, 152–55, 228n.19

Tabbs, John, 94–99

Tabbs, Mary Hannah, 94–99, 112, 209n.113, 214nn.50, 52

Kali N. Gross is assistant professor in the Department of History and Politics and Director of Africana Studies at Drexel University.

Library of Congress Cataloging-in-Publication Data
Gross, Kali N.
Colored amazons : crime, violence, and Black women in the City of Brotherly Love, 1880–1910 / Kali N. Gross.
p. cm. — (Politics, history, and culture)
"A John Hope Franklin Center book."
Includes bibliographical references and index.
ISBN 0-8223-3761-4 (cloth : alk. paper)
ISBN 0-8223-3799-1 (pbk. : alk. paper)
1. African American criminals—Pennsylvania—Philadelphia—History. 2. Female offenders—Pennsylvania—Philadelphia—History. 3. Crime and race—Pennsylvania—Philadelphia—History. 4. Discrimination in criminal justice administration—Pennsylvania—Philadelphia—History. 5. African American women—Public opinion—History. 6. African American women—Social conditions. I. Title. II. Series.
HV6795.P5G76 2006
364.3′7408996073074811—dc22   2006001659